Digital SLR Cameras & Photography

FOR

DUMMIES®

Digital SLR Cameras & Photography

FOR DUMMIES®

by David D. Busch

WILEY

Wiley Publishing, Inc.

Digital SLR Cameras & Photography For Dummies®

Published by
Wiley Publishing, Inc.
111 River Street
Hoboken, NJ 07030-5774
www.wiley.com

WILEY

About the Author

As a roving photojournalist for more than 20 years, **David D. Busch** illustrated his books, magazine articles, and newspaper reports with award-winning images. He has operated his own commercial studio, suffocated in formal dress while shooting weddings-for-hire, and shot sports for a daily newspaper and Upstate New York college. His photos have been published in magazines as diverse as *Scientific American* and *Petersen's PhotoGraphic,* and his articles have appeared in *Popular Photography & Imaging, The Rangefinder, The Professional Photographer,* and hundreds of other publications. He's currently reviewing digital cameras for CNet and *Computer Shopper.*

When About.com recently named its top five books on Beginning Digital Photography, occupying the number one and two slots were Busch's *Digital Photography All-in-One Desk Reference For Dummies,* and *Mastering Digital Photography.* His 80 other books published since 1983 include best-sellers like *The Nikon D70 Digital Field Guide, The Official Hewlett-Packard Scanner Handbook,* and *Digital Photography For Dummies Quick Reference.*

Busch earned top category honors in the Computer Press Awards the first two years they were given (for *Sorry About the Explosion* and *Secrets of MacPaint, MacWrite, and MacDraw*), and later served as Master of Ceremonies for the awards.

Dedication

For Cathy

Author's Acknowledgments

Thanks as always to senior acquisitions editor Steve Hayes at Wiley, who was quick to see that a book about digital SLR cameras should cover both the cameras *and* photography in depth. As both an author and avid consumer of *For Dummies* books, my special thanks go out to Wiley for publishing books like this one in full color, at a price anyone can afford. Technical editor Mike Sullivan, as usual, provided his sage advice from the viewpoint of one of the pioneers of digital SLRs, dating back more than a decade. Mike was also quick to come up with useful photos to illustrate particular points when my own portfolio came up short.

More thanks to project editor Rebecca Huehls and copy editor Virginia Sanders for keeping this book looking sharp. Working behind the scenes was my agent, Carole McClendon, who helped me work through a couple mini-crises that developed along the way.

Publisher's Acknowledgments

We're proud of this book; please send us your comments through our online registration form located at www.dummies.com/register/.

Some of the people who helped bring this book to market include the following:

Acquisitions, Editorial, and Media Development

Project Editor: Rebecca Huehls

Senior Acquisitions Editor: Steve Hayes

Copy Editor: Virginia Sanders

Technical Editor: Michael Sullivan

Editorial Manager: Leah Cameron

Media Development Manager: Laura VanWinkle

Media Development Supervisor: Richard Graves

Editorial Assistant: Amanda Foxworth

Cartoons: Rich Tennant (www.the5thwave.com)

Composition Services

Project Coordinators: Shannon Schiller, Maridee Ennis

Layout and Graphics: Melanee Prendergast, Heather Ryan

Special Art: Brian Drumm, Lauren Goddard

Proofreaders: Leeann Harney, Betty Kish, Joe Niesen, Dwight Ramsey

Indexer: Sherry Massey

Publishing and Editorial for Technology Dummies

Richard Swadley, Vice President and Executive Group Publisher

Andy Cummings, Vice President and Publisher

Mary Bednarek, Executive Acquisitions Director

Mary C. Corder, Editorial Director

Publishing for Consumer Dummies

Diane Graves Steele, Vice President and Publisher

Joyce Pepple, Acquisitions Director

Composition Services

Gerry Fahey, Vice President of Production Services

Debbie Stailey, Director of Composition Services

Contents at a Glance

Table of Contents

Introduction

*T*he digital single lens reflex (dSLR) is the great step upward for photographers who want to expand their creative horizons — or simply just get
better pictures. Whether you want to become a serious photo hobbyist, have
a hankering to turn pro, or want to take advantage of the improved control
digital SLRs give you over your photography, discovering how to use this tool
of the future should be high on your priorities list.

In the right hands, digital SLRs in the $600 to $1,000 range can outshoot the
$5,000 professional models of five years ago and are light-years ahead of even
the best point-and-shoot models of today. The dSLR provides more control
over what portions of your image are in sharp focus, boast lower levels of the
annoying grain effect called *noise,* and operate fast enough to capture the
most fleeting action. If that isn't enough, you can change lenses, too, adding
super-wide perspectives or the huge magnification possibilities of long, long
telephoto lenses to your repertoire.

Almost all the other advantages of digital photography come with your digital
SLR camera, too. You can review your image immediately, upload the photo
to your computer, make adjustments, and print out a sparkling full-color print
within minutes. You never need to buy film. You decide which images to print
and how large to make them. You can proudly display your digital photographic
work framed on your wall or over your fireplace. You can even make wallet-
sized photos, send copies to friends in e-mail, or create an online gallery that
relatives and colleagues can view over the Web.

About This Book

Technology and techniques — you find both in this book. Understanding
exactly how a digital SLR works can help you use its capabilities more fully.
By mastering the technology, you'll be better equipped to understand how
to use interchangeable lenses, set up speedy continuous-shooting burst
modes, apply selective focus, and shoot under the lowest light levels.
Understanding how a point-and-shoot digital camera works offers you little
advantage because such entry-level cameras don't give you the creative control that a dSLR does.

You don't need to understand internal combustion to drive a Porsche, but it helps if you know a little about double-clutching and limited-slip differentials. Technology also provides the grounding you need to work with advanced photographic techniques, such as the ones I discuss in this book. I fill these pages with basic information and tips you can use to hone your skills while you grow as a digital SLR photographer.

Foolish Assumptions

This book is written for both experienced and budding photographers who have a good grasp of using their computers and navigating the operating system and at least a cursory knowledge of the operation of their digital SLR camera. You needn't be an expert photographer — all you need is a desire to improve your skills and knowledge.

Because dSLRs are a more advanced type of digital camera, you might be making the upgrade from a conventional film SLR. At the very least, I assume that you aren't new to photography and have some knowledge of conventional photography. If so, this book helps you fine-tune your capabilities.

Although most of the emphasis in this book is on picture-taking, I offer a couple chapters on image-editing, too, so it would help if you have some familiarity with an image editor, such as Paint Shop Pro, Corel PhotoPaint, or Adobe Photoshop or Photoshop Elements.

How This Book Is Organized

Organization is your friend! All the chapters in this book are grouped together into parts that each address a broad general area of interest. If you're especially keen to know more about a particular topic, such as how to select the perfect dSLR or its accessories, turn to the part that includes that material. But you don't have to read this book in any particular order. You can absorb each part and chapter on its own. If I explore a certain topic, such as shutter lag or infrared photography, in more detail elsewhere in the book, I give you a cross-reference pointing to the relevant section in case you want more background. Read in any order you like. Skim through and study the photo examples, or examine only the odd-numbered pages if you prefer. It's your choice. I hope that eventually you'll wade through the whole thing, but my top priority is delivering the information you need right now to take better photographs.

Part I: Digital SLRs and You

Find out all the advantages of digital SLRs and why they beat the pants off both film and digital point-and-shoot cameras. Take a safari through the innards of a typical dSLR to track down the most-needed and most-desired features. Then, choose the accessories that will take your dSLR to the next level.

Part II: Oh, Shoot!

Digital SLRs bristle with controls and components that give you absolute sovereignty over virtually every feature and function. In this part, you work with those controls, master the mysteries of interchangeable lenses, and discover special features like image stabilization.

Part III: Beyond the Basics

It's time to take the next step and improve your photography by using more advanced features, such as the RAW format and your dSLR's action, sequence shooting, and flash capabilities. Then, apply the advanced features to get better compositions in a variety of settings.

Part IV: Fine-Tuning Your Output

Your creative possibilities don't end when the shutter snaps. After you transfer the photo to your computer, you can further enhance and refine your picture by using image-editing software. Then, make hard-copy prints you can show off, hang on the wall, or display on your mantel. This part shows you some of the things you can do with your prize (and prize-winning) photos.

Part V: The Part of Tens

There are just three (not ten) chapters in the Part of Tens, but each of them provides a-dozen-minus-two interesting things you can do to enjoy your digital SLR even more. You discover the ten best ways to improve your photography *right now,* ten fascinating things you probably never thought of doing with your dSLR, and ten online resources with more information and showcases for your digital dexterity.

Appendix

This handy glossary explains the trickiest terms you find in this book, as well as some that you don't, but which you might stumble over when exploring the world of digital SLR photography.

Icons Used in This Book

I use the following icons throughout the book:

The Tip icon marks tips (what a surprise!) and shortcuts that you can use to make working with your digital SLR easier.

Remember icons mark the information that's especially important to know. To siphon off the most important information in each chapter, just skim through these icons.

The Technical Stuff icon marks information of a more technical nature that you can normally skip over unless you have a special interest in the background info I discuss.

The Warning icon tells you to watch out! It marks important information that might save you headaches, heartaches, and even cash aches, especially when your dSLR starts acting in unexpected ways or won't do exactly what you want it to do.

Part I
Digital SLRs
and You

In this part . . .

The digital SLR difference is significant, as you discover in this part. I tell you exactly why dSLRs produce better results faster, and you master the technology behind these advanced cameras. You also discover how to select the best digital SLR for your needs and which accessories can help you do a better job.

Chapter 1 explains the advantages of dSLRs and outlines a few of the disadvantages — and why they don't matter. Chapter 2 takes you into the darkest recesses of your digital SLR camera, so you can understand sensors, shutters, and how exposure works. Then, in Chapter 3, you find a list of the features you need, want, and wish you had. Chapter 4 tells you about the accessories that any dSLR photographer must have.

The Digital SLR Difference

In This Chapter

▷ Discovering why digital SLRs are the next big thing

▷ Finding out how your shoot will change — big time!

▷ Exploring dSLR advantages

▷ Looking at downsides? *What* downsides?

*T*oday, the digital SLR (or dSLR) has become such a hot item among people who take pictures that virtually everyone, including your grandmother, probably knows that SLR stands for *single lens reflex.* However, your Nana — or you for that matter — might not know precisely what *single lens reflex* means. It's a camera (film or digital) that uses a marvelous system of mirrors and/or prisms to provide bright, clear optical viewing of the image you're about to take — through the same lens that is used to take the picture.

The key thing to know is that a dSLR is a very cool tool for taking photos electronically.

Welcome to the chapter that tells you exactly how smart you were when you decided to upgrade from whatever you were using previously to the future of digital photography. You find out how a digital SLR will transform the way you take and make pictures, why the strengths of the dSLR are important to you, and why the few downsides really don't matter. Getting in on the ground floor is great, and I tell you why.

dSLR: dNext Great Digital Camera

If you've already made the jump to a digital SLR, you've discovered that the dSLR lets you take pictures the way they were *meant* to be taken. After using other film or digital cameras, anyone interested in taking professional-looking photos notices why dSLRs stand out:

- ✓ **You can view a big, bright image that represents (almost) exactly what you'll see in the final picture.** No peering through a tiny window at a miniature version of your subject. No squinting to compose your image on an LCD viewfinder that washes out in bright sunlight. Nor do you have to wonder whether you've chopped off the top of someone's head or guess how much of your image is in sharp focus.

- ✓ **A dSLR responds to an itchy trigger finger almost instantly.** Forget about pressing the shutter release and then waiting a second or two before the camera decides to snap off the shot. Unlike most point-and-shoot digital cameras, dSLRs can crank out shots as fast as you can press the button.

- ✓ **You have the freedom to switch among lenses** — such as an all-purpose zoom lens, a super-wide angle lens, an extra-long telephoto lens, a close-up lens, or other specialized optic — quicker than you can say *170-500mm F5-6.3 APO Aspherical AutoFocus Telephoto Zoomexpialidocious.* (Best of all, you don't even have to know what that tongue-twister of a name means!)

Figure 1-1: Playing with lenses, lenses, and more lenses is one of the inevitable joys of working with a dSLR.

Just be prepared to succumb to *lens lust,* a strange malady that strikes all owners of dSLRs sooner or later. Before you know it, you'll find yourself convinced you *must* have optical goodies like the lens shown in Figure 1-1, a telephoto macro lens that's absolutely essential (you'll think) for taking photos of butterflies from enough of a distance to avoid scaring the timid creatures away.

If you're ready to say *sayonara* to film, *adiós* to poorly exposed and poorly composed pictures, and *auf Wiedersehen* to cameras with sluggardly performance, it's time to get started.

The sections that follow (as well as other chapters in this part) introduce you to the technical advantages of the digital SLR and how to use the dSLR's features to their fullest. When you're ready to expand your photographic horizons even farther, Parts II, III, and IV help you master the basics of digital photography, go beyond the basics to conquer the mysteries of photo arenas such as action, flash, and portrait photography, and then discover how you can fine-tune your images, organizing them for sharing and printing.

Improving Your Photography with a dSLR

The differences between digital SLRs and the camera you were using before you saw the light will depend on where you're coming from. If your most recent camera was a point-and-shoot digital model, you know the advantages of being able to review your photos on an LCD an instant after you took them, and you also know the benefits of fine-tuning them in an image editor. If you're switching to a digital SLR from a film SLR, you are likely a photo enthusiast already and well aware that a single lens reflex offers you extra control over framing, using focus creatively, and choosing lenses to give the best perspective. And, if you're making the huge leap from a point-and-shoot non-SLR film camera to a digital SLR, you're in for some *real* revelations.

A digital SLR has (almost) all the good stuff available in a lesser digital camera, with some significant advantages that enable you to take your photo endeavors to a new, more glorious level of excellence. Certainly, you can take close-ups or sports photos with any good-quality film or digital camera. Low-light photography, travel pictures, or portraits are all within the capabilities of any camera. But digital SLRs let you capture these kinds of images more quickly, more flexibly, and with more creativity at your fingertips. Best of all (at least for Photoshop slaves), a digital SLR can solve problems that previously required working long hours over a hot keyboard.

Despite the comparisons you can make to other cameras, a digital SLR isn't just a simple upgrade from a conventional film camera or another type of digital camera. A dSLR is very different from a film SLR, too, even though some vendors offer film and dSLRs that look quite a bit alike and share similar exposure metering, automatic focusing, and other electronics. If you look closely, you find that the digital SLR camera is different, and how you use it to take pictures is different.

In the sections that follow, I introduce you to the advanced features and inner workings so that you can begin getting the most out of your dSLR.

Composing shots with a more accurate viewfinder

With non-SLR cameras, what you see isn't always what you get.

Theoretically, the LCD on the back of a point-and-shoot digital camera *should* show exactly what you'll get in the finished picture. After all, the same sensor that actually captures the photo produces the LCD image. In practice, the LCD might be difficult to view under bright light, and it's so small (a few LCDs are only 1.5 inches diagonally) that you'll feel like you're trying to judge your image by looking at a postage stamp that's gone through the wash a few times.

The view through a non-SLR camera's optical viewfinder is likely to be even worse: tiny, inaccurate enough to make chopping off heads alarmingly easy, and with no information about what's in focus and what is not.

More advanced cameras might use an electronic viewfinder (EVF), which is a second, internal LCD that the user views through a window. EVFs provide a larger image that's formed by the actual light falling on the sensor and can be used in full sunlight without washing out. However, they might not have enough pixels to accurately portray your subject and tend to degenerate into blurred, ghosted images if the camera or subject moves during framing. They also don't work well in low light levels. An EVF is a good compromise, but not as good as a dSLR for previewing an image.

A digital SLR's viewfinder, in contrast, closely duplicates what the sensor will see, even though the image is formed optically and not generated by the sensor itself. It's all done with mirrors (and other reflective surfaces) that bounce the light from the lens to your viewfinder, sampling only a little of the light to measure exposure, color, and focus. As a result, the viewfinder image is usually bigger and brighter — from 75 percent to 95 percent (or more) of life size using a dSLR "normal" lens or zoom position, compared with 25 percent or smaller with a point-and-shoot camera's optical or LCD viewfinder. You see 95 percent of the total area captured, too.

Check out Figure 1-2 and decide which view of your subject you'd rather work with. Even the 2.5-inch LCD on the point-and-shoot model in the upper-left corner is difficult to view in bright light; the electronic viewfinder in the upper-right corner can be fuzzy, making it hard to judge focus. The digital SLR's big bright viewfinder (bottom) is, as Goldilocks would say, *just right.*

A dSLR shows you approximately what is in sharp focus and what is not (the *depth-of-field*), either in general terms (all the time) or more precisely when you press a handy button called the *depth-of-field preview.* Your digital SLR viewing experience is likely to be more pleasant, more accurate, and better suited for your creative endeavors.

Figure 1-2: A point-and-shoot LCD (upper left) or an EVF LCD (upper right) is no match for a dSLR's optical system (bottom).

Flexing the more powerful sensor

Digital SLR sensors are *much* bigger than their point-and-shoot camera counterparts, and this gives them a larger area for capturing light and, potentially, much greater sensitivity to lower light levels.

A dSLR's extra sensitivity pays off when you want to

- Take pictures in dim light.
- Freeze action by using shorter exposure times.
- Use smaller lens openings to increase the amount of subject matter that's in sharp focus.

Within the Canon digital camera line alone, you find digital SLRs with 22.2-x-14.8mm to 24-x-36mm sensors (the size of a 35mm film frame). Some of Canon's digital point-and-shoot cameras use a sensor that measures only 7.8 x 5.32mm. Put in terms that make sense to human beings, the dSLR sensors have 8 to 20 times more area than their Lilliputian sensor-mates. Figure 1-3 gives you a better idea of the relative sizes.

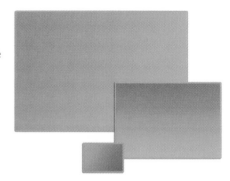

Figure 1-3: A dSLR's 24-x-36mm sensor (upper left), a dSLR's 22.2-x-14.8mm sensor (center), and a plain digital camera's 7.8-x-5.32mm sensor (bottom).

If you think of a sensor as a rectangular bucket and the light falling on it as a soft drizzle of rain, you see that the larger buckets are going to collect more drops (or the particles of light called *photons*) more quickly than the smaller ones. Because a certain minimum number of photons is required to register a picture, a larger sensor can collect the required amount more quickly, making it more sensitive than a smaller sensor under the same conditions.

In photography, the sensitivity to light is measured by using a yardstick called ISO (International Organization for Standardization). Most point-and-shoot digital cameras have a sensitivity range of about ISO 50 to ISO 100 (at the low end) up to a maximum of ISO 400 (at the high end). Fuji has introduced a compact digicam with its SuperCCD sensor that includes *two* light-sensitive areas per pixel, and it boasts an ISO 1600 maximum sensitivity, but virtually all other non-SLR cameras top out at ISO 400.

In contrast, digital SLRs — with their more sensitive sensors — commonly have ISO settings of up to ISO 800. Many are capable of ISO 1600 or even ISO 3200. There's a downside to this extra speed, as you see in the section "Reducing noise in your photos," but in general, the added sensitivity is a boon to people who want to shoot photos in dim light, take action pictures, or need to stretch the amount of depth-of-field available.

Reducing noise in your photos

Noise is that grainy look digital photos sometimes get, usually noticeable as multi-colored speckles most visible in the dark or shadow areas of an image. Although you can sometimes use noise as a creative effect, it's generally a bad thing that destroys detail in your image and might limit how much you can enlarge a photo before the graininess becomes obtrusive.

The most common types of noise are produced at higher sensitivity settings. That's because cameras achieve the loftier ISO numbers by amplifying the original electronic signal, and any background noise present in the signal is multiplied along with the image information. As you see in the Figure 1-4, a relatively low ISO value of 200 produces an image that's virtually free of the noise, but jumping the sensitivity to ISO 1600 produces a lot more noise — even though a person used a digital SLR for both pictures.

One reason why point-and-shoot digicams rarely have ISO settings beyond ISO 400 is that the noise becomes excessive at higher ratings, sometimes even worse than you see in the lower example at right. However, you can boost the information that the bigger dSLR sensors capture to higher ISO settings with relatively lower overall noise. I've used digital SLRs that had less noise at ISO 800 than some poor-performing point-and-shoots displayed at ISO 100. Obviously, the larger sensors found in dSLRs score another slam-dunk in the noise department and make high ISO ratings feasible when you really, really need them.

Figure 1-4: A noise-free photo shot at ISO 200 (top); a noisy photo shot at ISO 1600 (bottom).

Noise doesn't always result simply from using high ISO settings: Long exposures can cause another kind of noise. Although some techniques can reduce the amount of noise present in a photo (as you discover in Chapter 2), by and large, digital SLR cameras are far superior to their non-SLR counterparts when it comes to smooth, noise-free images.

Thanks to the disparity in size alone, all sensors of a particular resolution are *not* created equal, and sensors with fewer megapixels might actually be superior to higher-resolution pixel-grabbers. For example, most older 6-megapixel dSLRs produce superior results to the newest 8-megapixel non-SLR digicams. I've seen results from one $3,500 4.3-megapixel pro-level dSLR that run rings around the best images possible from an $800 EVF model with an 8-megapixel sensor. So no matter how many megapixels a point-and-shoot camera's sensor can hoard, that sensor isn't as big as a dSLR's. And when it comes to reducing noise, the size of the sensor is one of the most important factors.

Reclaiming depth-of-field control

Depth-of-field is the range over which components of your image are acceptably sharp. In general, being able to control the amount of depth-of-field is a good thing, because having more or less depth-of-field gives you creative control over what is sharp and what is not. You might prefer to zero in on a specific subject and let everything else remain blurry. Or you might want to have everything in your frame as sharp as possible.

To understand how dSLR cameras give you more control over depth-of-field, you need to understand the three factors that control this range, which I outline in Table 1-1.

Table 1-1	How Depth-of-Field Affects Photos
Factor	*How It Affects a Photo*
The distance between the camera and the ject subject	The closer your subject is to you, the greater the tendency for the objects in front or behind the sub- to be blurry.
The size of the lens opening (the *f-stop* or *aperture*) used to take the picture	Larger f-stops (smaller numbers), such as f2 or f4, produce less depth-of-field than smaller f-stops (larger numbers), such as f11 or f16. **Remember:** The size of the numbers are reversed because apertures are actually the denominators of fractions, so $\frac{1}{2}$ and $\frac{1}{4}$ are *larger* than $\frac{1}{11}$ or $\frac{1}{16}$.
The magnification (or *focal length*) of the lens	The shorter the focal length of the lens (say, 18mm or 20mm), the more depth-of-field is present. As the focal length grows longer (say, to 70mm or 100mm), depth-of-field shrinks.

Point-and-shoot digital cameras offer very little control over depth-of-field, because, unless you're shooting an extreme close-up (see Factor 1 in Table 1-1), virtually everything is in sharp focus (despite Factor 2). This condition (which can be a bad thing if you're trying to use focus selectively) is due to Factor 3: Non-SLRs use that tiny sensor, which calls for lenses of a much shorter focal length.

So, a point-and-shoot digital camera might have a 7.5mm to 22.5mm 3X zoom lens that provides a slightly wide-angle to slightly telephoto field of view. A digital SLR with the largest (24 x 36mm) sensor might need a 35mm to 105mm zoom to provide the same perspective.

Yet, depth-of-field is dependent on the *actual* focal length, not the equivalent. So that point-and-shoot camera's lens, even at its longest telephoto position, provides more depth-of-field than the dSLR's same-perspective zoom at its widest angle. So much is in focus with a non-SLR digital camera that, in practice, you have very little control over depth-of-field, except when shooting close-up pictures from very short distances.

Even if you're shooting relatively close with a point-and-shoot camera, as in Figure 1-5, judging and using depth-of-field can be tricky. The house in the background is too sharp, and because this particular digicam didn't have great close-up capabilities, the ice-covered berries in the foreground aren't sharp enough. Shooting the same scene minutes later with a dSLR equipped with a macro lens shows how control over depth-of-field can be used creatively to isolate a subject (see Figure 1-6).

Figure 1-5: A point-and-shoot yields too much depth-of-field.

Figure 1-6: A digital SLR makes it easy to isolate a subject with creative application of blur.

Because of the longer focal lengths mandated by the dSLR's larger sensors, these cameras offer the photographer an important creative tool.

In Chapter 6, I explain depth-of-field in more detail.

Taking photos faster

Everything about a digital SLR seems to work more quickly and responsively. That's important when you want to make a grab shot on the spur of the moment, or expect the camera to take an action photo *right now* when you press the shutter release at the peak moment. Most point-and-shoot digital cameras are downright sluggardly compared to dSLRs when it comes to performance. You can find improved speed in three key areas, which I explain in the following sections.

Wake-up time

A non-SLR digicam that can be powered up and ready to snap its first photo in as little as 2 seconds is considered fast. Many take 3 to 4 seconds to emerge from their slumber. Worse, because they consume so much power, these cameras go into stand-by mode or shut off completely if you don't take a picture for 30 to 60 seconds.

When you flip the power switch of a dSLR, the camera is usually ready to take the picture before you can move the viewfinder up to your eye. Some are ready to go in 0.2 of a second! Digital SLRs don't need to go to sleep, either, because they consume so little power when not in active use. I've left dSLRs switched on for days at a time with little perceptible draining of the battery. Certainly, the autofocus and autoexposure mechanisms go on standby a few seconds after you move your finger from the shutter release, but they're available again instantly with a quick tap on the button.

Shot-to-shot time

Conventional digital cameras have limits on how quickly you can take pictures in succession. Unless you're using the motor-drive-like _burst_ mode, one shot every second or two is about all you can expect. Even in burst mode, you'll be lucky to get much more than about one frame per second for 5 to 11 shots, max.

Digital SLRs have large amounts of built-in memory that temporarily stores each photo you snap before the camera transfers it to your memory card at high speed. You can probably take pictures in single-shot mode as quickly as you can press the shutter release, and for at least 8 to 10 shots before a slight pause kicks in. With faster dSLRs and some quality level settings, you can often keep taking pictures for as long as your finger (or memory card) holds out.

A dSLR's burst mode can capture 3 to 8 frames per second for 12 to 30 shots, depending on the speed of the camera and the quality level you've chosen (see Figure 1-7). No point-and-shoot camera comes anywhere close to that level of performance.

Shutter lag

When I've spoken before groups promoting my other books, such as _Digital Photography All-in-One Desk Reference For Dummies_ (Wiley Publishing, Inc.), the number-one question I get from new digital photographers is "What can I do about shutter lag!!?" This pause that distresses — between the moment you click and the moment the sensor captures a slightly different image — seems to be the thing that digicam owners like the _least_ about their shooters.

Digital SLRs experience shutter lag, too, but it's likely to be so brief — on the order of 0.1 to 0.2 of a second — that you never notice it. That's true only _most_ of the time, of course. Point your lens at a difficult-to-focus subject, such as the sky, or try to take a photo under low light, and your speedy autofocus lens might hunt back and forth while you gnash your teeth in frustration. (You discover some ways around this in Chapter 5.)

Figure 1-7: Digital SLRs make high-speed action sequences easy.

A dSLR works like a camera

Another reason why digital SLRs have improved performance is that they're easier to use, so you, as the photographer, can work faster as you shoot. Most point-and-shoot cameras have to be configured for consumers who are more interested in grabbing a quick snapshot than investing some artistry in creating a photograph.

Moreover, point-and-shoot cameras tend to be designed by an engineer who did a really, really good job adding photo capabilities to the vendor's cell phone line last year, and who obviously *must* be the best choice to cobble together a full-fledged digital camera. So, like a cell phone, non-SLR digital cameras tend to have most of the controls tucked away out of sight in the menu system where the average consumer never has to see them, and where the photo enthusiast has to hunt for them.

Digital SLRs, on the other hand, are always designed by a team of engineers with extensive photographic experience. They know which controls are essential and which can be buried away in the menus because you access them when setting up the camera and maybe once a month (if that) thereafter.

Digital SLR designers know that you don't want to go three levels deep into a menu to set the ISO sensitivity or adjust white (color) balance for the type of illumination you're using. You want to press an ISO or a WB (white balance) key and dial in the setting without giving it much thought. You don't want to activate an on-screen display to set shutter speed or aperture — you want to have separate dials for each. Nature intended zooming and manual focusing to be done by twisting a ring on the lens — not by pressing a little lever and letting a motor adjust the lens at its own pace.

Simply having a camera that operates like a camera instead of a VCR will make your picture-taking much easier and faster.

Getting more lens flexibility

With non-SLRs, the lens mounted on the camera is the one you use. Some models have add-on telephoto and wide-angle attachments, but those accessories tend to subtract a bit of sharpness even while they change the camera's viewpoint.

So point-and-shoot camera owners must decide at the time they buy the camera what kind of pictures they intend to shoot. If they want to take a lot of photos indoors or of architecture outdoors, they might need cameras with the equivalent of a film camera's 24mm wide-angle lens. (And if they need something even wider, they're probably out of luck.) Or, perhaps a photographer wants to shoot sports and would like a lens that's the equivalent of a 400mm lens on a film camera. Those are available, too, although not, generally, with cameras that also have wide-angle capabilities.

Digital SLR camera owners have fewer limitations. I own a 12–24mm zoom that's the equivalent of an 18mm to 36mm wide-angle lens. Other lenses I own cover every single focal length up to 500mm (750mm equivalent). I have two lenses designed especially for close-up photography and others with fast f1.8 apertures that are perfect for low-light sports shooting. I've far from exhausted the possibilities, either: Longer and wider lenses than what I own are available, along with specialized optics that do tasks such as canceling sharpness-robbing vibration caused by a photographer's unsteady hand.

Owners of dSLR cameras don't have to mortgage their homes to buy these lenses, either. Camera vendors offer some very sharp-fixed focal length lenses (*prime* lenses) for around $100. A versatile 28mm to 200mm zoom that I bought cost roughly $300. Because dSLRs can often use lenses designed for their film camera counterparts, hundreds of inexpensive used lenses are available, too. With a non-dSLR, if you want to expand your lens horizons, you frequently have to buy a new camera. You find out more about selecting lenses in Chapter 6.

Freeing yourself from image editors

Digital SLRs do more than change how you *take* pictures. They change how you *make* pictures, as well. Perhaps you're a seasoned image editor, accustomed to cropping images in Photoshop or Photoshop Elements to mimic the extreme telephoto perspective your previous camera couldn't duplicate. You might have used an image editor's Zoom Blur feature because your digicam's zoom lens didn't zoom fast enough to permit creating that effect in the camera, as shown in Figure 1-8. You've faked fish-eye lens effects because your camera didn't have a fish-eye lens, or you've manually added lens flare instead of trying to create the real thing.

Figure 1-8: Don't settle for fake zoom blur when you can have the real thing.

A closer look at shutter lag

Typically, the snapshooter can finally coax a niece or nephew into smiling, and press the shutter release to capture the moment. Or, a batter swings lustily at a fat pitch and lofts the game-winning run into the stands just as the photographer presses the shutter button. However, the crucial moment is never captured on pixels.

What happens instead is that the digicam's autofocus and autoexposure mechanisms make some last-minute adjustments, a bunch of electronic components process some algorithms, and, eventually, 2 or 3 seconds later (it seems), the camera takes the picture. This period of time is measured in *ohnoseconds,* ohnoseconds being the interval between when you *want* to take the picture and when you actually *hear* the shutter-click sound your camera emits. I've tested hundreds of digital cameras, and the actual elapsed time for non-SLRs ranges from 0.6 seconds to 1.2 seconds under bright, contrasty lighting conditions, or up to 1 to 2 seconds in dimmer lighting. It just *seems* even longer than that.

Or, you had to blur the background of your images in an image editor because your digital point-and-shoot camera always brought *everything* into sharp focus (an excellent trait when you *want* everything in focus, and not so great when you want to use focus selectively for creative effects).

Those limitations might be behind you now. A digital SLR can do lots of tricks that you had to fake in Photoshop in the past. Image editors are still helpful for some tweaks, as you discover in Chapters 11 and 12.

The Downsides That Don't Matter

Of course, the digital SLR isn't perfect — yet. I've found a couple downsides to using these *Wundermaschinen* that range from the annoying to the almost irrelevant. I address them in decreasing order of concern (at least for most photographers).

The lack or expense of super-wide lenses

Many high-end digital SLRs have sensors that are the same size as the 35mm film frame, so there are no equivalency factors to calculate. A 200mm lens provides the same magnification on a full-frame dSLR as it does on a film camera. More importantly, a 16mm or 14mm super-wide-angle lens retains its same wide field of view.

More affordable digital SLRs have smaller-than-full-frame sensors (more on *that* in Chapter 2), so the sensor crops the field of view of any lens you mount on the camera, to match the smaller sensor size. The *crop factor* ranges from 1.3 to about 2.0 for the current, er, crop of digital SLRs. In practice, that means that a 100mm telephoto lens mounted on one of these cameras will have the same field of view as a longer 130mm to 160mm telephoto lens on a 35mm film camera. Because you figure the effective field of view by multiplying the actual focal length by the crop factor, the figure is also sometimes called a *magnification factor*. That's inaccurate, because no magnification is taking place. The camera simply crops out part of what the lens sees. Your 100mm lens might *look* like it's been magically transformed into a longer 160mm optic, but the depth-of-field and other characteristics remain the same as the 100mm lens it really is.

Photographers who shoot sports and distant subjects love the crop factor, even though it gives them nothing they couldn't have achieved just by cropping a full-size frame. That's because the crop factor *seems* to provide a longer telephoto lens for the same money. The good news turns bad, however, when they mount 28mm wide-angle lenses on their beloved dSLRs and find they have the same field of view as a 45mm standard *(normal)* lens, or that their favorite 18mm super-wide lenses are now a 29mm ordinary wide-angle optics. (I use a 1.6 crop factor in all these examples.) In this case, you get a less wide view from a particular lens.

Fortunately, plenty of true wide-angle lenses are available for digital SLRs. Three different vendors offer 12–24mm super-wide zooms for my favorite dSLR, making it possible to shoot expansive shots like the one shown in Figure 1-9. Focal lengths down to 8mm to 10mm are available. None of these are particularly cheap. If you want to shoot wide and have a dSLR with a crop factor, prepare to spend a bit more money on lenses than you'd need to if you'd stuck to film.

On the positive side, however, most of these accessory lenses are considerably wider than the (current) widest-angle optics available for point-and-shoot cameras, which seem to get no wider than the equivalent of 24mm with a traditional film camera.

Fending off dirt and dust

For some dSLR owners, the bane of this category isn't the lack of wide-angle lenses, but the plethora of dust bunnies and odd particles of matter that seem to attach themselves to the camera's sensor at every opportunity.

Take extra care when changing lenses to keep dust from wending its way back to the sensor area (which is fully exposed only when you're taking a picture, anyway). You also need to know how to clean this dust off your sensor, a process that is much easier to do than it is to describe. You find out more about sensor cleaning in Chapter 4.

Figure 1-9: Panorama-like shots are possible with ultra-wide-angle lenses.

Some photographers have problems with dust seemingly on a weekly basis. Others go months without any infiltrations. Dirt and dust and digital SLRs might be a very small problem for you or loom larger, depending on your working habits, cleanliness, and willingness to stomp out a few artifacts from time to time in your image editor.

Working without an LCD preview

Non-SLR digital cameras are able to offer a live preview of the image as seen by the sensor prior to exposure. Almost all dSLRs can't provide such a preview because the mirror used to provide the optical view of the subject is in the way. It flips up just prior to exposure. A few oddball cameras from Olympus and Canon (you can find more about them in Chapter 2) use technologies such as dual sensors or a prism that splits incoming light into two paths (one for the sensor and one for the viewfinder). In most cases, however, when you use a dSLR, previewing images in an LCD viewer as well as the optical view just isn't possible.

You'll miss this feature in only a few cases. A digital SLR's larger optical viewfinder is usually a better choice for judging composition and depth-of-field and for framing fast-moving action. The following sections cover the key applications that *could* benefit from an LCD preview, if only your dSLR could display one on its back-panel LCD.

Live histograms stopped dead in their tracks

A *histogram* is a graph that displays the tonal range of an image and can be used to judge whether a photograph is or will be under- or overexposed. The trained eye can also see whether an image is likely to have excessive contrast or look particularly flat, based on the distribution of tones in a histogram.

You can make adjustments to lighting and exposure to improve the rendition of a shot. Lacking a live, real-time histogram that can be viewed prior to taking a picture (as found in most point-and-shoot digicams), the digital SLR owner must make these decisions after the fact and adjust for the next picture. You'll find more about the use of histograms in Chapter 5.

Déjà view with extended eye-points

The *eye-point* is the distance you can move the eye away from the viewfinder and still see all the image for framing. An extended eye-point is useful for sports and other applications where you want to keep an eye on what's happening outside the camera's viewfinder.

A live LCD preview lets you keep the camera a few inches from your face, or even at arm's length and still see what is going to be captured. Point-and-shoot digital cameras sometimes put the LCD on a swiveling mount so you can use it for framing with the camera held at waist level, overhead, or even facing you for a self portrait. Digital SLRs (except for a model from Olympus) don't have this kind of swivel LCD because they don't have the live preview that would make the capability useful.

Infrared imagery up to your imagination

Infrared photos call for a filter that blocks visible light. All you see through the optical viewfinder is a vast expanse of black, which makes framing your photo difficult. A live LCD preview would give you *some* type of image, at least.

Although this problem is annoying, you can work around it. Most people don't shoot infrared photos at all. Those who do find that exposures are so long, a tripod is a must. You have two options:

- Set up your camera on a tripod, frame your picture, and *then* mount the infrared filter.
- Frame the photo as best you can, take a shot, and then use the after-shot LCD review to make adjustments, as was done for Figure 1-10.

Neither solution is very satisfactory, but the lack of LCD preview in this case is likely to be annoying only for those who take a great many infrared photos.

Figure 1-10: You can't preview infrared shots in a dSLR's optical viewfinder, so the photographer often shoots blind.

Carrying that weight

With the exception of some tiny models from Pentax/Samsung and a few other vendors, digital SLRs are bigger, heavier, and clunkier than pocket-sized point-and-shoot digital cameras. The more you spend on a dSLR, the bigger it's likely to be, too, because vendors offer magnesium alloy bodies instead of the composite plastic used for entry-level digital SLRs. Tack on extra battery packs and special grips that let you shoot more comfortably in a vertical position, and the camera becomes even larger.

This "problem" is an annoyance only to someone who needs to travel light. For most photographers, the whole point of upgrading to a digital SLR is to gain access to the extra lenses and accessories that these cameras can use. The extra heft is part of the cost of the greater versatility. Many dSLR owners also purchase small point-and-shoot cameras to carry when weight and size are important to them.

Budding Spielbergs are out of luck

Most point-and-shoot digital cameras can capture motion picture clips with monaural sound. Many offer only poor quality clips at, say, a herky-jerky 10 or 15 frames per second (fps) instead of the standard 30 fps, and resolutions are as low as 320-x-240 or 160-x-120 pixels. You might be limited to 30- or 60-second clips, tops. Higher-end, non-SLR digital cameras might give you virtually TV-quality 640-x-480 resolution at 30 fps with decent sound, and recording times as long as the available capacity of your memory card. You can even find in-camera trimming and editing facilities.

Because a dSLR's mirror can't flip up and down 30 times a second, you won't find motion picture capabilities on any dSLR that I am aware of. That doesn't bother me. If I want to shoot digital movies, I take along a digital video (DV) camcorder. If I just want a few clips, I tote an old 5-megapixel digicam that shoots 640-x-480 clips up to 120 seconds long. Few people decide *against* buying a digital SLR because they can't also shoot movies with it.

Safari Inside a dSLR

*I*f digital photography is the greatest thing since sliced bread, the digital SLR is the toaster — a no-nonsense device that anyone can use to create tasty results. Even so, you can get better results if you know a little about how your favorite gadget works. You don't need to understand Ohm's law to make breakfast, but it's a good idea to understand a little about a toaster's innards before you poke a fork inside. In the same vein, understanding pixels and lenses and sensors can help you get better results from your photographic appliance.

This chapter takes you on a safari through the darkest recesses of the digital SLR to give you a little knowledge about how it works before you decide to poke a figurative fork inside.

Megapixels and Why dSLRs Have More of Them

If you've been working with digital images for a while, you know that pixels are your pals. They're the basic building blocks that make up an image. The term pixel is a *portmanteau,* a new word created by combining two old words, such as slimy and lithe to create *slithy.* In this case, pixel stands for *picture element* and came into vogue as computer imaging became popular.

However, you've seen pixel-like components outside the digital realm, in pointillist paintings, such as the illustrations Georges Seurat created for the Broadway musical, *Sunday in the Park with George.* You also see pixel-like components in newspaper halftone photos. All these are made up of tiny dots that you can see vividly up close, but those dots blend to create continuous tones and colors when you view them from a distance, as you can see in Figure 2-1. The difference between these picture elements and those used to represent digital photos is that the digital variety are all the same size and shape, varying only in brightness and hue.

In digital images, the pixels — tiny squares that can be seen individually only under magnification — are arranged in rows and columns like a checkerboard that happens to measure hundreds of squares on a side. Among current digital SLRs, this array is a minimum of 2,464 pixels wide and 1,632 pixels tall, for a total of 4.3 million pixels in all. The latest digital SLR cameras for consumers might offer 3,008 x 2,000 (6.1 million pixels) to 3,456 x 2,304 (8 million), but "pro" cameras go up to 4,288 x 2,848 (12 million) and 4,992 x 3,328 (16.6 million). That's a lot of pixels!

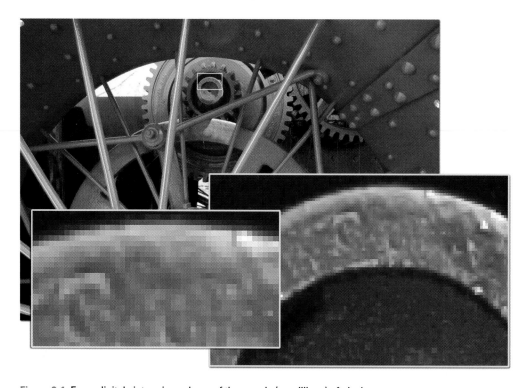

Figure 2-1: Every digital picture is made up of thousands (or millions) of pixels.

Those counts represent the number of light-sensitive areas in the digital camera's sensor, and the total is usually expressed in terms of *megapixels* (millions of pixels), and abbreviated MP. The precise dimensions might vary depending on the exact sensor used. For example, the Nikon D70s and D50 and the Konica Minolta Maxxum 7D and 5D use a 3,008-x-2,000-pixel sensor, but the original Canon Digital Rebel had a 3,072-x-2,048-pixel array. All three are considered 6MP dSLRs, even though the arrangement and number of pixels is slightly different.

Pixelementary, my dear Watson

Pixels, represented by individual light-sensitive areas in a sensor called *photosites,* are what capture the detail in your image. In general terms, the more megapixels the better, because as you add pixels, the ability of the sensor to capture more detail improves, and the effective *resolution* of the sensor rises.

It's like dividing a foot-long ruler into 1,200 increments rather than 120. In the former case, the ruler could measure things with $\frac{1}{100}$ of an inch accuracy; in the latter, the rulings could be used only in $\frac{1}{10}$ of an inch chunks. In the same vein, a sensor of a particular size with 12MP can show much finer detail than one the same size with only 6MP.

 As you can see in Figure 2-2, as the size of the pixels decrease, more of them can fit on a sensor to capture ever smaller details of the original image. However, there is more to image quality than resolution alone. Many 6MP dSLRs produce sharper and more noise-free results than 8MP non-dSLRs simply because the 6MP dSLR's sensors are physically larger, and each individual pixel is better. Some dSLRs even outperform other dSLRs with more resolution because of the quality of the sensors, lenses, or electronic circuitry. The raw number of megapixels is only a guide-line, even though more pixels is quite often better.

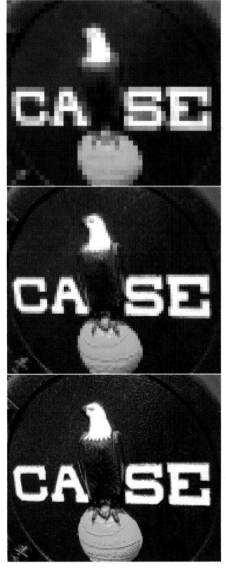

Figure 2-2: More pixels mean sharper images.

Deciding how many pixels your camera needs

People contemplating the purchase of a digital SLR often agonize over how many megapixels they should buy, even though other factors, such as ease of operation and the kind and quality of lenses available for a particular dSLR can be considerably more important in the long run.

Although more pixels usually equals more resolution and more detail in your pictures, the number of pixels you actually need depends on several factors:

- **How you'll be using the photo:** An image placed on a Web site or displayed in presentations doesn't need to have the same resolution as one that will be used professionally, say, as a product advertisement or a magazine illustration.

- **How much manipulating and cropping you plan to do:** If you'll be giving your images quite a workout in Photoshop or if you often crop small sections out of images to create new perspectives, you want all the spare pixels you can muster, because higher resolution images can withstand more extensive editing without losing quality.

- **How much you plan to enlarge the image:** Many people view most of their images on a computer display or in 4-x-6-inch to 5-x-7-inch prints. Any dSLR has enough megapixels for those modest applications. If you're looking to make blowups bigger than 8 x 10 inches, say, to make posters or prints displayed on the wall, you need a plethora of pixels.

- **The resolution of your printer:** Most digital images are printed on inkjet or dye sublimation devices with their own resolution specifications, usually from 200 dots per inch (dpi) to 300 dpi and beyond. Printers work best with images that more closely match their own ability to print detail.

If you primarily want to create prints, the following section can help you gauge which capabilities you need in your camera and printer so that you can get the best output possible.

Matching pixels to print sizes and printers

If nice-looking prints are important to you, you need to pay as much attention to your printer as the number of pixels in your digital SLR. In truth, printers with lower resolution don't benefit much from digital shots with high megapixel counts. They might produce *worse* results because they're forced to discard lots of that precious detail to squeeze the picture information into their available output pixels. You need a printer with lots of resolution to do the best job with a high-resolution photo.

Calculating the appropriate resolution for a particular printer/image size combination is easy. Just follow these simple steps:

1. **Multiply the printer resolution by the desired width of your image to get the number of pixels you need for an image that wide.**

   For example, if I have a 300 dpi printer and want an 8-x-10-inch print, $300 \times 8 = 2{,}400$ pixels.

2. **Multiply the printer resolution by the desired height of your image.**

   So, $300 \times 10 = 3{,}000$ pixels.

3. **Multiply the width in pixels by the height to get the number of pixels you need.**

   Keeping with my example, $2{,}400 \times 3{,}000 = 7{,}200{,}000$.

4. **Divide the total number of pixels by 1 million to get the number of megapixels your camera needs to collect for the print.**

   Technically, that's 7.2 megapixels in my case, but a ballpark figure of 6 megapixels will do. (The 6MP camera can hold as many as 3,000 x 2,000 pixels, which gives you a 6.67-x-10-inch print, so you can reasonably assume that a 6MP image is just about ideal for a print in the 8-x-10-inch neighborhood.)

Using an image of this same resolution (2,400 x 3,000 pixels), you can print in other sizes, of course, but your printer or the software that drives it must drop or add pixels by using a process called *interpolation,* also called *resampling,* which applies intricate computer calculations to come up with a reasonably good-looking representation of your original image at a different size.

✓ **Adding pixels (or *upsampling*):** Figure 2-3 shows you a highly simplified example of how new pixels are calculated from existing pixels during interpolation. In this case, *upsampling* is taking place; the two original pixels, one black and one white, are used to interpolate intermediate gray pixels. In sophisticated interpolation schemes, pixels in the rows above and below the original pixels and the actual colors of the pixels are also taken into account.

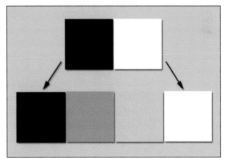

Figure 2-3: Software sees a black and a white pixel and guesses that gray pixels are needed between them.

✓ **Dropping pixels (or *downsampling*):** This is basically the same process as upsampling, but in reverse. Based on calculations by the software, some pixels are deleted to create the smaller image size.

Table 2-1 shows the nominal print sizes without the need for interpolation, for various camera resolutions at three different common print resolutions.

Table 2-1		Print Sizes at Various Resolutions		
Resolution	Megapixels	Print Size at 200 dpi (Inches)	Print Size at 300 dpi (Inches)	Print Size at 600 dpi (Inches)
3,008 x 2,000	6MP	15.0 x 10.0	10.0 x 6.7	5.0 x 3.3
3,456 x 2,304	8MP	17.3 x 11.5	11.5 x 7.7	5.8 x 3.8
4,256 x 2,848	12.1MP	21.3 x 14.2	14.2 x 9.5	7.1 x 4.7
4,536 x 3,024	13.7MP	22.7 x 15.1	15.1 x 10.1	7.6 x 5.0
4,992 x 3,328	16.6MP	25.0 x 16.6	16.6 x 11.0	8.3 x 5.5

These native print sizes represent only the dimensions you can get without interpolation. In practice, digital SLR cameras are capable of producing much larger prints with very little noticeable loss of quality. A 6–8MP camera should give you 11-x-14- to 16-x-20-inch prints that look great; a 12–16MP camera should be good for 20-x-30-inch enlargements and beyond.

Nothing's super about superfluous pixels

If you think you can never be too rich, too thin, or have too many megapixels, think again. There's a dark side, too, Luke. Unnecessary pixels lead to bigger image files, which are great when you actually need all those pixels, but a potential nuisance at other times. Few people have the problem of being able to afford a camera with a resolution significantly higher than we really need, but if you're in that elite class, consider these caveats:

- **Excess megapixels eat up your memory cards.** All dSLRs store images on solid-state memory cards. I own three cards for my 6MP camera, each of which can store about 100 pictures in the best high-resolution shooting mode. Most of the time, that's plenty of digital "film" for any day's shooting, and I can always drop back to a lower resolution mode to stretch my memory cards further. However, if I were using the same vendor's top-of-the-line dSLR, each of those cards would hold no more than an old-fashioned 36-exposure roll of film. I'd have to own a lot more memory cards to do the same work!

- **Extra resolution taxes your computer.** Fatter photo files take longer to transfer to your computer and call for faster processing speeds and extra memory to manipulate them in your image editor. That high-end digital camera you're lusting after might call for a high-end computer, too.

- **More pixels need more storage.** Very high-resolution files can be several times larger than your run-of-the-mill high-resolution image files. If you want to keep lots of them available on your hard drive, you need a large disk, and probably lots of extra CDs and DVDs to archive them to for permanent storage.

Touring Through a Digital SLR

Now is the time to explore the innards of your digital SLR as a way to better understand how to use all the nifty features your digital shooter includes. At best, these sections give you a better handle on why, sometimes, the results you get when you press the shutter release aren't exactly what you expected. At worst, you can find more convincing excuses to give when you goof.

In some ways, the basics of a dSLR have a lot in common with the conventional film SLR, or indeed, any film camera. All these picture-grabbers share some fundamental components, which I list in the general order of their arrangement inside your camera, as shown in Figure 2-4:

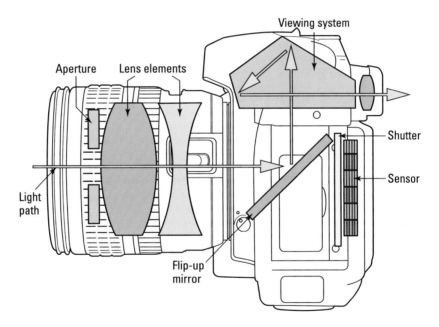

Figure 2-4: Components of a digital SLR.

✔ **A lens** — consisting of one or more optical components made of glass, plastic, or ceramic — which captures light and gathers it to a point of focus inside the camera.

✔ **A viewing system** that lets you see what the camera sees so you can compose your image and perform other functions such as evaluating depth-of-field.

✔ **An aperture,** or opening, inside the lens that you can (usually) adjust in size so that more or less light is able to sneak through into the camera.

✔ **A shutter or other mechanism** to control how long the light passing through the lens can expose the film or sensor.

✔ **A light-sensitive component,** either film or — with digital cameras — the sensor, which captures the illumination admitted through the lens by the aperture for the time duration allowed by the shutter.

✔ **A medium for storing the captured image** until it is removed from the camera. With a film camera, that medium is the film itself. For a digital camera, the storage is a solid-state film card.

Some of these components for film and digital cameras, especially lenses, are very similar. Indeed, many digital SLRs can use the same lenses built for their film counterparts. So, in this guided tour of the dSLR, I concentrate on the pieces and parts that are different. In the sections that follow, I explain each component listed here.

Sensorship

After a night on the town, you might find in the morning that you're extra sensitive to light. Well, a digital SLR's sensor is like that all the time. When exposed to an incoming stream of the light-bits called *photons,* a solid-state sensor scoops them up into little buckets, with one bucket for each pixel (except for certain Fujifilm cameras, which I describe in the sidebar, "Three exceptional sensor exceptions").

If each bucket, or *photosite,* collects enough photons to partially fill it to an imaginary line (called its *threshold*) seen as a line on the side of the bucket in Figure 2-5, that pixel registers something other than black. As more and more photons accumulate, the pixel's value gets lighter and lighter until, when the bucket is full, the pixel is deemed to be completely white. The intermediate tones are registered as grays or, in color pictures, as darker or lighter shades of a particular color.

If *too many* photons are dumped into the bucket, no further tonal changes happen to that pixel, but the excess light-bits can actually overflow to adjoining pixels, causing an unpleasant effect called *blooming.* After the exposure is completed, the bucket full of sloshing photons is converted to ice cubes. Well, not actually, but it might help to think of the process of analog (water) to digital (ice cubes) conversion that way. Your computer's bits and bytes can handle a discrete number of ice cubes (expressed in 1s and 0s) a lot more easily than it can work with an amorphous quantity of H_2O.

The bits are processed and then transferred to a memory card, making your camera ready to take another picture. All this can happen in $\frac{1}{2}$ to $\frac{1}{8}$ of a second or less (which explains why digital SLRs can take 2 to 8 or more pictures per second).

Figure 2-5: A photosite is like a bucket that collects photons.

Two (count 'em), two types of sensors

Two main types of sensors are used in digital SLRs today: CCD (charge-coupled device) and CMOS (complementary metal-oxide semiconductor) imagers. Although each type of sensor uses different technology to capture images, there is no inherent quality difference between them. Sony, Olympus, Nikon, and Pentax make great dSLRs based on CCD technology. In the CMOS camp are Canon and Sigma. With the introduction of the D2X, Nikon began exploring the CMOS arena as well. Note that while the Foveon sensor used in Sigma cameras is, in fact, a CMOS imager, it's of a special type that I describe in the nearby sidebar, "Three exceptional sensor exceptions."

Both CCD and CMOS imagers use metal-oxide semiconductors (although, apparently, the CMOS type is more complementary), and they have about the same degree of sensitivity to light. The main difference is in what each type sensor does with the light after capturing it:

> ✔ **The CCD sensor** is "dumb" to the extent that all it does is capture photons as electrical charges in each photosite/pixel. After exposure, the charges are swept off the chip to an amplifier located in one corner of the sensor. External circuitry converts the analog signal to digital form and handles storing it on your memory card.

✔ **A CMOS sensor,** theoretically, is a lot more complicated than its CCD counterpart. It includes solid-state circuitry at each and every photosite and is able to manipulate the data for each pixel right in the sensor. That's pretty cool because it gives the CMOS sensor the ability to respond to lighting conditions in ways that a CCD can't. However, sweeping all the photon information off a CMOS chip isn't necessary; every photosite can be accessed individually.

Piling on the components

Some interesting components are piled on top of both sensor types. These components include

✔ **Color filters,** which give the color-blind CCD and CMOS chips the ability to respond to various colors of light

✔ **Teensy microlenses** that focus the incoming light onto the photosensitive area in each photo site

✔ **A protective transparent layer** that might contain a special filter (called an *antialiasing filter*) that smooths out the incoming light signal by eliminating certain frequencies of light before they can clash

Only the color filters are likely to be of interest to the average digital photographer, because these filters make color photography possible. The sensors in dSLRs do a fairly good job of registering the brightness in a scene. However, these pixel grabbers are totally colorblind on their own.

So, each individual photosite is overlaid with a tiny color filter, as shown in Figure 2-6, that renders it sensitive *only* to a single primary color of light — either red, green, or blue. These colors can be combined to produce all the intermediate hues, such as yellow (red + green), cyan (green + blue), or magenta (blue + red). All three colors added together produce white. Your TV set and computer display use the same color system to show colors, and any image editor can manipulate them, which is highly convenient from the digital photographer's standpoint.

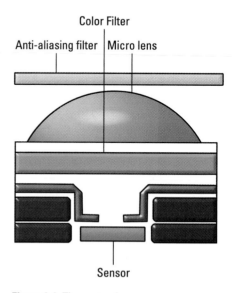

Figure 2-6: The parts of a sensor.

Three exceptional sensor exceptions

Although the majority of sensors on the market use the RGRGRG BGBGBG Bayer pattern (see the top half of the sidebar figure), a few exceptions totally mess up any attempt to generalize. These emerging technologies could fizzle out in the future . . . or blaze a trail for exciting new ways to capture images.

For example, some Sony sensors depart from the RGB model to add a fourth color, a shade of blue-green that Sony calls *emerald.* This RGB+E sensor technology (see the bottom half of the sidebar figure) supposedly deals with one quirk of human vision that changes the way we see certain red colors. The sensor contains 25 percent each of red, green, blue, and emerald photosites, and, most of the time, the emerald pixels respond more or less like the green ones to give the same overall effect. However, the camera can use the additional information gathered to correct those maverick red colors when they pop up.

Foveon has developed a special kind of CMOS imager that doesn't use the Bayer filter pattern at all. Instead, it has three separate photosensitive layers, one each for blue, green, and red (stacked in that order). During exposure, each pixel absorbs the blue light first (if present), then green, and finally red as the photons work their way through the layers. No interpolation is required, and each color of light can be detected by each and every pixel. Although Foveon technology sounds pretty cool (and it is!), some kinks still need to be worked out, not the least of which is that the highest-resolution Foveon sensors to date have only about 3.3MP of resolution. You could argue that 3.3MP without interpolation equals 10MP with interpolation, but that isn't necessarily the case.

Fujifilm stirs up the pot with its SuperCCD SR sensor, which uses two octagon-shaped photosites per pixel to capture images. One is relatively large and highly sensitive to light over a relatively narrow range. If you use buckets as an analogy for sensors, these high-sensitive photosites are containers with a wide mouth but a fairly shallow depth, so they can capture only a few different levels of photons before they fill. However, Fuji mates each high-sensitivity photosite with a smaller one that is lower in sensitivity but which can capture copious different levels of light (think narrow mouth, deep container). The information from both photosites, which is arranged in the standard Bayer pattern, can be used to capture images with lots of detail in both the inky shadows, bright highlights, and everything in-between.

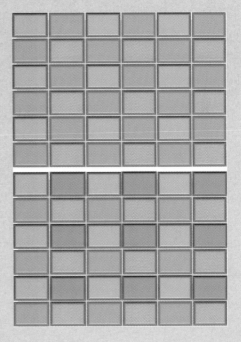

The (now) color-sensitive pixels are arranged in a matrix of alternate rows of red-blue-red-blue-red-blue photosites and blue-green-blue-green-blue-green photosites. Green gets twice as many pixels as each of the other two colors because of the way our eyes perceive color. (Humans are most sensitive to green light.) This arrangement is called a *Bayer pattern,* after the scientist who developed the process.

As you might guess, a green, red, or blue pixel might not be lucky enough to receive light colored its designated hue. So, the camera takes all the information and uses the color of surrounding pixels to calculate (or interpolate; there's that word again) the most likely true color of a particular picture element. With more than 6 million pixels to work with, this interpolation (called *demosaicing,* for any of you terminology nerds) generally provides a pretty good representation of the actual colors in a scene.

Understanding noise and sensitivity

You're driving along in your convertible with the top down, wind whistling in your ears, and the radio playing some cool tunes. This is pretty great, but it would be even better if you could *hear* the sounds coming out of the radio. So, you crank up the volume, only to find that you really can't hear the music much better. Welcome to the wonderful world of background noise. Unfortunately, digital photography has its own equivalent background noise.

In the digital camera realm, noise is what you get when you crank up the sensitivity of a sensor so it can capture the sparse population of photons that exist under dimmer lighting conditions. This sensitivity is measured in ISO settings, with ISO 800 being twice as sensitive as ISO 400, and ISO 400 having double the sensitivity of ISO 200.

When you amplify the signal created by actual photons striking the sensor, you also multiply the noise produced by random electrical charges generated in the sensor. At lower ISO settings, the sensor simply waits until a certain level of photons have been captured, and that number is enough to overpower the smaller number of random noise pixels.

In a digital camera, noise is worse at higher ISO settings; at longer exposures (because longer exposures provide more time for random pixels to be generated on their own); and in smaller pixels. I rhapsodize in Chapter 1 about how brilliant digital SLRs are at ignoring noise, chiefly because of their larger pixels, but remember that any digital camera is subject to this curse when you raise the ISO enough or take pictures with an exposure that is long enough.

Digital cameras can remove much of the noise caused by long exposures by taking a second, blank frame after the first picture is exposed, and then comparing the two. The camera can see which pixels appear in both versions and remove those that appear to be noise. Figure 2-7 shows a long exposure plagued with noise (left) and another interior photo in which the noise has been silenced with the dSLR's noise reduction feature.

Figure 2-7: Too much noise (left) and a much quieter photo (right).

You find more about noise reduction in Chapter 11.

The bits that control exposure

You need to understand the controls that adjust the exposure. What's exposure, you ask? A picture's exposure is nothing more than the amount of photons available for capture by the sensor. A good exposure requires exactly the right number of photons captured. Too few, and the image doesn't register at all. Too many photons, and the photo is overexposed.

As you might guess, if a lot of light is bouncing around a scene, a large number of photons can illuminate the sensor in a very brief time. If the light is dimmer, it might take longer for enough photons to reach the sensor. The important detail to remember is that for any given scene, an ideal exposure exists — one that provides just the right number of photos to capture the image.

Your digital SLR's exposure system is designed to improve your chances of getting that ideal exposure, either by adjusting the length of time the sensor is allowed to suck up photons or by modifying the number of photons that reach the sensor in any particular instant. You make these adjustments by using the camera's shutter speed and lens opening/aperture controls, which I describe in the following sections.

Your exposure time machine

Of course, in a digital SLR, the sensor isn't exposed to incoming light all the time. Instead, it sees photons for a brief interval, called the *exposure time,* usually measured in fractions of a second. The exposure time can extend for many seconds in the case of a *time exposure.*

The gatekeeper that controls these time slices, a sort of exposure-time machine, is called the shutter. The shutter can be a mechanical device (usually a curtain in front of the sensor that opens and closes very quickly) or an electronic mechanism that activates the sensor for a specific instant of time. Digital SLRs might have both, using a mechanical shutter for exposures measured in seconds from about $\frac{1}{180}$ to $\frac{1}{500}$ of a second and an electronic shutter for exposures in the $\frac{1}{500}$ to $\frac{1}{8,000}$ of a second range.

Longer shutter speeds let in more light but can produce blurring if the subject or camera move during the exposure. Shorter shutter speeds cut down the amount of light admitted, but they also reduce the chance that movement will cause blurriness.

An aperture is a lens opening is an f-stop

You can control photons by using the lens aperture (also called the *f-stop*). The aperture is the size of the opening through which the photons pass. You can think of an f-stop as a pipe: Larger pipes let more light flow in a given period of time, and smaller pipes restrict the amount of light that can pass. The aperture is a clever little adjustable mechanism that uses a sliding set of overlapping metal leaves to create an opening of the desired size, as shown in Figure 2-8.

To get the right amount of light for an exposure, you need to choose the right f-stop. And to choose the right f-stop, it helps to understand three confusing facts about f-stops:

Figure 2-8: Overlapping metal leaves create various sized lens openings.

- F-stops seem to be named wrong. That is, f2 is larger than f4, which is larger than f8. As the numbers get larger, the amount of light an aperture can admit gets *smaller*.

- F-stops don't seem to be properly proportioned. An f2 opening lets in four times as much light as f4, and f4 admits four times as much as f8. You'd think numbers like 2, 4, and 8 would represent double (or half) as much — not four times.

- F-stops use all these weird intermediate numbers that *do* represent halving and doubling the amount of light passed by the aperture. For example, between f2 and f4 is f2.8, which is exactly twice as large as f4, and half the size of f2. The actual sequence of f-stops, each half the size of the previous aperture, is this:

    f2, f2.8, f4, f5.6, f8, f11, f16, f22, f32

    What's going on here?

Everything becomes clear when you realize that f-numbers are actually denominators of fractions that represent the size of the aperture opening, just as ½, ¼, ⅛, or 1/16 represent ever-smaller quantities. So f11 allows your camera's sensor to collect more light than f16 because 1/11 is a bigger number than 1/16.

Two of one, half a dozen of the other

As far as the camera is concerned, f-stops and shutter speeds are equivalent. Cutting the shutter speed in half produces the same effect on exposure as using an f-stop that cuts the size of the lens opening in half. An exposure that is twice as long is the same as one exposed for the same length of time but with an f-stop that is twice as large.

So, if your camera's exposure system suggests an exposure of 1/500 of a second at f8, you could reduce the exposure to 1/1,000 of a second (half as long) at f8, or get the exact same exposure at 1/500 of a second at f11 (with the aperture half as wide).

Similarly, various combinations of f-stops and shutter speeds can produce the same exposure value. An exposure of 1/500 of a second at f8 is the same as 1/1,000 of a second at f5.6 (halving the shutter speed, but doubling the size of the lens opening), while 1/250 of a second at f11 (twice the shutter speed, but half the size of the lens opening) is the same, too. Although these reciprocal relationships might be confusing at first, they always seem natural after a few weeks using a camera.

Taking time out for viewing

Strictly speaking, your camera's viewfinder isn't part of the exposure process. It does have an important role, however, because the dSLR's viewing system is, with lens interchangeability, one of the reasons why people lust after these cameras in the first place.

Non-SLR digital cameras generally use an LCD on the back panel to provide a real-time image of what the sensor is seeing. This LCD view is often coupled with an optical viewfinder window that you can also use to frame the image, which is particularly handy under bright lighting conditions when the back-panel LCD is washed out. Some cameras, called EVF (electronic viewfinder) models (which might physically resemble dSLRs, even though their lenses can't be changed), have a second LCD inside, which you can view through a window. This EVF is easier to see in bright light.

Digital SLRs don't offer LCD previews in any form (except for a handful of specialized cameras). Instead, light admitted by the lens is bounced by a system of mirrors or prisms to a viewfinder window, making it possible to see exactly what the sensor will see. When it's time to take the picture, the mirror in a typical dSLR swings out of the way, blanking the viewfinder for a fraction of a second while the light is directed to the sensor to make the exposure.

Compared to the tiny LCD or optical view offered by non-SLRs, the big, bright optical display of a dSLR is easier to use to compose, evaluate focus, and judge how much of the image is actually sharp, as shown in Figure 2-9.

Figure 2-9: Digital SLR viewfinders show lots of information along with the big, bright view of your subject.

Through the looking glass

All cameras form their images by grabbing light through a lens, a series of precision-made elements of glass, plastic, or ceramic. The components are arranged to gather the light and focus it onto the film or sensor at a certain distance, called the *focal length*. Fixed-focal-length lenses, or *prime* lenses, always produce the same magnification. Other lenses have elements that can shift around in particular ways to change the magnification over a certain range. These are called *zoom* lenses. One of the coolest things about dSLRs is that you can remove a particular lens and replace it with one that provides a different zoom range or has other useful capabilities, such as the ability to focus extra close.

Inside the lens is a diaphragm that can dilate or contract, much like the iris of the eye, to change the size of the aperture. These f-stops not only control the amount of light reaching the sensor, but affect the amount of an image that is in focus. Smaller f-stops provide larger areas of focus (called *depth-of-field*), and larger f-stops offer a smaller sharp focus range.

The distance of the lens elements from the sensor also controls the overall focus of the picture. You can adjust focus manually by twisting a ring on the barrel of the lens itself, or automatically by using tiny motors inside the lens. Some lenses have additional motors that move the elements in response to camera shake or movement, producing a useful vibration reduction or image stabilization effect. I explain more special lens features in Chapter 3.

Storage

The very first electronic cameras of 30 years ago stored images on tape recorders! Fifteen years later, the $30,000 digital cameras that a few daring professional photographers used stored images on a bulky hard drive that had to be tethered to the camera by a cable. Today, you're much better off because you can use tiny solid-state devices called *flash memory* to store your photos until you can transfer them to a computer for permanent archiving. A dSLR's storage has two components you want to be aware of:

- ✔ **The buffer:** Your digital SLR takes the bits siphoned out of the sensor and conducts them to a special high-speed type of internal memory called a *buffer*. Thanks to the buffer, you're able to continue taking photos while the camera deals with transferring the most recent pictures to the film card.

  The size and speed of the buffer determines how many pictures you can take in a row. Digital cameras generally let you take 5 to 30 shots consecutively, and have continuous shot *(burst)* modes good for 2.5 to 8 frames per second for as long as the buffer holds out. A faster, larger buffer is better.

✒ **Memory card:** Memory cards have their own writing speed, which determines how quickly the card can accept images from the buffer. There's no standard measurement for this speed, so you can find memory cards labeled 40X, 80X, Ultra, or Extreme.

Most of the time, however, card speed limits your shooting only if you're photographing sports and want to take many pictures in a row. The rest of the time your dSLR is probably a lot faster than your trigger finger.

Digital SLRs today generally use either CompactFlash (CF) or Secure Digital (SD) memory cards, shown in Figure 2-10. They are mostly equivalent in speed, cost, and capacity, although SD cards are smaller than their CF counterparts. You'll also find miniature hard disk drives using the CompactFlash form factor.

Figure 2-10: Secure Digital cards (left) aren't all that secure, and CompactFlash cards (right) aren't compact.

Overcoming Quirks of the dSLR

If you're entering the digital SLR world from the realms of film cameras or non-SLR digital photography, you'll note some significant differences that can only be called quirks. They are idiosyncrasies of the dSLR that you must compensate for or grudgingly put up with. Some might even drive you crazy. The following sections offer some advice for contending with these quirks.

Out, out damned spot: Cleaning the sensor

Every time you remove your dSLR's lens to replace it with another, you could be admitting tiny specks of dust that might, if you're unlucky, find their way past the shutter when it opens for an exposure, and thence onto the sensor. It might take a few weeks or a few months, but eventually, you're going to end up with artifacts on your sensor.

You might not even notice this dust because it's most apparent when using the small f-stops that produce the largest range of sharp focus. (I explain why in "The bits that control exposure," earlier in this chapter.) If you take most of your pictures at f8, f5.6, or larger, any dust on your sensor might be blurry and almost invisible. In addition, if the dark dust spots happen to fall into dark areas of your image, they'll be masked.

So, if you own a digital SLR, you can plan on the need to clean your sensor from time to time. It's not particularly difficult, and cleaning kits are available at camera stores and online. Some tips to remember include:

✐ Point your camera downward when changing lenses to reduce the amount of dust that infiltrates.

✐ If possible, change lenses only in relatively clean environments.

✐ Do not attempt to clean your sensor with canned air, compressed air blowers, lens cleaning liquids, or other methods that seem to make sense, but which can damage your sensor. Bulb blowers and swabs intended expressly for sensor cleaning should be used.

✐ If you have any doubts about your ability to clean your sensor yourself, let your local camera shop or the manufacturer to it.

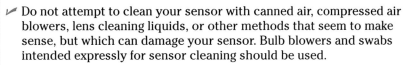

Multiplication fables: Working around the crop factor

Many digital SLR cameras use a sensor that is smaller than the 35mm film frame, even though they typically use lenses that were originally designed for full-frame cameras. The smaller sensor, in effect, crops out part of the image, so you're using only, say, 75 percent of the area produced, as shown in Figure 2-11. When you use a 100mm lens, say, only the center area is imaged by a smaller sensor, capturing an image with the same field of view as a 150mm lens.

This effect is sometimes called, inaccurately, a *multiplication factor* or lens *multiplier* because you can represent the equivalent field of view by multiplying the focal length of the lens by the factor. In truth, no multiplication is involved. A 100mm f2.8 lens used on a camera with a 1.5 multiplier is still a 100mm f2.8 lens and provides the exact same image. It's just being cropped down to a smaller rectangle by the camera. The correct terminology is *crop factor*. Common crop factors with today's dSLRs are 1.3X, 1.5X, 1.6X, and 2X.

The crop factor affects your picture-taking in two ways:

✐ **Your telephoto lenses seem to be magically converted to much longer focal lengths.** A 200mm telephoto lens becomes a 300mm telephoto lens; a 400mm-long lens is transformed into a 600mm super telephoto lens. Of course, your results would be identical to those you'd get taking the same picture with a full-frame camera and cropping the image, but it's a convenient fable even so.

✍ **The view of wide-angle lenses is cropped so that they no longer take
in as much of your surroundings as they would on a full-frame camera.**
A nice, super-wide 20mm lens on a camera with a 1.6X crop factor has
the same field of view as an ordinary 32mm wide-angle lens. A useful
35mm wide-angle lens view, like the one shown at upper left in Figure
2-11, becomes the mundane 56mm normal lens perspective, shown at
lower right. The crop factor means that, to get a true wide-angle view,
you have to purchase expensive, ridiculously wide lenses, such as the
popular 12mm–24mm lenses offered by Nikon, Sigma, and Tokina.

Figure 2-11: A wide-angle shot (upper left) loses its wide perspective due to the 1.5X crop factor
(lower right).

3

Tracking the Ideal dSLR

*W*hen you upgrade from your first digital camera to a digital SLR, the stakes increase dramatically. A dSLR generally costs quite a bit more than any point-and-shoot digital camera, so you want to make the right purchase the first time. You also want to buy into a camera product line that has all the accessories you'll want to buy in the future. Owning a very cool digital single lens reflex is little comfort if you can't find that special external electronic flash you need, or an underwater housing you absolutely must have.

The high stakes extend into the future, too. The dSLR you buy now will grow as you add lenses and other accessories, and you'll want to use those same add-ons with whatever camera eventually replaces your current pride and joy. SLR camera buyers have known for years that it's easy to get locked into a particular camera system, so selecting the right camera today is a little like choosing a spouse. If the photographic marriage doesn't last forever, starting over with a new mate can be expensive and full of heartache.

This chapter helps you choose your ideal dSLR now and ensures your future happiness.

Features for Now and the Future

Some have said that once, in the 1950s, a world-famous photographer was preparing to shoot a portrait of an important business executive. The captain of industry watched him set up and made conversation by observing proudly, "I see you use a Leica. So do I." Cracking a faint smile, the famed lensman replied, "I see your secretary uses a Royal typewriter. So does Hemingway."

The best camera in the world can produce mediocre pictures in the hands of a clumsy photographer. Conversely, a creative mind can produce stunning images when armed with the simplest of cameras. Figure 3-1 is far from a stunning photograph, but I took it with a $200 point-and-shoot camera and a pair of $10 high-intensity desk lamps for illumination. I didn't use any fancy close-up or macro lenses. You don't need an expensive camera to take good pictures.

Figure 3-1: A $200 camera took this photo. An expensive camera isn't a prerequisite for creative photography.

Of course, you don't have to tie one hand behind your back to make sure you concentrate on composition and capturing the decisive moment. So, consider the full range of available features when choosing your camera, recognizing that you might not be able to justify all of them right now. Divide the features you're considering into these three categories:

✏ **Features you need:** These are the capabilities you really must have for the kind of photography you do. Perhaps you shoot in low light levels and require a fast lens that lets you grab images without flash. Or, you specialize in sports photography and must have a dSLR with a 3–4 fps shooting rate or better. If you plan to shoot a lot of time-lapse photography, you probably want a camera that can take pictures while tethered to a laptop computer. Make a list of your must-have features and keep them in mind when searching for your ideal camera.

✏ **Features you want:** These are the features that aren't absolutely essential for the majority of your photography, but which could come in handy, or which might expand your picture-taking opportunities. Odds are, you'll consider how much extra you have to pay to get these features. You might want to take wildlife photos without a tripod, so the availability of long lenses with built-in image stabilization features could be nice. Still, if you can't afford such a lens, you could probably get by almost as well with a good tripod (despite the extra weight to lug around). Your nice-to-have features won't be deal-breakers, but they can tilt your preferences from one camera line to another.

✏ **Features you wish you could get, but can't (yet):** A few capabilities are totally out of your reach either because they're too expensive or not available for the camera models you're considering. Deposit these features in the What Ifs category: These features just might filter down to you someday — perhaps more quickly than you think. Perhaps you'd like image stabilization built into the camera itself so that just about every lens you own gains anti-shake capabilities. If that's what you want, you'll find it in an increasing number of cameras, including Sony Alpha and Pentax models.

Breadcrumbs on the Upgrade Path

The ability to upgrade your dSLR in the future can be tempting, like alluring breadcrumbs sprinkled on the path through the dark woods of the future. You can plan now to make sure these crumbs haven't been gobbled up by the time you choose to add to your own dSLR system.

TIP

The following tips can help you choose a camera with great upgrade potential:

- **Look at how particular vendors have handled the evolution of their lens systems as they've added features.** The Pentax line of dSLRs is capable of using KA and K mount lenses, older Pentax screw-mount lenses dating back decades, and even some lenses intended for medium format cameras if you have the proper adapter. The latest Nikon dSLRs can use virtually any Nikkor lens dating back to 1959, although some require slight modifications. Of course, automatic metering and focusing aren't possible in all cases for either Pentax or Nikon lenses built before these features were invented! While all Canon EF-series lenses work fine with any EOS camera (film or digital), the company's EF-S-series lenses must be used only on the latest consumer-oriented dSLR Canon models, such as the EOS 20D/30D or later, and the Digital Rebel/Rebel XT/Rebel XTi.

- **Explore how well a vendor supports its older model cameras and flash units.** Vendors are continually improving their dedicated electronic flash units. As a result, the latest speedlights might not be compatible with newer or future cameras. Some might not function with full through-the-lens metering, but can be operating in semi-automatic modes with exposure-measuring cells built into the flash itself. Others might not be usable in wireless mode without special adapters. For details on using electronic flash, see Chapter 9.

- **Figure out which filter size will fit the most lenses.** This is especially true before making an investment in polarizers, infrared filters, and close-up lenses that can be fairly expensive. A film SLR I worked with for many years used the same size filter on nearly all its lenses, so I could safely buy as many of these screw-on accessories as I wanted. I knew they wouldn't become obsolete when I added a new lens. Today, vendors might offer lenses that use a bunch of different size filters. You might own one lens that takes 62mm filters, another that calls for 67mm add-ons, and third that takes 72mm accessories. You might find that the clearest upgrade path is to buy the largest filters and then adapt them to other lenses by using step-down rings, as shown in Figure 3-2.

Figure 3-2: You might be able to use one set of filters on several different lenses.

Cameras of Today and Tomorrow

Only a few years ago, dSLR cameras came in only one category — expensive. You could expect to spend at least $5,000 for a digital SLR from Canon, Nikon, or Kodak, and be thankful the camera was that affordable. After all, it wasn't that long ago that digital SLRs cost upwards of $30,000, used a tethered 200MB hard drive, and gave you 1.3-megapixel photos!

Of course, dSLRs of the late 20th century were built on rugged professional camera bodies, and they housed very expensive sensors. The Kodak DCS 460 of a decade ago was basically a common Nikon body with a very, very costly 6-megapixel imager built in. Although some digital SLRs that cost as little as $2,000 (for the body alone) made an appearance, it wasn't until the original Canon Digital Rebel was introduced in 2003 at less than $1,000 (with lens) that the new category of basic consumer dSLR was born.

Although the distinct camera categories that I cover in the following sections have some overlap, these categories are still aimed at particular classes of buyers.

Basic dSLR cameras

The basic dSLR is the newest type of digital camera with interchangeable lenses. These cameras are stripped-down versions of more advanced digital SLRs, aimed specifically at photographers who are looking to step up from point-and-shoot models, but who don't necessarily want full-fledged systems with all the bells and whistles. Typical cameras in this class include the Nikon D40, the Pentax/Samsung models, and the original Canon Digital Rebel, which remained in the line even after the Rebel XT/XTi were introduced.

Priced at around $600 with lens, basic dSLRs compete directly with the more expensive point-and-shoot, non-dSLR cameras in the same price and megapixel range. The point-and-shoot cameras might have noninterchangeable zoom lenses with a longer range (12:1 or more) while offering a smaller and lighter package that's more portable.

The advantage of a $600 dSLR over a comparably priced point-and-shoot camera is usually faster operation and better image quality (even when matched in the megapixel department), plus the ability to exchange lenses. Those who never plan to buy additional lenses find the quality of the non-SLR adequate, and people who don't shoot demanding subjects like sports will be happy with the point-and-shoot models, especially the models that offer a bit of manual control. More serious photographers will take a basic dSLR at the same price every time.

Of course, these basic dSLR models do lack a few features that their more advanced brethren have — but, boy, are they affordable! You might be happy with one of these as your main camera or as a second camera body, particularly if your budget is tight.

What do you give up? Most of the basic dSLRs sacrifice a few features that you might never or rarely use. These include depth-of-field preview, higher shutter speeds, or the fastest continuous shooting bursts. Some of the cost-saving measures add some inconvenience: Your basic dSLR might have only one command dial, so you'd need to press a button to switch between setting the shutter speed and aperture. Or, the budget camera might use only SD memory cards, rather than the CompactFlash cards found in most dSLRs.

Still, what you give up to save several hundred dollars might be insignificant if it means you can get behind the wheel of an honest-to-gosh dSLR today.

Prosumer dSLRs

The term *prosumer* refers to the next step up in the digital SLR realm because these cameras are intended for advanced consumers/amateur photographers, but they have enough features to make them attractive to professionals as a second camera body. Indeed, some pros who have light-duty shooting requirements (perhaps because their work is more contemplative and they don't fire off thousands of shots a day) use them as primary cameras.

Prosumer dSLRs start at about $1,000 (for body only, or sometimes with lens) and range up to about $2,500. These models include the Nikon D80, Canon Digital Rebel XTi, Pentax *ist DS (shown in Figure 3-3), Sony Alpha DSLR-A100, and cameras from Fuji, Sigma, and others.

These cameras don't sacrifice many features; the corners are cut in ways that probably won't affect the typical photo enthusiast. For example, cameras in this class often are built around rugged polycarbonate bodies rather than the almost-indestructible magnesium camera bodies found in the pro cameras. They might lack built-in vertical camera grips and easy plug-in remote controls that professionals require. The viewfinder systems might use pentamirrors that are a little dimmer than the pentaprisms found in pro cameras, and magnification through the viewing system might be lower. It's common for these dSLRs to have much less sprightly continuous shooting modes, too.

For anyone who could never justify spending $5,000 or more on a dSLR, these prosumer models offer just about every needed feature with enough megapixels to produce very high-quality pictures, indeed.

Figure 3-3: Prosumer dSLRs start at less than $1,000 and have a full set of features.

Professional dSLR models

Although some older models are priced at less than $5,000, most professional dSLRs will set you back 5 to 8 grand, but if you're selling your work, the camera will be well worth the cost. Cameras in this class include the Nikon D2x, Canon EOS-1D Mark II N, Canon EOS 5-D, and Canon EOS-1Ds Mark II. These models take you all the way from 12 megapixels up to a lofty 16 megapixels and can, arguably, meet or exceed the image quality of the best film cameras.

What do you get for thousands and thousands of extra dollars? Here's a quick checklist of what your extra cash will buy:

✓ **Tank-like reliability:** Okay, I really have no experience with how reliable tanks are, but they must be pretty good if being "built like a tank" is a positive. Pro dSLRs have metal bodies, excellent sealing against the elements, and rugged controls and components like shutters that can be operated thousands of times without failing. A typical professional might shoot more pictures in a day than an amateur photographer takes in a year and can't afford to have a camera wimp out at the worst possible moment. So, many of these cameras are purchased for their ruggedness alone and *even then* true pros commonly buy multiple bodies in order to have a backup or two or three.

✔ **Faster operation:** Pro cameras generally have the most advanced auto-focus systems available from a vendor, so they're able to take pictures *right now* without delay or shutter lag. They have large internal memory buffers to suck up exposures as fast as you can take them, and the speedy digital image chips process the bits and bytes and write them to your memory card. Exposure systems, too, are top-notch, both in accuracy and speed. Professional dSLRs are veritable speed demons.

✔ **Faster burst modes:** Where prosumer dSLRs are considered speedy if they can capture continuous-mode pictures at three frames per second, pro cameras typically can grab four to eight frames per second without sweating. Those big memory buffers and digital signal processing chips make this speed possible.

✔ **More options:** Pro cameras let you set up multiple sets of shooting parameters and recall them at the press of a button, so you can tailor your camera's operation to particular environments. You might find other choices not available to lesser cameras, such as the ability to save images in either compressed or uncompressed RAW format, TIFF, and multiple levels of JPEG quality. (You find out more about file formats in Chapter 9.)

✔ **Bigger sensors:** Some pro cameras offer larger sensors, which can be an advantage to pro shooters. These sizeable sensors are available from Canon; several models offered by Kodak (before they were discontinued); and a few so-called medium-format dSLRs such as those from Mamiya and Hasselblad. In the case of the Canon and late, lamented Kodak models, the cameras used traditional 35mm-camera-style lenses, but imaged on a sensor that was the same size as a full 35mm frame. A chief advantage of this was the ability to use any existing 35mm camera lens with no lens crop factor applied. (Chapter 2 explains lens crop in detail.)

dSLR-like cameras — a waste of time?

A strange thing happened after the first low-cost digital SLR cameras emerged onto the market. The cameras positioned at the former high end of the amateur/photo enthusiast market suddenly began to be described as "SLR-like." These cameras happened to be priced about the same as the new dSLRs, but didn't have interchangeable lenses. They did have a form of through-the-lens viewing that lesser point-and-shoot cameras lacked, so they became "SLR-like." What's the story here?

In their time, cameras sporting internal electronic viewfinders (a miniature LCD inside the camera) were the next best thing and were all that serious photographers with limited bank accounts could afford. Their viewing systems were far superior to the optical viewfinder windows that supplemented rear-panel LCDs in point-and-shoot cameras. You could use these electronic viewfinders (EVFs) to compose your shots accurately even in bright sunlight and, with luck, monitor depth-of-field. Many of them were designed with real controls, including zoom rings, rather than the motorized gadgets and buttons the point-and-shoot cameras used.

But most EVF cameras are more "SLR-ish" than "SLR-like." Table 3-1 lists some of their advantages and disadvantages.

Table 3-1	The Pros and Cons of EVF Cameras
Pro	*Con*
EVF cameras are smaller. If ultra-compact size is important to you, a non-SLR might have the size you need.	The smaller sensors of EVF cameras produce more noise even at the reduced ISO range these models offer.
The typical EVF model offers excellent zoom range right out of the box, so you don't have to lug lenses around.	They don't have interchangeable lenses.
An EVF camera might have features that cost extra to add to your dSLR, such as built-in image shake technology.	It doesn't have SLR-fast response; shutter lag is still very much a problem with most EVF models.
You can shoot movies with a non-SLR, and you can preview an image on the LCD before you take it.	The LCD might offer a grainy, ghost-ridden view that's neither especially bright nor particularly useful for gauging depth-of-field.

If you're reading this book, you're probably irreconcilably biased towards a digital SLR. However, an EVF camera you already own or can pick up at a reasonable price can make a good spare camera or a fall-back camera for when taking your dSLR is undesirable or impractical.

Checking Out Key Features

As you approach your final purchase decision, look at the individual features of the cameras you're considering and how they affect you. I cover most of the main topics in the following sections in more detail in Chapter 2, and Chapter 7 has information on special features. The following sections just summarize what you need to know.

If you make a list of features and divide it into three categories, as I explain in "Features for Now and the Future" earlier in this chapter, this list can help you decide which camera best suits your needs.

Lenses

The ability to swap optics is the reason why the word *lens* is so important in the abbreviation SLR. Some factors to consider when choosing a camera include:

- **Lens quality:** Are the lenses of a particular vendor known for their quality, both optically and mechanically (what is known as *build quality*)? Does this vendor offer multiple lens lines with economy lenses that might be a little less rugged but affordably priced, as well as pro-style lenses with the ultimate in sharpness and ruggedness? Depending on the type of photography you do, trading off a little weight and replacing a few metal parts with tough plastic might be important. Or, you might require lenses that can take punishment and still deliver sparkling results.

- **Focal length ranges:** Some vendors are stronger in the telephoto lens department and weaker when it comes to providing wide-angle lenses. Some do a better job with certain kinds of zooms than others. Make sure that vendor of the camera you're contemplating offers lenses in the focal lengths and maximum apertures you require. If not, see whether you can fill in the lenses you require from third-party vendors, such as Tamron and Sigma. These manufacturers' optical offerings might be completely satisfactory — or they might not. It's best to see whether the lenses you will need are readily available at a price you can afford. Figure 3-4 shows a typical lens furnished with a digital SLR.

Figure 3-4: This lens is a little slow at f3.5/f4.5, but it covers a useful focal length range of 18mm to 70mm.

- **Special features:** Focal lengths, zoom ranges, and maximum aperture aren't the only features you want in a lens. You might need close focusing, fast autofocus (which is partially dependent on the design of the lens), or the ability to control the out-of-focus areas of an image. (Nikon, for example, has a line of DC lenses that are great for portraiture because you can control how the defocused areas look.)

Sensors and image processors

The sensor and digital signal processor has as much effect on your final image as the lens does, so be sure to check out the qualities of your dream camera's imager very carefully. In particular, look into the following:

- ✔ **The amount of noise it generates at low ISO settings (ISO 100 or ISO 200) and at higher ISO settings (ISO 800 and above):** Some photographers like the lower noise produced by the prosumer Canon digital cameras compared to that of competing Nikon dSLRs. Others find the Canon images so smooth they look plasticky and prefer the extra sharpness and texture of the Nikon sensor. Chapter 11 tells you more about noise.

- ✔ **The sensor's dynamic range:** Is there detail in both shadows and highlights? Are colors accurate? Do the images look sharp? If you answered "no" to any of these questions, you probably need to keep looking for the right camera.

CMOS and CCD sensors show little difference in quality these days, but significant differences exist among sensors from different vendors. Do some comparisons now so you'll be happy with your camera later.

Exposure systems

Exposure systems range from simple spot metering to center weighted to complex evaluative systems that examine a huge matrix of points to arrive at the correct settings. Often, all three systems dwell in harmony together in one camera. To better understand exposure systems and how they can affect your work, check out Chapter 5 before you select your camera.

Focusing systems

The focusing system of a dSLR is partially dependent on two factors:

- ✔ The mechanisms built into the lens, which move the lens elements to the proper position at the camera's direction

- ✔ The electronics in the camera that evaluate the contrast of the image to decide exactly where the correct focus point is

That's complicated stuff! Yet, if your image is out of focus, odds are that your picture is totally ruined. You can often partially or fully correct for improper exposure. Color-correction tools in an image editor can fix bad white balance. You can crop your photos to remove extraneous subject matter. But if your image is badly out of focus, you should end its suffering by pressing Delete.

You definitely want a camera with an efficient autofocus system, one that focuses accurately. You sometimes need to specify what point the camera should use as the point of focus, especially when your main subject is *not* in the center of the viewfinder. It's a good idea to be able to specify that the camera locks focus when you press the shutter release halfway down, or that it can continue to seek a focus point for moving subjects right until the instant of exposure.

You might appreciate a camera that can *predict* where the focus point *will* be when a moving object is racing towards or away from the camera.

You might want the ability to switch quickly to manual focus by using a switch like the one shown in Figure 3-5. Some kinds of photography, particularly macro photography, work best when the photographer has complete control over focus.

Figure 3-5: A convenient switch on the camera or lens enables you to quickly change from automatic focus to manual focus.

Special features

Digital SLRs are rife with special features. There are enough of them, in fact, that I devote all of Chapter 7 to describing things like image stabilization, time-lapse photography, and so forth.

If you have specialized needs, you might have special requirements. For instance, if you like to photograph the progress of blossoming flowers or construction, you might require the ability to connect to a computer, as shown in Figure 3-6. Or, perhaps you've discovered that the vibration of the flip-up mirror in an SLR spoils your critical close-up or telephoto shots, and want a camera with preshot mirror lock-up. Maybe you want to be able to instantly transmit your photos to a laptop computer for immediate review by an assistant. If infrared photography is your most important application, you need a camera that's especially sensitive to infrared illumination.

Figure 3-6: The ability to connect your camera directly to a laptop can be essential for time-lapse photography.

If you do have special needs, pay particular attention to how well your potential new digital camera fills them. Nothing is more frustrating than having a hard-to-fulfill requirement while owning a camera that's just a little less than what you require in that department.

Accessorizing Your dSLR

*R*emember how cool it was to pick out your school supplies every August before classes began? You got to choose the exact notebook and paper you wanted. You likely selected your pencils and book covers with the greatest of care. If you're younger than I am, you probably spent a lot of time deliberating over which Trapper Keeper to get. If you're my age, the big decision was which quill pen to buy. If you own a digital SLR, you can experience the same joy of buying school supplies — but all year 'round!

That's because one of the best things about dSLR cameras is that they're almost infinitely expandable. Hundreds of different lenses are available, of course, but that's another whole level of accessorization. I'm talking about add-ons that let you focus closer, operate your camera more efficiently, hold your camera steady for long exposures, or do things that you otherwise couldn't do at all.

I'm sure you already know about some of the accessories in this chapter. Some are a bit more obscure, though. Only a few of them, such as memory cards, are absolutely essential for taking photos. However, you might take comfort in knowing that so many tools are available if you want them. This chapter shows you some of the basic items to consider.

Memory Cards in a Flash

Most digital SLRs are furnished without any memory card at all, so you need to buy one as soon as you get your camera. Of course, even entry-level point-and-shoot digicams frequently come without a card, too, or are furnished with a useless 16MB card, so this omission should come as no surprise.

Whereas low-end cameras come with no card to save costs, more sophisticated cameras like your dSLR lack a memory card because it's highly unlikely that the vendor will know exactly what kind of card you'd prefer. By not including any memory card at all, your camera vendor is upholding your right to choose the card that exactly suits your needs. So, when choosing a memory card for your digital SLR, here are the key factors to consider:

- ✔ **Type:** It behooves you to buy the type of card that fits your camera. For most cameras, this means you choose either flash or hard disk.

- ✔ **Write speed:** Perhaps you shoot a lot of sports and want to use only high-speed memory cards that can suck up bursts of shots as quickly as you can take them.

- ✔ **Capacity:** With most dSLRs, a 256MB or sometimes even a 512MB card is almost useless because of its low capacity. Who needs a card that holds as few as 40 RAW shots? You might not want to bother carrying around any card smaller than 1GB in capacity.

- ✔ **Form factor:** This is one factor you usually *don't* need to consider — unless you have a camera that accepts more than one type of media. Maybe your digital SLR accepts both CompactFlash (CF) and Secure Digital (SD) memory cards. A few do, and at least one camera accepts both SD and xD cards. In both cases, you might prefer SD cards because you can also use them in an MP3 player.

In the following sections, I explain the three main considerations in more detail.

Choosing between flash and hard disks

Most memory cards use solid-state flash memory to store information. Also, a limited number of cards are actually miniature hard drives, descended from the original microdrives developed by IBM and eventually taken over by Hitachi.

Compared to flash memory, microdrives are relatively cheap. I've seen 8GB microdrives on sale for $129, which works out to $16 per gigabyte. (I expect prices to change during the life of this book, but as I write this, that is a very good price!) But before you act now on this low, low rate, keep in mind that you might just get what you pay for. In terms of quality, the drives sometimes don't quite stack up against flash memory:

✔ Drives are generally slower and require more power than flash memory cards.

✔ Some dSLRs can't use microdrives at all.

✔ You can't find any solid data on the reliability of these drives, but like any hard drive, they're likely to be less rugged than a solid-state card.

From reading photographer forums and newsgroups, I'd guess that reliability is lower; I've seen many reports from users of hard drives failing right out of the box or after a short period of time. Dead-on-arrival flash memory cards, on the other hand, seem to be comparatively rare. Keep in mind that only the folks with problems are likely to complain publicly, so there might be millions of happy microdrive users.

The right write speed

Memory cards operate a little bit like hard drives in the sense that some of them can write data faster than others. Although cards don't have the rotating platters that hard drives have, they do have electrical properties that limit the speed with which they can accept and store information.

Real-world write speeds typically range from about 0.75MB/second to about 8MB/second, and they depend greatly on the speed of your digital camera. That is, a particular card might be usable at 3MB/second in one camera and at 8MB/second in another. However, the speeds are proportional: A card rated as a better performer works faster in all the dSLRs it is used with, regardless of the actual speed.

Fast memory cards can help if your digital SLR has a small buffer that can hold only a few shots. The faster your card can accept images, the more quickly you can resume shooting. Some digital single lens reflex cameras can't shoot and write at the same time, so this can be critical. For more info about memory cards, check out Rob Galbraith's Web site (`www.robgalbraith.com`).

Finding the key to the (capa)city

You must weigh technical, cost, and practical considerations when choosing memory card capacity:

✔ **Technical:** Some dSLRs can't use memory cards (neither solid-state nor microdrive) with capacities of more than 2GB, because they aren't compatible with the file system used for larger cards. (Check with your vendor in case there has been a firmware update that fixes this.) You might find some 4GB cards with a switch that transforms them into a pair of 2GB cards-in-one, but this is a poor solution. If your camera is limited to 2GB storage, that's the largest you should buy.

✔ **Cost:** If a 2GB card costs more than twice as much as a 1GB card, it isn't an economical buy — unless you really need a 2GB memory card rather than two 1GB modules, like those shown in Figure 4-1. If you must have the higher capacity to keep from switching cards often or if you plan to upgrade to a higher resolution dSLR in the future and want to use the same cards, you might be willing to spend more per gigabyte for the components you buy now. As I write this, 2GB cards cost almost exactly double the 1GB versions, but 4GB cards are roughly four and eight times the cost of their 1GB counterparts.

✔ **Practical:** Some photographers are nervous about putting all their photo eggs in one basket. They fear having a card failure or, more commonly, losing the card altogether. Using a smaller number of higher-capacity media does put you at risk of losing a chunk — or even all — of your vacation to Paris if something bad happens. Only you can weigh the risks. However, as you see in the following section, you can take steps to minimize picture loss.

Figure 4-1: A selection of memory cards lets you keep your photo eggs in multiple baskets.

Storing Your Images

You won't keep your images stored on your flash memory cards for very long. The first chance you get, you'll want to copy them to your computer's hard drive for reviewing, editing, and printing. The second chance you get, you'll want to copy them to more permanent storage for archiving. So, backup media should be high on your list of accessories for your dSLR.

Exploring options for backup media

The most common way to store images is on CDs or DVDs. All commercial computers built today, even laptops, have some sort of CD or DVD burning capability.

You can also purchase battery-operated burners and hard drives with 20–40GB of storage to offload your images while you're traveling. Personally, I prefer the portable DVD burners over the portable hard drives because the hard drive solutions are subject to the same potential problems that any hard drive can suffer. Non-rewriteable optical media that's verified when originally written should remain readable for at least long enough to copy it to additional backup discs when you return.

If you own an Apple iPod, consider buying one of the card-reader adapters available from several vendors. You can use these to copy your images to your iPod. Then you can transfer them to your computer later.

Creating image archives that last

According to the National Institute of Standards Technology (NIST), current DVD/CD technology is suitable for archiving images, for "tens of years" at a minimum.

Of course, not just any media will last that long. Nor should it need to. Within 10 to 20 years, a newer, better storage medium likely will come along, and you'll be able to transfer all your image files to that medium just as you copied your floppy-disk files to CD as floppies faded from use.

To improve your chances of retaining your priceless images for the ages, you need to use media that resists the rigors of aging and protects your discs from rough handling, heat, humidity, and direct light. Although rewritable CDs and DVDs are fine for temporary storage, for archiving images you're better off with write-once CD-R and DVD-R/DVD+R media rather than the RW/+RW variety.

Maximizing the life of your CDs and DVDs

By taking a few precautions, you can avoid losing your archived images unnecessarily through age. Here's the regimen to follow so you get the most from your CD or DVD archives:

- Don't flex or bend your discs, and store them vertically in a cool, dry area as much as possible.

- Never use a solvent-based marking pen in the data area. The safest place to jot information about your disc is in the clear center area around the hub.

- If you use labels, make sure they adhere perfectly. Irregularities such as bubbles can imbalance the disc and cause tracking areas.

- If you must remove dirt or fingerprints from the read side of the disc, use a CD or lens cloth and wipe in straight lines out from the center. Never use a circular motion or wood-based products such as facial tissue. You can use isopropyl alcohol, clear water, or soapy water to clean a grimy disc, but never use acetone or antistatic agents.

- Make multiple copies of your photo discs and store at least one copy off-site.

Of course, CD-Rs and DVD-R/DVD+Rs aren't necessarily permanent, either. The organic dyes, like the dyes in color film and papers, change over long periods of time as part of a natural process that can be accelerated when they're exposed to high temperature and humidity. These dyes are also sensitive to UV illumination and fade on exposure to direct sunlight.

In the case of CDs, the technology is fairly stable, so after you locate a name brand that purports to have the permanence you're looking for, you can generally stick with it. The technology for recordable DVDs is a little more fluid because vendors regularly increase the recording speed of the media with more sensitive dyes, and they switch to double-layer systems to boost capacity.

Even the worst optical media will last a year or two if treated gently. After a period of time, a few bits here and there will be lost as the disc degrades. You might not even notice, at first, because error correction routines can usually reconstruct limited amounts of unreadable data. When a disc starts developing uncorrectable errors, the end is near. For tips on keeping your discs in good shape, see the nearby sidebar, "Maximizing the life of your CDs and DVDs."

Filtering Factors

Filters are those glass or gelatin disks or squares that are affixed to the front of your camera's lens, changing the light that passes through the lens in some way. Filters were *really* popular before the advent of digital photography because some of the effects you could get with them weren't possible (or easy) to achieve in the darkroom. I own dozens of them, including some types, such as a complete set of decamired color-correction filters, that many photographers have never heard of.

Glass and gelatin filters are less used today among casual photographers because you can achieve many of the effects they provide within Photoshop. Yet, not all filtration effects are possible in the digital darkroom. Here's a description of the most essential filter add-ons:

  ✔ **Infrared:** Many digital SLRs are capable of taking photographs by using only infrared illumination, which produces a spectacular effect outdoors. You can get dark skies, vivid clouds, and ghostly white trees in your landscape shots and strange, pale complexions with your photographs of humans. However, you must buy an infrared filter that blocks visible light, and be prepared to shoot at slow shutter speeds (because very little light is left for the exposure). Also, you can't preview your shot (because an SLR viewfinder turns black when an infrared filter is mounted). For more on infrared photography, see Chapters 7 and 15.

  ✔ **Polarizers:** Polarizing filters, like the one shown in Figure 4-2, can reduce the glare bouncing off shiny surfaces in your photos. Simply attach the filter and rotate it until the glare disappears. These filters can also help deepen the contrast of the sky from certain angles.

Be certain to buy a *circular* polarizer rather than a *linear* polarizer for your dSLR. (All polarizers are round; circular refers to the way in which the filter handles light.) Circular polarizers won't interfere with the auto-exposure mechanism of your camera as linear polarizers can.

  ✔ **Neutral density:** The third kind of filter that every digital SLR photographer should own is a neutral density (ND) filter, so called because it blocks light but is neutral in color. ND filters come with various assigned filter factors, such as 2X (reduces the light by 1 f-stop), 4X (reduces light 2 f-stops) and 8X (cuts down 3 f-stops). As with most filters, they can be stacked to combine the effects of more than one, as long as the additional filters don't become visible in the image, thereby cutting off corners. Neutral density filters also come in a split variety — the top half (or bottom half or one side, if you rotate it) has neutral density, and the other half is clear.

✔ **Special Effects:** Lots of different filters produce special effects, including star-like points on highlights, prisms, special colors, and so forth. All the leading filter vendors offer these, but the 140 spectacular filters offered by Cokin (www.cokin.com) are in a class by themselves. Check them out. If you're interested in making your own filters, flip to Chapter 15.

Figure 4-2: Polarizing filters can reduce glare in many situations.

Things to do with ND filters

You can do a lot of amazing things with a neutral density (ND) filter, including rendering objects invisible! All ND filters decrease the amount of light reaching the sensor, so you need to use a longer exposure than you would without the filter (or let your camera adjust the exposure for you automatically). Here are the key applications you'll want to take advantage of:

✔ **Use the large f-stop you prefer.** Sometimes, there is too much light to use the large f-stop you want to work with (in order to reduce depth-of-field). Some dSLRs have ISO settings no lower than ISO 200, so in bright sunlight, even a ¼,₀₀₀ of a second shutter speed means that the largest f-stop that you can use is about f4. Add a 2X or 4X ND filter, and f2.8 or f2 are available to you.

✔ **Use the slow shutter speed you want.** Perhaps you want to get the classic blurry-water effect possible when photographing a flowing stream at a slow shutter speed while the camera is mounted on a tripod. At ISO 200, using f22 gives you a shutter speed of $\frac{1}{100}$ of a second under bright sunlight. If, as is likely, your mountain stream isn't in bright sunlight, it's still unlikely you'll be able to use a shutter speed any longer than about $\frac{1}{30}$ to $\frac{1}{15}$ of a second. An ND filter can give you the half-second to several-second exposures you need for truly cool-looking water effects, like the one shown in the following figure, which I further enhanced in Photoshop.

✔ **Make moving objects vanish.** The moving cars and people in your scene distract from the image of the building you're trying to capture. No problem. Use an 8X or heftier neutral density filter (stack several filters if you need to), mount the camera on a tripod, and shoot an exposure of 30 seconds or even longer. Unless a traffic light halts traffic, it's unlikely that any individual person or vehicle will be in the image long enough to register. If you have enough ND filter power at your disposal, this trick works in full daylight, so you can create your own ghost town.

✔ **Balance the sky and foreground.** In most scenes, the sky is much brighter than the foreground. A split ND filter, with the dark portion rotated so it's on top, can even out the exposure for the two halves, making those washed-out clouds visible again.

The Tripod: Your Visible Means of Support

One way to tell the casual photographer from the serious photographer is the size of her tripod. (Snap-shooters don't have any tripod at all and are probably none the worse for it.) Casual photographers rarely shoot the longer exposures that need help from a tripod, and the lenses of their digicams aren't long enough to require a tripod's steadying influence. That's all for the better because photographers who aren't serious photo enthusiasts are likely to purchase flimsy tripods that don't do what they're supposed to in any case.

As a shooter evolves into a photo enthusiast, the real value of a tripod becomes evident. The first step is to spend $100 on a "really good" tripod, which will turn out to be not so really good after all. However, the money isn't totally wasted because experience with inadequate tripods provides a valuable education that comes in handy when it's time to buy the real thing.

You know you've met a serious photographer when he unfolds a beautiful work of art made of carbon-fiber or magnesium alloy, topped with a quick-release grip-ball head that allows him to pivot the camera in any direction in seconds. Such a tripod is likely to be larger and steadier than the amateur jobs (which frequently have tell-tale leg braces because they *need* them) but still weigh a lot less thanks to the exotic materials used in its construction. Although a really good tripod can cost $500 (don't gasp; I wanted to say $800, but didn't think you'd believe me), but can be a once-in-a-life-time investment. I bought my own tripod when I was in college, and it has served me ably ever since. If enough of you buy this book, I am planning to replace it with a new one, but only because current tripods have a few features my original one doesn't have, and weigh about 75 percent less.

Putting a tripod to good use

A tripod is much more than a three-legged camera stand. They can do a lot for you and let you take pictures you couldn't get otherwise. Their key uses are:

- **Holding the camera steady:** If you need a long shutter speed for a picture in dim light, a tripod reduces the loss in sharpness from camera shake. Notice I said *reduces*. You might still have camera shake when using a tripod if the tripod itself is unsteady or is jiggled during the exposure. A steady camera is essential when shooting longer exposures in dim light or when using a telephoto lens, which magnifies vibrations along with your image. Few people can hand-hold a camera for $\frac{1}{30}$ of a second or slower with a normal or wide-angle lens. Fewer can get good shots at a shutter speed slower than the reciprocal of the effective lens focal length — for example, $\frac{1}{300}$ of a second with a 300mm lens (which might actually be a 200mm lens before a 1.5X crop factor).

✏ **Serving as a camera stand:** Perhaps you'd like to get in the picture, too, or do something else besides stand behind the camera as the photo is taken. Even if the shutter speed is going to be high enough that you won't need the tripod's steadying influence, the tripod fixes the camera in one place long enough for you to take the picture with the self-timer, a cable release, or remote control device.

✏ **Providing precise, stable positioning:** A tripod lets you frame a shot exactly and then take several pictures with the same framing. This capability can be useful for landscapes, portraits, or any other shot that you want to be repeatable. Stability is almost essential for close-up pictures when precise depth-of-field or focus considerations come into play.

✏ **Keeping the camera level for multiple shots in a panorama series:** Some tripods can be fitted with a panorama head that can help you provide the precise positioning and proper overlap for these photos.

The chief disadvantage of tripods is that you have to carry them along when you need them, and sturdy-but-light-weight tripods can be expensive. An alternative is to use a tripod substitute, which can vary from a simple clamp-like device to beanbags to monopods.

I always, without fail, carry my tripod clamp in my bag, and most of the time carry along a monopod, too. I have a 170mm–500mm zoom lens that I like very much, but I've found that it's virtually impossible to use without, at the very least, a monopod. At 500mm (750mm after applying the crop factor), I've detected visible camera shake in my photos even when using a $\frac{1}{2,000}$ of a second shutter speed. Who wants to jump up to ISO 1600 to be able to get a decent aperture while freezing camera motion when a tripod or monopod lets you do the same thing at ISO 400 or ISO 800?

Choosing a tripod

The thing that all tripods have in common is that they have three legs, except if they have only one leg, in which case they're not called tripods at all but, instead, *monopods*. Some tripods can also have only two legs, but that's because their third leg is removable and can be used as a monopod. Ordinarily, they're one or the other because a bipod has very little practical use. Here are some considerations for you to think about:

✏ **What you see and what you get:** Tripods always look nice in the catalog, but what is shown might include several optional components that you don't get unless you order them with your tripod. For example, higher-end tripods tend to come as a set of legs, only, with a center column that cranks up or down to extend the height of the tripod beyond what you get from extracting the legs. If you want a tripod head to attach your camera to, that might be $100 extra (don't wince; I wanted to say $200–$300, but I held back for your sake). Other necessary parts, including quick-release plates that help you mount and dismount your camera speedily, might be shown but cost more.

✔ **Leg style:** The legs might be cylindrical, cylindrical but flat on one side, open-channel, or some other shape. They might open from three to five different sections. The more sections, the more compact the tripod is when folded up, but the smaller the inner sections have to be to fit inside the others. The important thing is that the legs are as sturdy as possible when extended. They should not bend or flex, and the extended tripod should not sway in the breeze.

✔ **Leg height:** Your tripod should extend up to at least eye-level without the need to crank up the center column (which is best used only for minor height adjustments, when you require the absolute maximum height, or if the column swivels and can be used to vary the shooting angle). My own tripod goes up much higher than that, so I need to stand on a ladder or stool to use it at its maximum height. That's great for shooting photos from a higher vantage point. At the other end of the scale, you want some way of shooting from low angles too, which can be accomplished by retracting the legs of a tripod with multiple sections or by swiveling or reversing the center post.

✔ **Leg lock and positioning:** Check out the method used for locking and unlocking the legs, and note the range of movement available. The best designs let you lock or unlock all the sections of a particular leg simultaneously rather than one at a time, as shown in Figure 4-3, and they allow you to position the legs at independent angles so you can use your tripod on uneven ground.

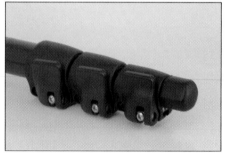

Figure 4-3: Well-designed legs let you grip all the locks at once and operate them simultaneously.

✔ **Use your head:** The head is the part you attach your camera to. The most common type is the pan/tilt head that allows you to pan the camera on one axis and tilt it on another. Fluid heads have a long handle that you can twist to release the head so you can pan and tilt simultaneously. Increasingly popular are joystick and ball heads, which let you tilt the camera at any angle.

✔ **Fast release:** Some heads come with quick-release plates or can be fitted with them. One part of the plate fastens to the tripod socket of your camera. The other part attaches to the tripod. Instead of screwing and unscrewing the camera from the tripod each time, you press a control and slide it off.

Electronic Flash in the Pan

Digital SLRs that cost $2,000 or less — for the body only — generally have a built-in electronic flash, or *speedlight.* (The exception to this rule as I write this book is the inexpensive Foveon-based dSLRs from Sigma.) Digital SLRs that cost $2,000 or more usually *don't* have a built-in flash (except the Fuji pro-quality S series dSLRs).

Professional photographers probably wouldn't use a built-in speedlight on their high-end cameras, usually because such units aren't powerful enough for anything other than fill flash, and provide the kind of direct lighting that pros abhor. I've been paid for my photos and seen them used on the covers and inside magazines, but not every picture I take is destined for the cover of *National Geographic Magazine* (okay, *none* of them are). Like you, I find it quite handy to be able to pop up my dSLR's internal flash when I want to take a quick shot and/or don't have my fully laden shoulder bag handy. I *like* having a flash built-in and always available.

However, like you, I'm serious about photography, and I'm glad I have my more powerful and flexible external flash units available to provide additional and supplemental lighting. In the following sections, I offer tips on the types of flashes you'll likely find useful. I also explain different ways external flash units work with your camera, and I cover any pros and cons you'll want to be aware of. In Chapter 9, I explain using a flash for various effects.

Perusing different types of flash units

Flash units come in several types. I have a whole bunch of them, and you can probably use any of these types of flash with your dSLR:

- **A fancy sort of flash:** My $350 super-sophisticated unit can communicate with my camera and do fancy tricks such as zooming its coverage to match the camera lens's zoom setting. It also reports to the camera the exact color temperature it uses, which results in more accurate hues, and adjusts its exposure by reading the light that actually goes through the lens. In wireless mode, I can use it off-camera with no connecting cable.

- **Do the mashed potato:** I have a big monster of a "potato masher" flash with massive output for sports photography. I use this beast when I want to, say, illuminate a fullback on the opposite sideline. It attaches to an external battery powerpack, so it lasts forever, and I never ask it to do anything fancy. Although it has an automatic mode, I don't use that all the time, because I often want to get the maximum output. The only zoom coverage available is through built-in wide-angle and tele filters that modify the light.

- **Studio flash dance:** I probably get the most use out of my studio flash, though, which consists of a pair of large *monolights* (AC powered flash units with power built into the flash head) and two smaller electronic flash units used as background and hair lights.

Tools for triggering the flash

To use an external flash, your camera needs to have some way of triggering the supplemental flash unit. You can do this in four ways:

- ✔ **Slave operation:** Perhaps the external flash can be set to function as a slave unit, which means it has a photocell that detects the firing of the camera's main flash, and the external flash triggers in response. In this mode, you can use any slave-compatible external flashes, including those with an add-on trigger. The problem with using slave flash is that you might not want both the built-in flash and the external to illuminate your scene. If you're able to cut the power of the internal flash, you might be able to reduce its impact on the photo, relegating it to a fill-flash effect.

- ✔ **Wireless mode:** Some dSLRs are able to communicate with the same vendor's electronic flash units in what is called wireless mode. You might expect something called *wireless* to involve radio waves or, at the very least, some sort of infrared signal, but it can be much simpler than that. For example, Nikon's flash units "talk" to compatible Nikon dSLRs by using almost imperceptible preflashes that take place an instant before the flash fires. The camera's own flash tells the external flash details such as the zoom setting of the lens, the correct exposure to use, and most importantly, when to fire. The external flash, in turn, responds with information like the color temperature of the illumination it provides. This data exchange can take place when the two flashes aren't connected or even without the built-in flash providing part of the main exposure.

- ✔ **Hardwired PC connection:** You can find some dSLRs with a standard PC connection for attaching standard electronic flash units. (PC stands for Prontor-Compur, pioneering shutter manufacturers, rather than personal computer.) That means you can plug in studio flash and speedlights made by other vendors, assuming that the triggering voltage of the flash units isn't high enough to fry the circuits of your dSLR. (An add-on device called a Wein SafeSync isolates your camera from the flash's voltage. I use one to connect my studio flash to my digital cameras.) A PC connection, if you have one, works only with non-dedicated flash units that aren't able to communicate with the camera. The only signal that is exchanged between the camera and the flash is the trigger that fires the external unit.

- ✔ **Hot shoe connection:** Modern cameras, including dSLRs, tend to use more sophisticated dedicated flash units that require full communication between the camera and speedlight. These require special connectors, usually in the form of a *hot shoe* on top of the camera, like the one shown in Figure 4-4. The shoe has multiple contacts. You can plug in a flash unit designed to work with these contacts or use an adapter that allows connecting a flash with a cable instead.

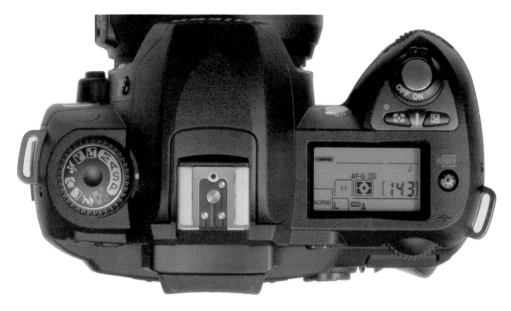

Figure 4-4: Dedicated electronic flash units use hot shoe connections.

Other Must-Have (Or Maybe-Have) Gear

After you've collected the most essential accessories your digital SLR needs, if you have any money left over you might want to consider some of the add-ons I discuss in the following sections.

A second camera

I've gone to Europe on vacation and taken along only a single camera and lens. But now that I think about it, that wasn't a smart thing to do. When people are paying me money to take pictures, I *always* have one or two spare camera bodies, extra lenses, multiple flash units — duplicates of any essential piece of equipment. I learned early in my career that "sorry, my camera broke!" is *not* an excuse that clients find acceptable. So why was I so dumb to go overseas and risk arriving with no way to take photos? Umm . . . I wanted to travel light?

Sooner or later you'll discover that a second camera body makes sense for you, too. Even if you aren't 3,000 miles from home, can you really stop taking photos for a few weeks while your dSLR is off in the shop? Haven't you been in situations where you wanted to alternate between taking photos with a wide-angle and a long telephoto lens? Having an extra body, one for each lens, can be just what you need.

You don't have to break the bank to buy your second camera body. Your existing lenses will fit just fine if you buy another model from the same vendor, but you don't need an identical camera. You can purchase a Nikon D50 or Pentax *ist DL to supplement more expensive bodies from the same manufacturer. Or, you might find yourself with an extra camera body when your favorite vendor comes out with a new model and you decide to buy it and keep your old camera as a spare/second camera.

Sensor cleaning kit

Like it or not, if you remove the lens from your dSLR, sooner or later you're going to have to clean dust and grime off the sensor. Available gear to do this include blowers, swabs, and special liquids, like those shown in Figure 4-5. Taking that first swipe at your sensor can be terrifying, but cleaning is actually simple and relatively safe.

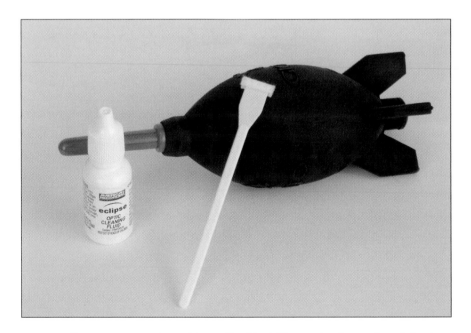

Figure 4-5: Keep your sensor clean with gear like this air blower, cleaning swab, and cleaning liquid.

Close-up equipment

Lots of available add-ons can help you focus closer, including filter-like close-up attachments that screw onto the front of the lens, as well as bellows accessories that fit between the camera and lens.

Extension tubes, like those shown in Figure 4-6, are an inexpensive and versatile solution. These tubes are installed between the camera and lens, and they provide the additional distance needed to focus closer. Single tubes are available for as little as $50, but you can pay $150 or more for a complete set of fully automatic tubes in multiple lengths.

The extension tubes that couple with the camera's automatic focus and exposure mechanisms are your best bet from an ease-of-use standpoint.

Figure 4-6: Extension tubes let you focus closely.

Part II
Oh, Shoot!

In this part . . .

*A*ll those controls! What to do with them? It's true that digital SLRs give you great control over every camera feature and function. In this part, you find out how to work with those controls, master the use of interchangeable lenses, and work with special features such as image stabilization.

In Chapter 5, I explain Shutter Priority and Aperture Priority modes, various programmed exposure features, how to adjust your exposures with histograms, and the mysteries of autofocus. Chapter 6 tells you everything you need to know about choosing and using lenses, including special-purpose optics such as macro lenses. Chapter 7 explores special features that some — but not all — digital SLRs have.

Taking Control of Your dSLR

*I*n terms of buttons, dials, and controls, comparing a typical point-and-shoot camera with a digital SLR is like comparing a hang glider to a Boeing 767 cockpit. Certainly, the more sophisticated option has more controls, but most people find it easier to flip a switch and shift a control than to yank on a lever, lean to the right, and pray.

Because you can do so many different things with a dSLR, the learning curve is a bit steep. You might have four or five exposure modes to choose from, a half-dozen different ways to focus, and the ability to fine-tune details such as white balance, sharpness, contrast, and color. Because you're a more serious photographer, those options are probably the reason you bought a digital SLR in the first place.

Okay, champ. You've got this incredibly versatile gadget in your hands. How are you going to make it work? This chapter helps get you started with the toughest of the tough: exposure and focus.

Discovering the Secrets of Exposure

If you're lazy or not up to using your brain on any given day, you can set up your digital SLR to operate much like a glorified point-and-shoot camera. Turn on autofocus, set the exposure control to Auto, and fire away. As you depress the shutter release, your camera tries to guess which subject in the frame is most important, and it focuses on that. The camera attempts to ascertain what kind of picture you're shooting (landscape, portrait, close-up, for example), and it chooses an exposure that is probably fairly close.

Clever little algorithms choose a shutter speed that eliminates subject- or camera-related blur (most of the time) and an f-stop that provides a decent compromise between depth-of-field and proper exposure. It's almost a given that your $1,000+ dSLR then produces pictures just as good as a $200 snapshot camera.

But that isn't what you bought your digital SLR for. Auto is the mode you use when you hand your camera to your fumble-fingered brother-in-law and ask him to take a picture of you and your kids. You'd rather maintain control over your exposures so you can apply f-stops and shutter speeds creatively.

Understanding why exposure is tricky

In a perfect world, your dSLR's sensor would be able to capture all the photons that reach it from your subjects. Dark areas would be represented by photosites (the individual picture elements) that received few photons, and light areas would be registered by photosites that captured lots and lots of photons. All the intermediate tones would fall somewhere in between.

But it doesn't work quite that way. Some dark areas might produce too few photons to produce an image at all; some very light areas might be represented by so many photons that excess light overflows from one pixel into adjacent pixels, causing a light smear known as *blooming*. (I introduce this in Chapter 2, where I explain how sensors work in more detail.)

Proper exposure helps ensure that the sensor receives enough light to capture detail in the dark areas of an image, but not so much that light areas are washed out. Figure 5-1 shows some of the choices you might have to make. Exposing for the shadows provides lots of detail in the top version (the original version of this image), but the highlights are completely washed out. The bottom version uses improved exposure to trade off some of the brightness in

Figure 5-1: Expose an image so highlights don't wash out; they are impossible to retrieve.

the shadows for more highlight detail. (Actually, I played with the exposure by using an image editor on the RAW version of the file, but this represents real-life choices nonetheless. You can find more information on using RAW files in Chapter 8.)

It's generally a good idea to try to preserve highlight details; they are impossible to retrieve if washed out. Brightening dark shadows is a lot easier than retrieving lost highlights.

Achieving such an ideal exposure can be tricky, because sensors have a fixed *dynamic range,* which is the range over which detail in both light and dark areas can be captured. No sensor's dynamic range covers the full gamut of illumination levels that you're likely to encounter in everyday photography, so the "right" exposure is likely to be a series of compromises.

The first compromise comes when the continuous range of brightness and darkness in an image is converted from that analog form into digital bits and bytes. During the conversion, an infinite gradation of tones is sliced up into a limited number of different shades — 256 different shades per color in the case of the 24-bit "full" color you probably work with in your image editor. Your digital SLR might capture more different tones than that — as many as 4,096 variations if your camera captures 12 bits per color channel — but you still end up with a measly 256 tones for each color in Photoshop (except if you're working with an HDR, high dynamic range, image).

Your mission, if you choose to accept it, is to make sure that the available tones are the *right* tones to represent your image. You don't have many to spare. Perhaps you're shooting a night scene and have lots of detail in the shadows that you want to preserve, but there are also some details in highlights illuminated by a street lamp. How can you even guess how the camera will capture each of these details? Let the histogram be your guide.

Getting exposure right with the histogram

Digital SLRs include a kind of display called a *histogram,* which is a chart shown on your LCD that displays the number of tones being captured at any brightness level. The number of pixels at each brightness level is shown on the histogram as a vertical bar, and there are 256 of these bars. The far-left position represents the darkest tones in your image, and the far-right slot shows the tones in the very lightest parts of your image.

Typically, a histogram looks something like a mountain, as shown in Figure 5-2. Most of the tones are clustered in the middle of the image because the average image has most of its detail in those middle tones. The bars are shorter at the dark or light ends of the scale because most images have less detail in the shadows and highlights. However, images that have a great deal of detail in the dark or light portions can have histograms that look very different, reflecting that particular distribution of tones.

Figure 5-2: With a well-exposed image, the histogram looks like this.

It isn't really possible to manipulate the shape of the histogram in your camera. For that, you need to use an image editor. What dSLR owners can do with a histogram display is use it to judge whether the current exposure is correct for the image. That's fairly easy to do:

1. **Take your picture.**

   You have to take the picture first because, unfortunately, dSLRs can't display a histogram "live" (in real time). The sensor doesn't see the image until the exposure is actually made. (Point-and-shoot digital cameras might show a live histogram.)

2. **Examine the histogram with your picture review function.**

   • If an image is overexposed, the graph is shifted towards the right side of the histogram, with some of the pixels representing lighter tones clipped off entirely, as you can see in Figure 5-3.

   • An underexposed image has the opposite look: The tones are crowded at the left side, and some of the shadow detail is clipped off, as in Figure 5-4.

3. **If you see either condition, compensate by changing the f-stop, shutter speed, or EV (more on these later in this chapter) to correct the exposure error.**

   If you're shooting RAW (see Chapter 8 for more about that), you might be able to adjust exposure and contrast when importing the image into your image editor. However, most of the time you'll want to get the exposure correct in the camera.

Figure 5-3: An overexposed image clusters all the information at the right side of the graph.

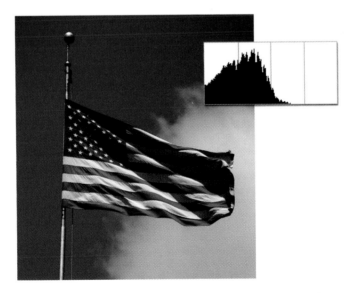

Figure 5-4: An underexposed image moves all the picture information to the left side of the histogram.

Fine-Tuning Exposure with the Metering System

Your camera's exposure metering system is a tireless friend that keeps plugging away, calculating its reckoning of the correct exposure (based on parameters you set) regardless of whether you choose to pay attention. It's available whether you're setting exposure manually or using one of the programmed or priority modes. You can't really turn off the exposure meter completely when the camera is on — although it might go to sleep after a few seconds of inactivity. Even then, as soon as you tap the shutter release button, a sleeping meter wakes up, looks at the current view through the lens, and reports its findings.

Like any true friend, your metering system is on its best behavior when you're around. It responds with the metering mode you prefer and calculates exposure based on your particular guidelines. What more could you ask for?

In the following sections, you find out how metering works, and you get a tour of all the main metering options on your dSLR to help you choose the optimum setting for the type of picture you want to take.

Metering works how?

The reason why dSLR exposure meters are so accurate is that they interpret the actual light passing through the lens, which is flipped upward by the mirror toward the viewfinder (or sideways in the case of cameras like those in the Olympus E series). Some of the light is used for viewing, and some is used to measure the exposure. If you zoom the lens (which often changes the amount of light passing through) or place a gadget like a filter in front of the lens to modify the light, the meter sees the results and takes them into account. The metering system is also linked to the shutter speed and aperture controls, so it understands the effects of both on the recommended exposure.

Choosing a metering scheme

Metering schemes on your dSLR enable you to configure the photosensitive elements of the exposure system (which can number from a dozen or so to thousands of individual light sensors) so that the exposure system interprets the incoming light in a specific way. Table 5-1 explains how photographers typically use the most popular schemes.

Table 5-1	Metering Schemes	
Scheme	**What It Does**	**Best Used For . . .**
Center weighting	This system looks at the entire frame, but tends to emphasize the portion of the image in the center, assigning a center weighting determined by the vendor, but which usually amounts to about 80 percent for the center and 20 percent for the rest of the image.	Scenes in which — d'oh — the most important subjects are in the center of the frame. Perhaps you're shooting portraits or close-ups of flowers and, naturally, want to center your subject. Center weighting zeroes in on those subjects and isn't influenced by very bright or very dark areas outside the center.
Spot metering	This method makes its exposure recommendations based only on a center spot shown in the viewfinder which might measure 6mm to 12mm. Illumination outside the spot is ignored. Your dSLR might allow you to choose the size of the center spot.	Subjects that don't dominate the frame, and which are surrounded by areas of misleading brightness or darkness. If you were at a Bruce Springsteen concert and wanted to capture him during a spot-lit acoustic set, you could use spot metering to collect exposure information from the Boss alone. Figure 5-5 shows the relative areas used by typical spot and center weighted metering schemes. (Sorry, I don't have any photos of Bruce Springsteen.)
Multipoint metering	This mode is the default metering mode for most dSLRs. It collects exposure data from many points on the screen (usually *not* shown in the view-finder) and uses sophisticated algorithms to decide which points to use in calculating the correct exposure.	Any scenes that don't require the special treatment provided by the other two methods. In other words, you'll use multipoint metering almost all the time.

More versatility with metering options

Your digital SLR has several options that can increase your exposure versatility:

✔ **Lock in settings with exposure lock control.** When you press the button, the current exposure (or focus, or both) is locked until you press the button again or take a photo. This lock gives you the freedom to set exposure and then reframe the photo any way you like without worrying that the preferred settings will change. This option is different from the normal system of locking exposure and/or focus when you press the shutter release partially because you don't have to keep your finger on the release button. Exposure lock control is sometimes combined with a focus lock adjustment.

✔ **Shoot a series of photos at different exposures by setting your dSLR's *bracketing* system.** The camera takes the first picture at the metered exposure, and then it takes the second and third at, say, one-third stop less exposure and one-third stop more exposure. You can set the exact increment, choosing to bracket by half or full stops if you want. You can also bracket parameters other than exposure, such as white balance and flash. Your camera might allow you to bracket more than one of these, and in the order you choose.

✔ **Adjust the shutter speed and/or aperture combination in use without changing the exposure at all.** If the camera chooses $\frac{1}{250}$ of a second at f8, spinning the command dial to the right might switch to $\frac{1}{500}$ of a second at f5.6, or to the left to change to $\frac{1}{125}$ of a second at f11. All these exposures are the same, but they provide different useful combinations of shutter speeds and f-stop sizes.

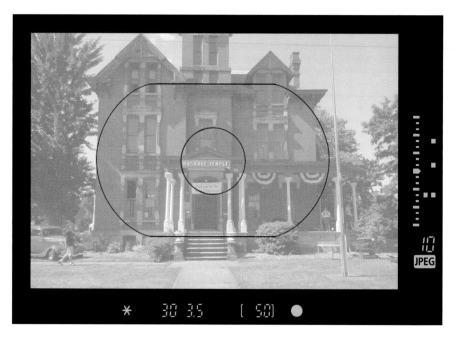

Figure 5-5: A spot metering area (center of the image) and a center-weighted zone (the larger oval area).

The Many Ways to Choose Exposure

The available exposure options — both automated, manual, and semiautomatic — must be used in an intelligent way if you want to get the best results. Whether you're choosing Auto, Programmed, Aperture Priority, Shutter Priority, Manual, or one of the programmed Scene modes, give some thought to what you want to accomplish and choose the mode that's best suited for your planned picture-taking session.

The following sections offer tips for selecting the right mode.

Adjusting exposure the easy way

Digital SLRs include a simple way of bumping exposure up or down called EV (Exposure Value). You can use EV as a way of referring to equivalent shutter speed and aperture settings that produce the same exposure. For example, if the correct exposure for a scene is ½₅₀ of a second at f11, exactly equivalent exposures would include ½₀₀ of a second at f8 (a shutter speed half as long, but an aperture twice as large) and ⅟₁₂₅ of a second at f16 (a shutter speed twice as long, but an aperture half as large). All three exposures would have the same EV.

If you bumped up exposure by one EV, you could change the shutter speed to ⅟₁₂₅ of a second while keeping the f-stop at f11, or you could use the equivalent exposure of ½₅₀ of a second at f8. Reducing exposure by one EV works in the opposite direction: You can shorten the shutter speed or make the aperture smaller. It doesn't matter. EV is a quick way to add or subtract exposure without fiddling with the shutter speed or aperture controls directly.

Your digital SLR has an EV button somewhere. Press it and use the corresponding EV control (usually a command dial or cursor pad button) to adjust the EV up or down one increment. This adjustment overrides your camera's auto-exposure setting. In effect, you're giving your image more or less exposure than the exposure meter indicates when you change the EV.

Whether the camera adjusts the aperture or shutter speed is determined by your current shooting mode:

- If your camera is set in a Programmed exposure mode, the camera might adjust either value. It's that simple.

- If you're using Aperture Priority mode (you set the f-stop and let the camera determine the shutter speed), making an EV change bumps the shutter speed up or down.

- If you're using Shutter Priority mode (you set the shutter speed and the meter sets the f-stop), an EV adjustment makes the aperture larger or smaller.

In the following sections, I discuss these modes (Program, Aperture Priority, and Shutter Priority) in more detail.

Giving up control (in Program mode)

If you don't want absolute control over your exposure, you have an alternative to the dreaded Auto setting. It should suit you to a P, and that's where this option is usually found on the mode dial. P stands for *programmed* exposure. It's an automated exposure system but, unlike Auto, the Program setting lets you fine-tune the exposure settings it selects. Auto generally locks you out of most useful adjustments completely.

Program mode is smarter than Auto. Most dSLR cameras have a built-in data-base of tens of thousands of photos that have been analyzed and reduced to numbers that characterize their optimum exposures. In Program mode, your camera can look at the image in your viewfinder, compare it with this database, and come up with an image that probably is a pretty good match. It can then apply the exposure parameters to your picture.

For example, the camera decides it has a landscape picture on its hands and attempts to maximize depth-of-field. Or, the camera determines that it's working with a portrait and, therefore, *less* depth-of-field might be in order. The algorithms might dictate that high shutter speeds are used to counter camera shake or subject motion, and the program switches to lower shutter speeds only when the aperture is deemed too small for the correct exposure at the current speed.

Carried to the extreme, programmed exposures can include settings that are optimized *only* for a specific type of picture, such as portraits, night photography, beach or snow photos, sports, or macro photography. These are called *Scene* modes, and they're useful when you want to take a partic-ular kind of picture and want to inform the camera of what you're doing, but don't have the time to set up the camera yourself. Scene modes can include more than exposure settings, too. They might adjust saturation to give you more vivid landscapes or decrease contrast to cope with bright snow scenes.

Figure 5-6 shows an image that would have benefited from using the Sports Scene mode. The default shutter speed selected by the camera produced a good exposure, but it wasn't fast enough to stop the moving softball and bat. Although a little blur can be useful in action photography (as you see in Chapter 9), in this case it was too much. (Shutter priority, which I discuss later in this chapter, would have helped, too.)

Both Program and Scene modes are useful shortcuts for photographers in a hurry. However, most of the serious photographers I know use the options in the next section — Aperture Priority, Shutter Priority, and Manual Exposure modes — almost exclusively.

Figure 5-6: The Sports setting could have improved this action photo by freezing the ball and bat, limiting the amount of blur.

Taking control

One of the joys of gaining expertise with your dSLR is knowing what's best for a particular type of photo and making the necessary choices, even if you let the camera's electronics do most of the work. That's why Aperture Priority, Shutter Priority, and even Manual Exposure modes are so popular among digital SLR owners.

Here's how to choose among them.

Getting your aperture and shutter priorities straight

Your camera doesn't know you're taking photographs of a soccer game, but you do. You know that you sometimes want to use $\frac{1}{1,000}$ of a second to freeze the action, but other times you'd prefer to use $\frac{1}{125}$ of a second to introduce a little blur into the mix.

With *Shutter Priority mode,* the shutter speed is your choice. After you select the shutter speed, the camera locks it in. The autoexposure system varies *only* the aperture.

You also see the selected aperture in the viewfinder so that you, the all-knowing photographer, can decide when, say, the f-stop is getting a little too large for comfort and you want to accept a slower shutter speed to gain a smaller aperture. Should light conditions change enough that your selected shutter speed won't produce a correct exposure with the available f-stops, you're alerted with a LO or HI indicator in the viewfinder or, perhaps, a flashing LED.

Aperture Priority mode is the flip-side of Shutter Priority mode. Perhaps you want a small aperture to maximize depth-of-field or a large f-stop to minimize it. It's your choice. You set the aperture you want, and the metering system sets the matching shutter speed. Again, if you notice that the shutter speed is too slow or high, you can opt to adjust the f-stop you've dialed in to one that's larger or smaller.

Shutter and aperture priority let you use your photo smarts to set a basic parameter suitable for the photo you have in mind, and then the camera takes over to intelligently make the other adjustments.

Doing exposure yourself

Sometimes if you want something done right, you just have to do it yourself. Manual Exposure mode allows you to set both the shutter speed and aperture by using the camera's built-in meter for guidance. After you switch to Manual mode, the dSLR won't touch either setting, but it continues to evaluate the scene for the correct exposure and provide information in the viewfinder showing that you're over or under its recommendation, or right on.

I'm no technological Luddite, but I did resist exposure automation for an interminable period. Why did I resist? Well, Manual Exposure mode has some distinct advantages:

- **Special effects:** Suppose you want to create a silhouette effect, as in Figure 5-7, or underexpose a sunset to cloak your image in deep shadows. Maybe you'd like to overexpose a bit to wash out unwanted detail. Any automatic exposure mode stubbornly tries to correct for the lighting, effectively blocking you from applying your special effect. Simply switching to Manual Exposure mode and making the settings yourself is usually a lot faster than trying to override your camera's autoexposure mechanism.

- **Balancing lighting:** You have a subject that's illuminated by several different light sources, say, two or more studio lights, or outdoors, by sunshine and fill light from your flash or a reflector. Manual Exposure mode lets you control exactly how exposure is set for these multiple light sources.

- **Older optics:** You might have an older lens that doesn't couple with your dSLR's autoexposure system. In that case, setting the exposure manually might be your only option.

✓ **Noncompatible flash:** I use Manual Exposure mode quite frequently when I connect my dSLR to some studio flash units. The camera can't control the flash, and it has no way of adjusting exposure automatically. So, I use a flash meter and set the f-stop manually. If you're using a flash that isn't built specifically for your dSLR or you want to use the flash in Manual mode (say, to make sure it always uses its full power), manual exposure setting can work for you. Chapter 9 covers working with flash in more detail.

Figure 5-7: Manual settings let you use creative exposure for special effects.

Focus Pocus

Focusing your image correctly is arguably the most important technical aspect of taking pictures because even a small focus error might ruin an image beyond redemption. You can often correct exposure problems or fix bad color balance in an image editor. You might be able to fix clumsy framing with some judicious cropping. You can even retouch images to remove particularly ugly subject matter. But if an image is badly focused, you can sharpen it a little, but most likely not enough to bring a blurry shot back from the dead.

Oddly enough, focus is something that is both a benefit and bane of the dSLR. Focus isn't usually much of a worry for point-and-shoot photographers except when taking close-up pictures. Nor is *selective focus* (placing parts of an image out of focus to emphasize other portions) much of a creative tool. That's because the very short focal lengths required by the tiny sensors in those cameras put virtually everything in sharp focus, regardless of zoom position, f-stop, or distances (other than close-ups). A telephoto shot taken with the lens wide open is likely to be sharp from a few feet to infinity.

That isn't so with dSLRs and their lenses. You can throw parts of your scene, such as the background in a portrait shot, out of focus to emphasize your subject. Unfortunately, you can also accidentally throw your subject out of focus if you aren't careful, producing unintended results.

Digital SLRs offer two different ways of achieving focus: manual and automatic. Each method has its advantages and disadvantages. Read on for details.

Focusing manually

Manual focusing sounds easy, but it's more difficult than it sounds. All you need to do is twist a ring on the front of the lens, and the image pops into sharp focus, right? If only it were that simple! Manual focus is, unfortunately, rather slow when compared to the automatic focus features of digital SLRs. It works well when you're doing thoughtful work such as macro (close-up) photography, where your subject sits there patiently while you fiddle with the camera (often locked down on a tripod) and focus until you get everything exactly right.

Manual focus isn't so good when you're photographing fast-moving sports or if you're shooting in a rush for any reason. The big problem is that our brains have a very poor memory for sharpness. You don't really know for sure that sharp focus has been achieved until you've passed it and your image starts to blur again. Then you have to jog back and forth until you're convinced the image is sharply focused. This jostling takes time, and you might not have that much time to waste.

Focusing an image becomes more difficult when your scene is darker or lower in contrast. That's true for both you and the camera's autofocus mechanism, but at least when the camera's doing the job you don't have to fret in frustration.

Still, manual focus might work for you in several situations:

- ✏ **Zeroing in on one subject:** When you want to focus on a particular object that the autofocus system won't readily lock in on, focus manually. Perhaps you have three chess men set up in a diagonal row on a chess board and you want to focus on the center one, as in Figure 5-8. Most autofocus systems can be aimed, but it might simply be faster to do the focusing yourself.

- ✏ **Shooting action pictures:** In some action situations, autofocus systems can be fast, but they might focus at lightning speed on the wrong subject. Sports photographers can sometimes use Manual mode to focus ahead of time where they know the action will be, dispensing with the uncertainty.

- ✏ **Avoiding total confusion:** Autofocus systems are totally confused by some kinds of situations, such as subjects posed against plain backgrounds. For example, I've found that when photographing seagulls in flight, I often have to focus manually, unless I'm lucky enough to have a bird blunder into one of my camera's autofocus zones.

- ✏ **Photographing through glass:** Sometimes an autofocus system fixates on the glass itself rather than the subject behind it, so you might be better off focusing manually.

Oughta' autofocus

Digital SLRs focus automatically by selecting the focus point at which the highest image contrast is achieved. When a subject is out of focus, it looks blurry and lower in contrast. When the subject is in focus, the lack of blur translates into higher contrast that the focus system can see.

Of course, that means that a low-contrast subject or one that's poorly illuminated can give an autofocus system fits. (I recommend manual focus in such cases.) Sometimes a *focus assist lamp* built into the camera or a dedicated flash unit can put a little light on the focus problem.

Figure 5-8: It might be easier to focus on the center chessman manually.

One nagging problem with autofocus is how the system decides what to focus on. Most digital cameras have five to nine (or more) focus sensors grouped around the viewfinder screen, and the cameras evaluate the contrast of the image in each of them to select the zone on which to base focus. To gain a little more control over the focal point of a shot, you might have the following options:

- **Switching zones manually:** You might be able to switch from one zone to another manually by using your camera's cursor pad. That's useful if your subject isn't smack in the center of the frame but still lies within one of the other focus zones. The zone you select is highlighted in the viewfinder and remains in that position until you move to another zone.

- **Switching zones under camera control:** If you don't choose a focus zone yourself, your camera does it for you by using a scheme such as *dynamic focus area* (the zone switches around as the camera detects subject motion) or *nearest subject* (the zone is locked into what the system determines is the closest object to the camera). You might be able to allow the autofocus system to set the focus point for you, yet still override its decision without resorting to full manual focus.

✔ **Locking out focus ranges:** Another option is the ability to lock out certain focus ranges, such as extreme close-up or distant focus, so your autofocus system won't hunt over the full range when seeking correct focus.

Most of the time, you can let your camera focus for you, choosing between two primary focus modes:

✔ **Continuous autofocus:** After you press the shutter release halfway, the camera sets the focus but continues to look for movement within the frame. If the camera detects motion, the lens refocuses on the new position. Use this option for action photography or other subjects that are likely to be in motion. Remember that if your subject moves faster than the autofocus system can keep up, you might take an out-of-focus picture. That isn't as bad as it sounds, though: Sometimes you'd rather capture a picture — any picture — even if it's slightly out of focus than miss the shot entirely.

✔ **Single autofocus:** Press the shutter release halfway, and focus is set. It remains at that setting until you take the photo or release the button. This mode is best suited for subject matter that isn't likely to move after it's been brought into sharp focus. However, you won't be able to take a photo at all until focus is locked in, so you end up either with a sharp photo or none at all.

6

Mastering the Multi-Lens Reflex

*I*n one sense, the term *single lens reflex* is a misnomer. I don't know *anyone* who owns a dSLR who has only a single lens. And, buying extra optics for one of these cameras is more than a reflex — it's a passion! Add-on lenses are probably the most popular accessory for digital SLRs.

Of course, you probably know that the term SLR refers to a camera design that uses the same lens to take the picture for reflex viewing (that is, by reflection with mirrors or a prism) as opposed to a "twin-lens reflex" that pairs two lenses of the same focal length for separate viewing and snapshooting. These days, however, dSLR owners are more likely to be single-minded about acquiring accessory lenses.

This chapter helps you choose which lenses to add to your collection based on your needs — both real and imagined. You also find out how to use them effectively.

Optical Delusions

Unless you happened to purchase a compact 12mm–400mm f1.4 zoom lens with your dSLR (they don't exist), you're deluding yourself if you think you couldn't use an accessory lens to improve your photography. Lenses don't make you a better photographer, of course, but they do increase your opportunities and enable you to take pictures you simply couldn't grab with the lens that came with your camera.

In the following sections, I discuss just some of the things that an accessory lens can do for you.

Shooting in lower light

The do-everything zoom lenses furnished with dSLRs often have maximum apertures of f3.5 to f4.5:

- ✔ The Canon Digital Rebels, Nikon D40, and Pentax models all are furnished in kit form with 18mm–55mm f3.5/f5.6 zooms. (I'm sensing a trend here.)

- ✔ The Nikon default package lens for the D70 is an 18–70mm f3.5/f4.5 lens.

- ✔ The Olympus E-300 is often sold with a 14–45mm f3.5/f4.5 lens.

- ✔ The Sony Maxxum 7D and Maxxum 5D dSLRs are generally offered without a lens, but the existing 24–100mm f3.4/f4.5 and 17mm–35mm f2.8/f4 zooms are popular. New AF DT 18mm–70mm (shown in Figure 6-1), and 18mm–200mm zooms designed especially for the digital frame size are other options.

Figure 6-1: An 18mm–70mm zoom range seems to be the most popular basic lens for dSLRs.

You can't compare the focal length ranges directly, of course, because these popularly priced dSLRs have different crop factors, ranging from 1.5X (for Nikon and others) to 2X (for the Olympus line). (See Chapter 2 for details about crop factor.) But you can compare maximum apertures, and you'll see that f3.5 or slower is common among every vendor's "starter" lenses. That's where your add-on lenses come in.

Whereas zooms with large maximum apertures are expensive, fixed-focal-length ("prime") lenses that are fast can cost very little. For example, a 50mm f1.8 lens from a major camera manufacturer might cost less than $100 even though it's two f-stops faster than an f3.5 lens and three stops better than an f4.5 optic.

If you're willing to spend a little more, you can buy 28mm, 35mm, 50mm, or 85mm f1.4 lenses from the larger lens companies, or you could get speedy third-party lenses like the Sigma 30mm f1.4. Those extra notches on the aperture ring let you take hand-held pictures in darker environments, as shown in Figure 6-2, without resorting to detail-robbing higher ISO ratings. An indoor concert that calls for an exposure of ⅕ of a second at f4 and ISO 100 might work just fine at ⅟₁₂₅ of a second at f1.4.

Figure 6-2: Wider apertures allow shooting in dim light without mounting the camera on a tripod.

The fastest lenses are generally designed to produce good results wide open, too, so you needn't fear using f1.4 with a prime lens, even though you've gotten poor results with your zoom at f4.5.

Improving your shutter speed

That wider aperture also pays dividends in the shutter speed department. The difference between f1.4 at ⅟₁₂₅ of a second and ⅕ of a second at f4 can be quite dramatic from a sharpness perspective, as you discover in Chapter 4. Chapter 7 tells you more about making the most of slow shutter speeds by using image stabilization technology.

Producing sharper images

You might be able to get sharper images by switching lenses, too. That's not to say that the lens you purchased with your camera is unsharp. However, your do-all lens is built on a foundation of compromises that don't necessarily produce the best results at all zoom positions and all apertures. Other lenses you add to your collection might provide better results at specific focal lengths or f-stops. For example, that 50mm f1.8 lens you pick up for less than $100 just might be the sharpest lens you own. Or, you might buy a close-up lens that's optimized for macro photography and produces especially sharp images at distances of a few inches or so.

The lens you bought with your camera is probably very good, but that doesn't mean you can't get sharper pictures with another set of optics, particularly when you're swapping a general-purpose zoom lens for a fixed-focal-length prime lens designed for exactly the kind of photo project you're working on at the moment.

Taking a step back

Wider lenses let you take in a wider field of view, in effect, stepping back from your subject even in situations where there really isn't room to move farther away. It's likely that the lens you bought with your camera provides a field of view no wider than that of a 28mm lens on a full-frame film SLR. That isn't really very wide. You can achieve some very interesting perspectives with ultra-wide lenses, including the 10.5mm fish-eye view provided by one Nikkor lens (particularly because Nikon offers a utility that can defish the curved image to produce a more *rectilinear,* or straight line, version). Your particular dSLR might have wide-angle lenses available with the equivalent of a super-wide 18mm lens, or better. Third-party vendors also offer some interesting wide-angle choices, such as the Sigma 10–20mm f4/f5.6 optic that offers the equivalent of a 15mm–30mm zoom on a dSLR with a 1.5X crop factor.

It's understandable if you've been lusting after longer and longer lenses, particularly if you shoot wildlife or sports, but if you haven't worked extensively with wide-angle lenses, I urge you to give them a try. It's a whole new world. If you want to get your whole Little League team in one shot, or shoot a striking vertical picture, a wide angle might provide just the perspective you're looking for.

Getting closer

The inverse of a wide-angle lens is the telephoto lens, and the longer focal lengths of a telephoto lens let you bring distant objects that much closer to your camera. The lens that came with your camera probably provides only a moderate telephoto effect, perhaps around 70mm, which, with a 1.5 crop factor, is the equivalent of a 105mm short tele on a full-frame 35mm film camera.

Longer lenses are easy to find and can be very inexpensive because telephoto prime lenses and telephoto zooms are generally simpler to design than their tricky wide-angle counterparts. You can find 70mm–300mm zooms for many dSLRs for only a few hundred dollars. Prime lenses can be even cheaper. I picked up an ancient nonautomatic (focus, exposure, and aperture) 400mm lens for about $79. It's great for shooting the moon (as in Figure 6-3) or wildlife, especially if you can mount the camera or lens on a tripod.

Figure 6-3: Shoot for the moon — if you have a long enough telephoto lens.

Focusing closer

Your add-on lens might be able to focus much more closely than the lens that came with your camera, making it a macro lens. If you're new to close-up photography, you'll soon find out that the *magnification* of the image is more important than the close focusing distance.

You can get the same size image with a 200mm lens at 8 inches that you get with a 50mm lens at 2 inches, and you might even be better off. The closer you get, the harder it might be to get good lighting on your subject. You simply don't have a lot of room to apply effective lighting when you're faced with a gap of only a couple inches between the front of the lens and that tree frog you're snapping. Worse, the tree frog might get skittish at the proximity of you and your camera, making that 200mm lens and the extra distance it provides an even better idea.

Choosing Your Prime Lens or Zoom

In the olden days, fixed-focal-length prime lenses were all photographers used most of the time. Zoom lenses were slow, often expensive, and had limited zoom ranges. In the 1960s and 1970s, photographers used zoom lenses only when they absolutely couldn't swap lenses to get the focal lengths they needed, and even then they were more likely to tote around three or four camera bodies, each mounted with a prime lens of a different focal length. Zooms were also good for special tricks, such as the infamous "zoom during exposure" effect. In 1966, Nikon introduced one of the first decent zooms with a practical zoom range and acceptable sharpness — a 50mm–300mm f4.5 zoom lens that seems fairly tame today, but which was revolutionary and horrendously expensive at the time.

Today, zooms are sharper, smaller, faster, and less expensive. The 28mm–200mm zoom I have mounted on my dSLR right now cost around $300, measures about 2.7 x 2.8 inches, weighs 13 ounces, and focuses down to 1.3 feet at 200mm. It's truly an all-purpose lens. You can find other zooms that meet your needs or, perhaps, fill out your arsenal with a few prime lenses. In the following sections, I explain some of the main options.

Prime time

Prime lenses can be faster (both in aperture and autofocusing speed), sharper, and much lighter in weight than zoom lenses. If you're looking for the ultimate in image quality, a good prime lens or two might be exactly what you want.

Here's a list of some common applications and the prime lenses that might be especially suitable for them:

In all cases, when referring to recommended focal lengths, I use the actual focal length but assume that your camera has about a 1.5X crop factor. That's a good number that works for the majority of consumer-priced dSLRs on the market, and it isn't too far off for people with 1.3 to 1.6X crop factors.

- ✓ **Architecture:** Wide-angle lenses in the 18mm to 30mm range (depending on how much of the wide view your system's crop factor clips off). Most of the time you'll be shooting stopped down to a relatively small aperture to gain depth-of-field, so an f2 or f1.4 maximum aperture isn't as important, even when shooting indoors under low light levels. A tripod can serve you better. If you shoot a great deal of architecture, you can purchase a *perspective control* lens that compensates for the "falling back" effect that results when you tilt the camera back to capture the upper reaches of a tall structure. You can find out more about perspective problems in Chapter 10.

- ✓ **Indoor sports:** You'll want a moderately wide angle of roughly the equivalent of 30mm focal length for indoor sports, such as basketball and volleyball, with longer lenses for shooting from up in the stands.

Large apertures can be useful for available-light sports, but only if you can focus carefully on a single subject or two, because depth-of-field will be limited.

- **Outdoor sports:** Longer lenses are useful for shooting outdoor sports, and primes in telephoto focal lengths often offer an excellent combination of reach and speed. The 100mm to 200mm lenses, or longer, are great for capturing football, baseball, soccer, and other outdoor sports. Apertures of f2.8 to f4 let you use faster shutter speeds to freeze the action (assuming that you or your camera's autofocus system make the most of the available depth-of-field).

- **Portraits:** If you're taking head-and-shoulders shots, a 50mm to 70mm prime lens offers the same flattering perspective as the traditional 75mm to 105mm portrait lenses used with 35mm full-frame cameras (with a 1.5X crop factor on the dSLR). Such prime lenses usually come with f1.8 or faster maximum apertures, which are useful for limiting depth-of-field when you want to concentrate on your portrait subject's face. Longer focal lengths can produce a flattening effect on the features, and shorter focal lengths can make ears look too small while enlarging noses if used up close.

- **Macro photography:** Prime lenses, such as the ever-popular 50mm f1.8, although not intended for close-up work, can still do a great job. You might have to purchase extension tubes or other accessories to focus close enough to get pictures like the one in Figure 6-4.

- **Landscapes:** Wide-angle prime lenses (18mm to 24mm) can give you landscape photos that are sharp enough to blow up to 16 x 20 inches or larger as framed pictures to grace your walls.

Figure 6-4: Even an inexpensive 50mm lens can shoot great close-ups.

Of course, the only problem with using prime lenses is that you must be willing to swap lenses whenever you decide to shoot something else or when you need a different perspective that you can't get by stepping closer or farther away. Digital SLRs have one additional consideration: If you're working in a dusty environment, you might not want to change lenses a lot because each time you take off a lens you're letting some dirt invade the camera body, and that dirt might end up on the sensor. You can read more about sensors and dust in Chapter 2.

Zoom, zoom, zoom

Zooms are good, too. Honest. I might be a little biased because most of my lenses have always been primes, with only a lone zoom that I didn't use much. Today, most of my work is with 12–24mm, 18–70mm, 28–200mm and 170–500mm zooms, so you can see I'm no optical Luddite. But I still get a lot of use from my new 60mm and 105mm macro lenses, as well as older prime lenses I own, including a 16mm fish-eye lens that functions as a quirky 24mm lens with a heck of a lot of barrel distortion (even after the crop factor has trimmed the image). I also regularly use my prime 50mm f1.4, 85mm f1.8, 105mm f2.5, and 200mm f4 lenses when I want a little extra sharpness or aperture speed.

But those applications are in the distinct minority. Like you, I rely on zooms most of the time. You have several broad categories of zooms to consider:

- **Wide-angle zooms:** These are strictly designed for wide-angle perspectives, and if designed for dSLRs, might include ranges like 10–20mm or 12–24mm. You'll find wide-angle zooms that were originally created for full-frame 35mm cameras, too, with ranges like 17–35mm. On a camera with a crop factor, such lenses are actually closer to wide-to-normal in range, but they're likely to be very sharp (and sometimes very expensive).

  Before purchasing a wide zoom for your dSLR, you might want to check it out carefully because the widest of the wide often have serious distortion and aberrations.

- **Mid-range zooms:** The lens furnished with your camera is likely to be a mid-range zoom, with a focal length at the wide end of about 17–18mm, extending out to 55mm to 70mm at the telephoto end. Such lenses are inexpensive, not very fast, but reasonable in cost. You can also find some upscale versions in the same focal lengths, with greater sharpness and larger maximum apertures. These are usually designed for finicky full-frame 35mm film camera users. They're usually worth the extra expenditure because they often have a fixed maximum aperture throughout the zoom range. That is, a 17–55mm f2.8 lens has a constant f2.8 aperture and doesn't vary between, say, f2.8 at the wide-angle position and f4 at the telephoto position, which is common with less expensive models (like the one that came with your camera).

- **Short tele to telephoto zooms:** These lenses might start out at 50mm to 70mm and extend out to 200mm to 300mm or more. One vendor's 50–500mm zoom is especially popular because it provides such a huge range of focal lengths in one lens. Of course, it's also possibly the largest and heaviest 50mm lens on the planet, so you'd want to own such a beast only if you plan on actually needing its 10X zoom reach.

- **Telephoto zooms:** These lenses start long and go longer. My 170–500mm zoom falls into this category, and it's able to *really* reach out and touch someone, as shown in Figure 6-5, which shows a stone carving that was almost 50 feet out of reach behind a high fence. You'll also find 200–400mm zooms or even longer lenses from various vendors. As with any lens of more than about 200mm, you'll want to seriously consider using these optics with either the lens or the camera mounted on a tripod.

- **Macro zooms:** Several vendors offer lenses with zoom ranges in the medium telephoto range (out to about 200mm) that also offer macro focusing. They're especially useful for wildlife photographers who photograph big beasts and small.

Figure 6-5: Easily capture subjects that you can't get close to with a long lens, like the 500mm zoom used to capture this shot.

Special (lens) delivery

I touch on special-purpose lenses in this chapter and describe them in more detail in other sections of this book. Just to make things neat and tidy, here's a list of the special kinds of lenses you might encounter (or want to acquire):

✓ **Optical image stabilization lenses:** These lenses counter camera or photographer shake by shifting lens elements around just before exposure. They give you the power to shoot at shutter speeds about 4X as long without producing camera-induced blur. Konica Minolta builds the anti-shake feature into the camera itself, so, with only a couple exceptions, *all* your lenses can be used with image stabilization. (I discuss these lenses further in Chapter 7.) Figure 6-6 shows two flower close-ups, one taken with image stabilization and one without. I took both shots at ¹⁄₃₀ of a second with a 105mm lens.

✓ **Perspective control lenses:** These optics shift to improve the perspective when photographing buildings or other subjects that converge in the distance.

✓ **Macro lenses:** These are prime or zoom lenses designed especially for close-up photography, offering extended focusing, better sharpness, and, often, extra-small apertures (such as f32 or f45) to maximize depth-of-field.

✓ **Focus control portrait lenses:** Nikon offers a series of DC lenses with *defocus control,* which lets you adjust how the out-of-focus background appears in portraits or similar kinds of single-subject pictures.

Figure 6-6: The image-stabilized version (top) is significantly sharper than the unstabilized shot (bottom).

✓ **UV lenses:** If you're a scientist photographing subjects with ultraviolet light, you probably want to scrounge around for one of these rare, expensive optics — which don't filter out UV in the same way as lenses built of conventional glass elements.

Understanding How Film Lenses Work on a Digital Camera

Ideally, lenses used on dSLRs should be designed to meet the special needs of digital cameras. That isn't always possible. Most digital SLRs use lenses that were originally designed for film cameras, which might not work as well on a digital camera. Some vendors, such as Pentax, Nikon, and Olympus, offer lenses that work exclusively with their digital cameras. That's a better solution, in my book.

Sensors aren't what engineers might describe as "plug compatible" with film. You can't rip out the film transport mechanism and substitute a digital sensor and expect the same results (even though that's exactly how some of the original dSLRs were designed).

Sensors are smaller than film frames, introducing the infamous crop factor I'm forced to drag into about half the shooting discussions in this book. Only part of the image formed by a lens designed for a full frame sensor is captured by a sensor that's smaller than 24 x 36mm. The crop factor might be 1.3X, 1.5X, 1.6X, or even 2.0X. This can be (seemingly) good for telephoto pictures, but not such a great effect if what you really wanted was a wide-angle view. A 100mm lens might have the field of view of a 150mm lens, but a 20mm wide-angle lens ends up with the viewpoint of a 30mm lens.

If you're using a lens that was originally designed for a film camera, you might just be using the best part of the lens. Because a smaller portion of the lens coverage area is used when the lens is attached to a dSLR, the smaller sensor crops out the edges and corners of the image, where aberrations and other defects traditionally hide.

Now vendors are producing lenses designed expressly for smaller sensors, which means that their reduced coverage area must be extraordinarily even in terms of sharpness and light distribution.

But wait, there's more! Sensors don't respond to light the same way film does. Film grains absorb light in roughly the same manner regardless of its angle of approach to the film surface. A sensor's photosites, on the other hand, are little pixel-nabbing wells that collect photons best when the photons drop directly into the well, rather than coming in from a steep angle. With lenses designed for film, some of the light can hit the side of the well or spill over into adjacent pixels. Unwanted patterns and light fall-off can also result, along with flare that results when photons bounce off the shiny sensor surface, hit the equally shiny rear-lens elements, and then reflect back onto the sensor. Ugh!

Although camera and lens designers have found ways to counter these problems with equipment designed expressly for digital photography, optics created for film cameras might not produce the same uniformly good results. Image quality can vary from lens to lens, based on how well the design meets the needs of digital imaging.

Going for Bokeh

Obsessing over the bokeh (the quality of the out-of-focus areas of an image) that a lens produces has become a fixation of its own in recent years. Some lenses are prized for their wonderful bokeh, but others are reviled because their bokeh stinks. You can find endless discussion of this topic in the photographic forums online. So what does it all mean?

The word *boke* means "blur" in Japanese, I'm told. English speakers insisted on rhyming it with "broke," so the silent *h* was added to the Western spelling of the term to help ensure that the language-challenged folks would properly pronounce it as if it rhymed with "mocha."

Bokeh describes the points of light in the background that become fuzzy disks when rendered out of focus by inadequate depth-of-field. Various lenses render these disks in different ways. Some create uniformly illuminated disks. Others generate disks that are dark in the center and lighter at the edges, which makes them stand out like a sore thumb or, actually, a frosted doughnut. The reverse effect, a nicely illuminated center that fades to a darker edge, is ideal because the disks tend to blend into each other. Lenses with the very best bokeh characteristics display almost no disk shapes at all.

If you shoot close-ups, portraits, or long telephoto shots that have out-of-focus backgrounds, be sure to very carefully examine the bokeh characteristics of any lens you're considering. You might not even be aware of the deleterious effects of bad bokeh (except when using a so-called *mirror* or *catadioptic* telephoto lens, which generates the mother of all doughnuts around each point of light). But you'll eventually notice that some out-of-focus backgrounds are more harmonious than others, or in the worst case, your bokeh-aware photographer friends will make fun of you. Figure 6-7 shows examples of both good and bad bokeh.

Figure 6-7: With bad bokeh (top), out-of-focus light points produce obvious disks that are darker in the center than at the edges. With good bokeh (bottom), you get a smooth out-of-focus background.

Using Lenses Creatively

Working with a lens involves more than simply adjusting to its greater or lesser field of view. That is to say, a wide-angle lens is much more than just a wider perspective, just as a telephoto lens has a lot more going for it than the ability to pull objects closer to your camera. The following sections show you some of the techniques you need to know to work with wide-angle and telephoto lenses creatively.

Creative use of wide angles

Wide-angle lenses have some special characteristics. Those characteristics can hold some special pitfalls that you'll want to avoid, but they also offer some creative advantages if you use them properly.

Here are some of the ways you can use the wide-angle lens's special qualities in your photography:

- **Increase depth-of-field.** Sometimes you want what cinematographers call *deep focus*. Akira Kurosawa was a master of the technique of sharply focusing on subjects both very close to and more distant from the camera. You can do it, too. At any given aperture, wide-angle lenses provide more depth-of-field than telephoto lenses, allowing you to picture a larger range of subject matter without distracting blurriness of objects in the foreground, background, or both.

- **Emphasize the foreground.** If you want to put extra emphasis on subjects in the foreground while de-emphasizing the background, use a wide-angle lens. For instance, you might want to emphasize a lake or meadow while de-emphasizing the mountains in the background.

- **Distort the foreground.** Although wide-angle lenses tend to exaggerate the size of objects closest to the lens, you can effectively use this form of perspective distortion to create an interesting viewpoint in your picture.

- **Add a unique angle.** When you get down low and shoot up with a wide angle, the combination of perspective distortion and the unusual angle can be used creatively, as shown in Figure 6-8. The same is true when shooting down from high angles.

A low angle with a wide-angle lens is a dual-edged sword. The perspective is interesting, but you run the danger of having tall structures appear to be falling backward.

✐ **Use slower shutter speeds.** Just as telephotos magnify camera shake, wide-angle lenses tend to minimize it. If you can hand-hold your camera with a normal lens (or zoom setting) at ⅟₆₀ of a second, you just might be able to pull off ⅟₃₀ of a second exposures, or longer, with a wide-angle lens.

✐ **Show more stuff.** Indoors or outdoors in tight quarters, you can show more of your scene with a wide-angle lens. That's great when you want to picture most of a building or all of a room indoors, but you can also use this expansive view when photographing people in their environment.

Figure 6-8: If you start feeling queasy, take a deep breath and *don't* hurl on the book.

Don't be lulled by the creative opportunities wide-angles lenses offer. You need to avoid some pitfalls, too:

- **Avoid skewed horizontal and vertical lines.** Watch the horizons and vertical lines of buildings so they don't look skewed in your photos. Keep the camera level as much as possible.

- **Watch proportions.** Because wide-angle lenses exaggerate the relative size of objects that are close to the camera, you can end up with weird proportions in your photos. You don't want your spouse's nose to appear twice its normal size (even button noses don't benefit from optical plastic surgery), so keep the possibilities of distortion in mind when framing your photos.

- **Don't let lens defects ruin your photos.** Wide-angle lenses might be subject to distortions that change the shape of vertical and horizontal lines at the edges of the photo. Or, such lenses might have chromatic aberrations that add purple or cyan glows around backlit subjects.

- **Avoid vignetting.** Filters, lens hoods, and other add-ons might actually intrude into the picture area with wide-angle lenses, causing the dark corners known as vignetting. Use thin filters, avoid stacking too many of them together, and use only lens hoods designed for a particular lens.

- **Watch that flash.** Your digital SLR's built-in electronic flash might not spread wide enough to cover the full frame of a wide-angle lens. Use a diffuser or wide-angle adapter over your flash. Some dedicated flash units actually "zoom" their coverage to match your lens's zoom position. Also, make sure that your lens or lens hood doesn't cast a shadow when shooting close-up subjects with flash.

Creative use of telephoto lenses

Telephoto lenses have their own set of creative strengths and dangerous pitfalls. Keep these tempting applications in mind when working with your longer lenses and tele-zooms:

- **Compression:** Telephoto lenses compress the apparent distance between objects, making that row of fence posts appear as if each post is only a foot or two distant from the next. (Moviemakers use this effect all the time to make the hero appear to be racing bravely between speeding cars while crossing the street, when actually none of the vehicles come closer than five or ten feet.)

- **Isolation:** The reduced depth-of-field of tele lenses lets you apply selective focus when you want to isolate your subjects from the foreground or background.

- **Sports action:** A telephoto lens brings you into the middle of the huddle, right in the center of the action around the goal, and a lot closer than you ever wanted to get to the periphery of a scrum.

✔ **Nature's bounty:** A telephoto can take you closer to your photographic prey, including animals of all shapes and sizes, while letting you stay far enough away that you don't become prey yourself, as shown in Figure 6-9.

✔ **Macro photos:** You might not need a macro lens to shoot macro photos. A telephoto lens with enough reach that focuses reasonably close might be all you need.

Figure 6-9: Don't get too close! Use a telephoto lens and live to shoot another day.

Telephoto lenses don't have an unusual number of pitfalls, but be aware of them nevertheless. Here are the crucial troubles to watch out for:

- **Flash coverage:** Like wide-angle lenses, telephoto lenses have some potential problems with electronic flash coverage, except that the problem is *depth* rather than *width*. The electronic flash built into most dSLRs isn't powerful enough to reach more than 10–20 feet, so if you're photographing a running back who's 50 feet away, you'll end up with a very underexposed photo.

   If you do a lot of sports photography, you might want to consider buying a powerful external flash to provide the extra light you need.

- **Too-slow shutter speeds:** Because longer lenses magnify the shakiness of lightweight cameras or lightweight photographers, you want to use a shutter speed that's high enough to counter the vibration. If you can't use a higher shutter speed, use a tripod or monopod.

- **Reduced depth-of-field:** Telephoto lenses have less depth-of-field at a given aperture. If you need the maximum amount of depth-of-field, use a smaller f-stop.

- **Atmospheric conditions:** Even when smog doesn't fill the sky, the air is full of enough haze or fog to reduce the contrast of your long telephoto shots enough to affect your pictures. Sometimes a skylight or haze filter helps, or you can boost the contrast and color saturation in your camera or image editor.

- **Flare:** Telephoto lenses have a narrow field of view, allowing bright light outside your image area to affect your image with flare, which reduces contrast. Use your lens hood without fail.

7

Special Features of dSLRs

*E*veryone loves watching movies on DVD more than on videotape, premium cable, or maybe even in a theater. Why? Because of those special features! It's a kick to press a button and hear the director's commentary, watch out-takes, or listen to Ben Stiller and Owen Wilson banter in French or Japanese.

The special features built into your digital SLR are even cooler. These are the functions built into some dSLRs, but not all. They let you do some very interesting things, such as take pictures in virtual darkness or shoot the unfolding of flowers through time-lapse photography.

This chapter describes what you can do with some of these special features. There are no movie stars chattering in a foreign language among these options, but if you have your heart set on gibberish, your dSLR probably has a setting for switching your menus to any language you like. While you're at it, I'll keep busy exploring some of the more useful features of digital cameras.

Feel the Noize at Night

All digital SLRs can take fine pictures at night, but some do a better job than others, thanks to special features built into them to handle long exposures and noise (or, as Quiet Riot and Slade fans call it, *noize*). This section describes the key components you need to work with so that your night shots are sparklingly clear.

A fast lens . . . or not?

As you discover in Chapter 6, a lens with a large maximum aperture (generally, anything faster than f2.8) is a must only if you're hand-holding (that is, shooting without a tripod) your night photos or, perhaps if you want to shoot with flash and need your speedlight's illumination to reach as far as possible. An f2 or f1.4 lens might let you take some night pictures at 1/30 of a second hand-held or, with image stabilization (which I discuss in the next section), at slightly slower shutter speeds.

The more sane shooters take night photographs with the camera securely mounted on a tripod, so that you can use virtually any lens at any desired f-stop and still get a clear photo. Correct exposure in such cases is simply a matter of using a sufficiently long shutter speed. That said, using a long shutter speed isn't always an option, as I discuss in the next section.

Taking night shots at short shutter speeds

You might want to avoid very long shutter speeds and prefer the shorter shutter intervals a higher sensitivity (higher ISO setting) affords for any number of valid reasons:

- Perhaps you don't want to spend 30 seconds or more making a single exposure because of time constraints or physical conditions (rain, muggers, and so forth).

- You might want to take as many photos as possible in available darkness.

- Or, you'd rather avoid the light streaks from moving cars or other illuminated objects that a long exposure is likely to produce.

Bumping up the ISO can let you take your night photo with a reasonably short exposure. Some dSLRs have ISO settings no higher than ISO 800, but others go up to ISO 1600, ISO 3200, or higher. A few cameras top out at a specific ISO notch but include "push" settings, which elevate the effective sensitivity a notch or two more and you can use in a pinch. You can also adjust your camera's EV controls to underexpose an image (effectively providing a higher ISO setting) and then try to salvage the photo in your image editor.

Of course, high ISO settings tend to amplify non-image signals in an image, producing extra noise. That's where your camera's noise reduction circuitry comes in, reducing the annoying speckles produced. See the next section for more about using noise reduction.

Noise Reduction Made Easy

You'll want to consider using noise anytime you take photos at night using long exposures or high sensitivity settings, because of the objectionable texture that overlays unprocessed images.

Noise comes from several sources. One might be the amplification of the weak signal that the sensor produces under low light conditions. The sensor itself also produces noise as it inevitably heats up during a long exposure and some of that heat is mistaken for incoming photons. So, noise can be generated at high ISOs with exposures of any length and at relatively low ISO settings with long exposures.

To cancel out some of those noisy speckles, digital SLRs include internal noise reduction circuitry. It works by making *two* exposures: an actual picture of your subject and a blank or dark exposure for the same length of time. This second picture contains only noise, of the same type that appears in the real picture. The camera's noise reduction circuitry compares the two and zaps the pixels that are common to both (the noise). This solution is along the order of the sculptor who starts with a block of marble and removes everything that doesn't look like a statue.

Figure 7-1 shows two versions of an image taken in the early evening at an amusement park, using a relatively short exposure (⅟₆₀ of a second), but with the ISO setting cranked up all the way to ISO 1600. A lot of noise is visible in the upper version. (The upper version is actually a little exaggerated to make it visible on the printed page.) The lower version is the same shot with noise reduction applied. The difference is quite dramatic.

Figure 7-1: The upper version badly needs noise reduction. You can see the results in the lower version.

Because the noise reduction feature works by taking two shots, any photos taken with the noise reduction feature turned on take twice as long. You'll scarcely notice the delay with shutter speeds of about one second or shorter, but when you're snapping off 30-second exposures, you'll definitely notice the extra half-minute pause during this "dark frame subtraction" process. If you're in a hurry or forgot to switch on the noise reduction, you can also perform some post-shot noise reduction with an image editor such as Photoshop (as shown in Figure 7-2) or with a third-party application such as Neat Image (www.neatimage.com) or Noise Ninja (www.picture code.com).

The Reduce Noise filter in Photoshop lets you control the strength of the noise reduction, how much detail to preserve, whether to eliminate color noise, and how much sharpening of the remaining detail should be applied. For an introduction to image editors and image editing, see Chapters 11 and 12.

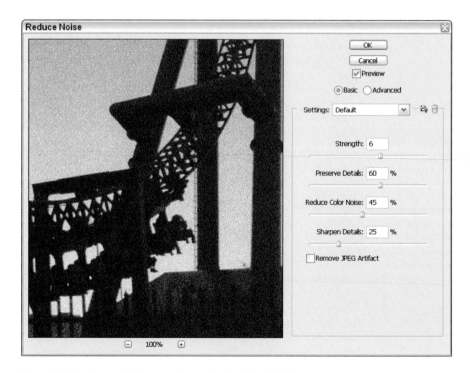

Figure 7-2: Photoshop CS2 has a noise reduction filter built in.

Shake, Shake, Shake

Whenever photographers get together, one of the inevitable topics of conversation is each shooter's prowess at hand-holding a camera for incredibly long exposures. Oddly enough, these are the same photographers who might swear by an emerging camera-steadying technology known as image stabilization.

"I get razor-sharp images at ⅟₃₀ of a second, even with telephoto lenses!" one will boast. "I can squeeze off shots at ¼ of a second with no problem!" another will counter. "I have a special technique for bracing my arms that lets me take time exposures of up to two seconds without a tripod!" a third will assert, leaving the others to wonder whether he's joking or just filled with braggadocio.

No matter how experienced a photographer you are, and whether or not you apply arcane breath-control and body-steadying practices to your techniques, you only *think* you're steady enough to shoot long exposures with short lenses, and reasonably long exposures with telephotos.

In the sections that follow, you find out some of the common myths about camera shake, identify the point where you *really* need to switch from hand-held shots to a tripod, diagnose shake-related problems in your photos, and discover ways to fix those problems.

Leaving camera shake myths behind

In camera shake lore, you might have come across two misleading assumptions:

- ⮑ **If you don't see the shake, it isn't there.** The slowest shutter speed at which you *think* you can reliably shoot sharp images is probably the speed at which you can't detect the blurriness that appears at normal levels of enlargement. Crop a small section out of the center, or make a huge enlargement, and you'll likely be able to see the difference. A surprising number of your shots very likely would be sharper if you used a tripod.

- ⮑ **Use a shutter speed that's the reciprocal of the lens's focal length (for example, ⅟₂₅₀ of a second with a 250mm lens).** This is more of a rough-guideline-of-thumb than a rule, because it doesn't take into account the crop factor some dSLRs produce. That is, your 250mm lens is effectively a 400mm lens (if your camera has a 1.6X crop factor). No, you're *not* multiplying the focal length of the lens (as I emphasize over and over), but you *are* filling the frame with less subject area, magnifying any camera shake just as if you'd made an 8-x-10-inch print instead of a 4-x-6-inch print.

And remember, some people are shakier than others, so a ⅟₄₀₀ of a second shutter speed that can be used successfully by one photographer might be woefully inadequate for another. To figure out the point where you personally need to switch from hand-held shots to using a tripod, see the next section, "Testing for tremors."

It goes without saying, of course, that this discussion is concerned *only* with blurriness caused by camera/photographer shake. Blurs derived from moving objects is another issue entirely, although they, too, can be fixed by using higher shutter speeds.

Testing for tremors

Before looking at the latest technological cure for shaky hands, try this exercise to see just how bad you have the affliction:

1. **Find a scene that contains sharp pinpoints of light, preferably at night so you'll have a dark background, such as a scene with streetlights.**

2. **Switch your camera to Manual mode so you'll be able to vary both the shutter speed and f-stop independently.**

3. **Take several pictures at a fixed f-stop but vary the shutter speed for each picture.**

   Use various shutter speeds you think are test-worthy. For example, ⅟₆₀, ⅟₃₀, ⅟₁₅, or ⅛ of a second.

4. **Calculate your exposure with your digital camera's metering system.**

   Exposure needn't be precise, as long as you vary only the shutter speed during the tests. If you change f-stop or focus, you can change the size of the points of light, although the greatest effect will be on any out-of-focus points.

   If you're shooting over a great range, change the ISO setting of your camera so you can maintain the same aperture while varying the shutter speed.

5. **When you're finished, open your shots in your image editor and examine the camera shake by enlarging the light points enough that you can study their shape.**

   The appearance of the round disks of light in your images will let you judge fairly accurately how steady you were able to hold the camera during the tests:

   • **If the disks are perfectly round,** like those shown in Figure 7-3, you used a shutter speed that's fast enough to stop action at that focal length.

   Keep in mind that if you zoom in to a longer focal length, you need a higher shutter speed. Telephotos *magnify* the effects of camera shake.

   • **If the disks are elongated vertically,** the camera has been shaken up or down (or both).

Figure 7-3: The spots of light in the lower-right and upper-left corners are round; the shutter speed was fast enough to stop camera shake.

- **Should the disks be elongated in a diagonal direction** (usually a diagonal pointing from upper left to lower right), you've jerked the camera, probably by punching the shutter release button too aggressively. Why that particular direction, since you tend to press down and to the right, not the other way around? Remember that an image is recorded on your sensor *upside-down,* so the direction of any camera movement is reversed.

- **If the disks are elongated from side to side,** your camera shake formed some panning-style blur. Again, the direction of the blur is reversed, so if you jerked the camera slightly to the left, the blur will appear to the right in your final image.

- **If you're *really* shaking, you might find the blurs create a streaky pattern,** like the one shown in Figure 7-4. That shutter speed is *way* too low for hand-held exposures.

Figure 7-4: Really streaky photos mean that you need a *much* faster shutter speed if you want to hand-hold your camera.

Everyday solutions for shakiness

After you determine what your minimum practical shutter speed is for hand-holding (keeping in mind that this speed can vary because of lens focal length and other factors), you can attempt to sharpen your photos. To cease the shakes, try using

- Higher shutter speeds
- Better shooting ergonomics (that is, bracing yourself)
- Aids like tripods, monopods, or beanbags (see Chapter 4)
- Techie tools, including image stabilization

Image stabilization: The ready-steady-shoot technology

Leave it to the techno-wonks to come up with stunning new technologies just because they can. Camera-steadying technology has been around since 1976 in the motion picture industry when the Steadicam was introduced. This device produces gyroscope-like stability through an exquisite application of gimbaling and balance. By 1995, Canon had introduced an electronic form of image stabilization (or IS), which is now offered by Nikon, Sony, Pentax, and others under names like Vibration Reduction, Anti-Shake, or Image Stabilization.

Nikon and Canon build IS into individual lenses; Sony, Pentax (the only other vendors offering the technology for digital SLRs) incorporates their image stabilization into the cameras, such as the budget-priced Maxxum 5D model shown in Figure 7-5. They all operate by using similar principles: The device (lens or camera) senses motion and then shifts components in the opposite direction(s) to compensate — those components being elements of either the lens or the sensor. You can turn off the vibration-reduction feature when you don't need it. An anti-shake on/off switch is shown in the lower-right corner of Figure 7-5.

Figure 7-5: Turn off anti-shake technology when you don't need it.

The mechanics of image stabilization work very quickly, although not quickly enough to avoid slowing down camera operation a tad. That's why IS is best suited for countering camera shake when taking pictures of relatively slow-moving subjects, when using longer exposures, or for shooting with telephoto lenses without a tripod. Although many photographers use IS for sports photography, the small delays it introduces can be annoying — the dSLR equivalent of shutter lag.

IS allows you to hand-hold your camera at shutter speeds roughly four times longer than you'd be able to manage without image stabilization. If you can hold your camera steady at $\frac{1}{60}$ of a second, you can get the same results with IS at $\frac{1}{15}$ of a second. Those extra two stops of exposure might mean the difference between not being able to take the picture at all and getting a well-exposed shot at a decent aperture.

The following scenarios offer a close-up look at how image stabilization works in different circumstances:

- Suppose you're shooting a poorly lit subject, and you need an exposure of $\frac{1}{60}$ of a second at f2. Oops! Your zoom lens has a maximum aperture of f5.6. With image stabilization cranked up, you can go ahead and shoot at the equivalent exposure of $\frac{1}{15}$ of a second at f5.6, and expect the same amount of sharpness from a camera steadiness perspective.

   Of course, if your *subject* is moving too much for capture at a slow shutter speed, that's another story. I took photos of my son's high school stage performance last fall by using the $\frac{1}{15}$ of a second and f5.6 combination. I ended up capturing razor-sharp scenery, but the expressive hands, arms, and mouths of the actors were often lost in blur!

- Using long lenses and shutter speeds that are high, but not quite high enough, such as if you're shooting wildlife (or even sports, if you can put up with the slight delay). In this case, IS can offer extra steadiness to compensate for the shake that long lenses can introduce. For example, you might find that shooting at $\frac{1}{500}$ of a second at f16 and ISO 400 with a 500mm lens is correct from an exposure standpoint, but your front-heavy lens causes enough wobble to blur photos even at that shutter speed. With IS, you can retain the $\frac{1}{500}$ of a second shutter speed and the depth-of-field provided by the f16 aperture, but with enough steadiness to make your image tack sharp. Figure 7-6 shows a pair of images shot with a 400mm lens at $\frac{1}{200}$ of a second, both with and without image stabilization. Tracking this bird in flight made holding the camera steady difficult at $\frac{1}{200}$ of a second (top), but I got a sharp image at the same speed with image stabilization turned on (bottom).

Figure 7-6: Image stabilization made it possible to shoot this bird hand held with a long lens.

Time Waits for Someone: Creating Time-Lapse Sequences

Walt Disney didn't invent time-lapse photography, but some of the most memorable nature sequences ever filmed were early Disney films of flowers blossoming or the sun marching across the sky in the Painted Desert. Today, time-lapse imaging is so easy that people use it for transitions and segues in television shows. Just set up a motion picture or video camera, pop off a frame every minute or hour or day, project the sequence at the normal 24 or 30 frames per second, and you have a time-lapse movie.

Your digital SLR can easily produce the same kind of sequences. You can snap off pictures at preset intervals to document a flower opening, a butterfly emerging from its chrysalis, or the construction project across the street. All you need is a willingness to tie up your camera for the necessary period of time and some means of tripping the shutter at the proper times. Of course, you can trip the shutter manually if you have the patience.

Some non-SLR digital cameras have built-in timers that will trip the shutter for you. With digital SLRs, however, it's more common to tether the camera to a computer with a USB cable and allow computer software to take the exposures. This method makes sense for several reasons:

- **Time-lapse photography uses a lot of juice.** Consequently, it's a good idea to keep the camera close to a computer and an AC power source. If your sequence takes more than an hour or two, your camera's battery probably won't be able to supply the power needed to take the photos. So, you'll want to connect your camera to an AC adapter plugged into the same power that keeps the attached computer running.

- **Long sequences tax your camera's internal storage.** If you want to use the maximum resolution your dSLR offers, you might find that a single memory card fills up before your sequence is done. Systems that tether the camera to a computer save the images directly onto the computer's hard drive.

- **Computer-driven time-lapse photography can be more sophisticated.** Most of the software programs used for this kind of work can automatically assemble your finished shots into a movie.

Experiment with time-lapse photos to see your world from an entirely different perspective. It's fun!

Better Infrared Than Dead

Feel like your creativity is on its last legs? Looking for a real challenge? Do a little research and see whether your particular dSLR can handle one of the unexplored frontiers of digital photography — infrared imaging. It's dark territory (quite literally — you'll be shooting blind), but it's worth a long look.

Infrared (IR) photos have a particular, other-worldly look. Skies are dark, clouds stand out in sharp relief, and foliage appears ghostly white, as you can see in Figure 7-7. Human faces are pale and lack texture. The pictures are grainy and sometimes seem to glow with an inner light. You'll either love or hate these effects after you take the time to explore them for yourself.

Some digital SLRs are better suited to IR photography than others. That's because most models include an IR-blocking filter called a *hot mirror* to filter out most of the longer wavelengths of light that encompass the infrared band. As luck would have it, digital sensors are quite sensitive to infrared, but that sensitivity leads to poorer photographs in visible light. Thus, you need an IR-blocking filter.

Figure 7-7: Infrared images are other-worldly in appearance.

Luckily for photographers interested in infrared imaging, some of these filters do a worse job than others in blocking the IR illumination. Your own dSLR might be one of those capable of taking infrared pictures. A quick way to tell is to point a remote control at your lens and snap off a picture with a button on the remote depressed. If you can see the glow of the remote control's IR burst, you're in business.

In addition to the hot mirror, watch for infrared blockers on your lens, too. A few lenses from Canon and other vendors have an anti-IR coating that can produce a bright spot in the center of your image. If you have this problem, switch to a different lens, or try to correct the spot in your image editor.

To start taking infrared photos, all you need is a special filter and some patience:

- ✔ The filter blocks visible light but lets infrared light though. (Don't confuse this infrared filter with the hot mirror I just mentioned.)

- ✔ Patience is essential because even with the most IR-worthy dSLRs, most of the infrared light is still filtered out. Enough infrared light remains to take a picture, but you'll have to use long exposures for best results. I've taken IR photos at $\frac{1}{30}$ of a second with my lens wide open and ISO set to 1600, but they've been fuzzy and lacked depth-of-field.

For better results, use normal ISO settings and mount your camera on a tripod. The tripod helps because you'll be shooting blind. Any IR filter you use removes virtually all visible light, so the view through your viewfinder is totally black. Digital SLRs generally don't provide an LCD preview, so you can't frame your photograph that way.

In Chapter 15, you find details on choosing a filter and steps that walk you though taking infrared photos.

Many photographers thought their IR prayers were answered when Canon introduced the Canon 20Da model, a special-purpose camera for astrophotography. This camera has a special low-pass filter that allows light in the 656 nanometer band through, and it provides a black-and-white preview image on its rear-panel LCD. Unfortunately, infrared photography involves wave lengths longer than 700 nanometers, and these are still blocked by filtration system in the Canon 20Da. This camera is best suited for astrophotography, not infrared photography.

Part III
Beyond the Basics

The 5th Wave   By Rich Tennant

"If I'm not gaining weight, then why does this digital image take up 3 MB more memory than a comparable one taken six months ago?"

In this part . . .

Moving on up . . . taking your digital imagery to the next level by putting your digital SLR's advanced features to work. In this part, you find out how to work with the RAW format and marshal your dSLR's action, sequence shooting, and flash features. I show you how important composition is, too.

Chapter 8 explains the fuss over formats and shows you how shooting RAW can give you extra flexibility when it's time to manipulate your images. Chapter 9 offers a solid grounding in action and flash photography — because the two often work hand-in-hand. Then, in Chapter 10, you discover how to arrange all the elements in your photo in pleasing ways by using compositional rules that were meant to be broken (after you understand exactly how they work).

8

Working with RAW and Other Formats

*Y*ou can find many bones of contention in the digital SLR world, but the choice of file format is one of the boniest. Some photographers swear by RAW, an "unprocessed" format that supposedly retains all the information the sensor captures. Others scoff at RAW, feeling that the JPEG format is the key to taking pictures most efficiently, with a minimum of after-shot processing required. Old-school photographers might insist that TIFF format is the only way to go, despite the fact that a decreasing number of digital SLRs even support that option.

This chapter removes the mystery surrounding RAW and other formats and helps you choose which one is right for you in any particular situation. Should you shoot RAW, JPEG, or *both* at the same time? In the following sections, I explain what you need to know.

So Many Formats, So Little Time

The proliferation of file formats started with image-editing software. There are dozens of different schemes for saving image files, and most of the leading image editors are forced to support just about all of them.

Unfortunately, digital cameras brought back the revenge of the format proliferators, and it helps to get the lay of the land before you venture out to do what should be so simple: Choose a format for saving an image.

Along came a proprietary format

Did you know that Photoshop gives you the option to save your images in almost two dozen different formats right out of the box? Do you know what RLE or PXR or TGA formats are or what applications create or need them? Or why these formats exist at all?

I'm sure each of the various file formats must have seemed like a good idea at the time. The ostensible reason for creating a particular format is that the software vendor wanted to add special features, such as the layers in the Photoshop PSD format, which weren't possible in other formats. Presto! A new file format is born that includes support for the new feature.

Of course, back in the dark ages of computing, another reason for creating a proprietary format existed: It tied buyers to the particular application that relied on that particular format. If you liked PixelPaint (I'm not making the name up; it was a Macintosh program that flourished in the early 1990s), you used the PixelPaint format, and after you'd accumulated a few thousand images in that format, you were pretty well locked into that program. That is, until a new, spiffier application came along, offering support for the PixelPaint format and negating the advantages of the proprietary feature.

Before long, most of the non-compatible formats fell into disuse (although they remain as shadows in many Save As menus). Virtually all image editors support the Photoshop PSD format, plus JPEG (created to provide extra-small file sizes) and TIFF (the closest thing to a standard high-quality format not tied to one vendor). Image editors still have their own proprietary formats, but users of those programs are more likely to archive processed images as PSD or TIFF.

Digital SLRs today (except for a couple quirky cameras from Sigma) all support JPEG because that format lets you squeeze more images onto memory cards that have limited amounts of space. A few, chiefly higher-end, dSLRs also let you capture images in TIFF format, which is great at retaining detail but not great at compressing photos down to a reasonable size. All dSLRs, including those from Sigma, have the option for saving images in a *proprietary* RAW format that, supposedly, preserves all the image detail and parameters captured by the sensor.

What!? Am I telling you that *each* digital camera vendor uses a different RAW format? If only it were that simple! As it turns out, some camera makers have created several different versions of their RAW format, each incompatible in some way with earlier versions, so that instead of a dozen RAW variations, you have to deal with *several* dozen. For example:

- The different RAW formats for Canon dSLRs include CRW and CR2.
- Nikon has some slightly different variations of its format, including its latest trick of *encrypting* the white balance information of its newest cameras so that third-party RAW tools can't interpret it.
- Other vendors might use one RAW format for their dSLRs and another for their high-end point-and-shoot models.

This mess was Adobe's cue to get into the act, producing yet another format, DNG (digital negative), which purports to support all the features of all the other RAW versions, as a sort of standard. Adobe even provides a free Digital Negative Converter, shown in Figure 8-1, should you want to change all your current RAW files to the new format.

Things get even more interesting when you realize that there is no standard for naming the formats used within digital SLR cameras. Instead, the cameras use names like Fine, Basic, Superfine, Good, and so forth, providing no real clue to which format you're actually choosing. The Superfine option might represent TIFF on one camera, and JPEG with minimal image loss on another. Choosing the right format is difficult, but the following sections help clear things up.

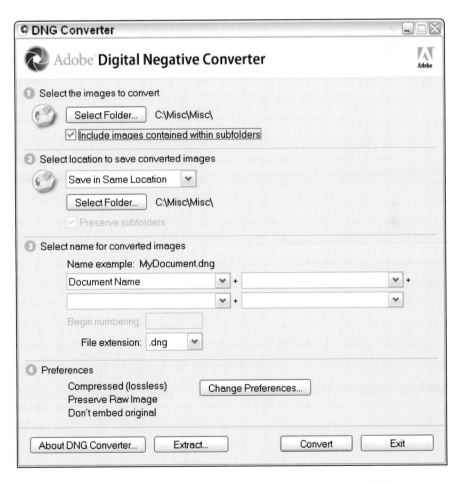

Figure 8-1: Adobe's free Digital Negative Converter transforms your current RAW files into the new Adobe DNG format.

Worth the Fuss: Understanding the Main Formats

I ignore the file formats used only within image editors and for applications outside of digital cameras, such as Web pages. These formats include GIF, PNG, PICT, PDF, and BMP. Nice formats. Not relevant. B-b-b-bye!

When you're trying to decide what format to shoot with, you need to look at only TIFF, JPEG, and RAW, because that's what digital cameras work with. Each of these formats has its advantages and disadvantages, and that's what you really need to know about to make a wise selection.

Don't get TIFFed

This format originated in 1987 with a company called Aldus, which developed pioneering graphics and layout programs such as Freehand and PageMaker. Intended as a standard file format for images, TIFF (Tagged Image File Format) includes the ability to incorporate descriptors called *tags,* which you can use to provide the parameters for any special features included in the file. Theoretically, an application could include any kind of information it liked in a TIFF file, such as layers, objects, special color information, and selections, and tell any other application attempting to read that TIFF file how to retrieve the special data.

In practice, the TIFF format's versatility ends up making it possible to create "standard" files that can't be read by all the applications that need to work with them. TIFF files run the gamut (ha!) from RGB, CMYK (cyan, magenta, yellow, black), and L*a*b color models to black/white and grayscale images. It supports both 24-bit and 48-bit (high dynamic range) color depths, and it can be squeezed down without losing any picture information by using optional Huffman encoding, LZW, or PackBits. (If you don't know what some of these are, consider yourself lucky; they aren't important for day-to-day shooting.) Adobe acquired Aldus in 1994, and today offers options for saving Photoshop layers and selections right in a TIFF file.

To make things even more interesting, some of the RAW formats I discuss a bit later in this chapter are actually TIFF files with some headers that transform them from standard TIFF into a vendor-specific format that requires special software to read.

Here are the two most important TIFF file facts for you to keep in mind:

✔ **TIFF files are *lossless*** (that is, they don't discard any of your image information).

✔ **TIFF files are much larger than JPEG and RAW files.** The larger size can increase the time it takes for your camera to store them on a memory card. In my tests, files that take only a few seconds to write to a memory card in RAW format can take 20 seconds or more as TIFF files.

The third most important thing to keep in mind is that fewer dSLRs offer a TIFF option these days; most that do are professional-level cameras, such as the Nikon D2X, as shown in Figure 8-2.

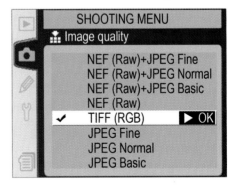

Figure 8-2: Pro-level dSLRs still offer TIFF file options, as shown in this camera menu.

JPEG o' my heart

Virtually every dSLR currently on the market can create JPEG (Joint Photographic Experts Group) files. About 15 years ago, a consortium of the same name created this format. (The consortium originally consisted mostly of vendors such as Eastman Kodak Company, but it's now overseen by an international standards body.) The goal of devising the JPEG format was to create files that are significantly smaller than is possible with formats like TIFF, which compresses files somewhat without discarding image information. The first JPEG-capable applications reduced the time needed to transmit images by telecommunications links. (The Internet wasn't in wide use by the public at that time.)

JPEG can reduce files by a factor of 20 or more by throwing away some of your hard-won image data in a series of processes that are intended to reduce the size of the file by eliminating excess or redundant information.

JPEG compression first divides your image into *luminance* (brightness) values and *chrominance* (color) information, on the theory that human eyes are less fussy about color than they are about brightness. (That is, if you see a stop sign that's a slightly odd shade of red, you'll notice that less than if the same sign were darker or lighter than you'd expect.) It's the excess color information that's discarded.

The process slices up your image into cells, say 8 x 8 pixels on a side, and then the process looks at each of the 64 pixels in the resulting chunk individually. Using mathematical trickery called Discrete Cosine Transformation (DCT), pixels that have the same value as those around them are discarded. (You don't have to remember things like *Discrete Cosine Transformation* unless you're trying to impress someone at a party.) Next, quantization occurs, during which pixels that are nearly the same color are converted to a common hue, and the picture information that's left is transformed into a series of numbers, which is more compact than the original information. (It's a bit like writing 1,500 instead of *one-thousand five-hundred.*) If everything is done properly, the process compresses the image by 5X to 20X or more.

Because JPEG doesn't keep all the image information, it is referred to as a *lossy* format. Each time you load a JPEG image, make changes, and then save it again, you run the danger of losing a noticeable amount of information because the JPEG process occurs all over again. The loss might be very slight at first, but it can accumulate, as you see in Figure 8-3, which shows a photograph that has lost sharpness after repeated savings

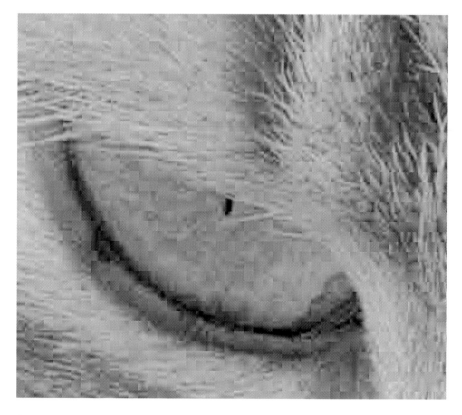

Figure 8-3: Repeatedly saving JPEG images can introduce artifacts into your photos.

What's cool about JPEG is that you can dial in the amount of compression you want, using lots of compression to produce very small file sizes (with an attendant loss in quality), or very little compression to preserve quality at the cost of larger files. What's *not* cool is that there is no standard way of referring to the amount of compression. Digital cameras tend to use discrete steps with names like SuperFine, Fine, Normal, Good, and Basic. Image editors might let you choose a continuous compression/quality range from, say, 0 to 15 or 0 to 20. The Nigel Tufnels in you might wish that your editors offered a 21 setting for when you need just that little bit of extra quality, but unfortunately, the designers of these applications apparently have never seen the movie *This Is Spinal Tap.*

Instead, in-camera JPEG compression is a little like a box of chocolates: You never know what you're going to get.

The RAW deal

RAW isn't really a file format. It's the broad term applied to all the proprietary formats created by each digital camera vendor for its particular product line. Every RAW format is different, which means that in order to access a RAW file, you must have either

- Special software from your vendor designed especially for its RAW format

- A third-party utility, such as Adobe Camera RAW (furnished with Photoshop and Photoshop Elements), that is compatible *with your particular camera's* RAW format

Not all utilities support all RAW formats (not even the Adobe DNG converter), so your choices for reading these files might be somewhat limited.

You can consider RAW files to be your digital negatives because they haven't been subjected to the usual manipulations mandated by your camera settings when the raw image data is converted to JPEG or TIFF. (Actually as you find out later in this chapter, that isn't precisely true.) See the section "Using RAW Files as Digital Negatives" for more details.

Choosing a File Format

So, your choices boil down to TIFF, RAW, and JPEG (or, with some cameras, saving in RAW and JPEG simultaneously). Which do you select? Your decision might hinge on how you shoot and what you plan to do with your files after you've transferred them to your computer. Your available storage space might also figure into the equation.

If you get good results most of the time by using your camera settings, don't want to do a lot of processing in your image editor, and are taking lots of pictures, you might opt for TIFF or JPEG. TIFF gets the nod if you want the best image quality, but JPEG might be preferable if you're on a trip and want to make your memory cards stretch as far as possible. RAW could be best if you plan on doing a lot of tweaking. These next sections explore these options in a little more detail.

TIFF enuff

If your camera has a TIFF option, here are some factors to consider:

- **Highest quality:** Use TIFF if you want the highest-quality image in a standard file format. This lossless format produces image files that are theoretically and practically better than even the least compressed JPEG image.

- **Minimum of post-processing:** TIFF is a good choice when you're generating large numbers of images for distribution and want to apply a minimum of post-processing. Perhaps you're shooting a wedding or other event and don't want to laboriously apply individualized settings to each photo with your image editor. If you carefully select your camera settings so your TIFF files already have the exposure, color balance, sharpness, and other attributes you want to end up with, you can safely save your files in TIFF format and expect all or most of them to be good to go right out of the box.

- **Limited editing:** TIFF is fine for images that will be manipulated in Photoshop for improvements that don't involve "unprocessed" RAW file attributes. For example, if you'll be retouching portraits to minimize facial flaws or compositing several images into one, you really don't need to work from RAW images. TIFF will serve just as well.

- **Too slow for sports:** TIFF might not be the best choice if you're shooting sports or doing continuous shooting and your dSLR takes a long time to save such files to your memory card. Most digital SLRs store JPEG and even RAW files much more quickly than they do TIFFs.

- **Takes lots of memory:** TIFF is a poor choice if your memory card space is limited. If you're on vacation and have only a few 1GB cards to use between opportunities to offload your images, you'll find that TIFF files fill up the available media with alarming speed. (Your camera's best JPEG setting will produce image quality that's almost as good while consuming perhaps 10 percent of the storage space.)

JPEG Junkies Unite!

JPEG is a highly popular alternative to TIFF (for cameras that offer that option) and RAW. Some JPEG junkies use nothing else for their original photos. The format is compatible with virtually all applications, making it as much of a standard as TIFF, and much more compatible than RAW formats.

Of course, JPEG has that nagging loss-of-quality issue. You have to decide on your own how important that is. Here are some points to ponder when considering JPEG:

✔ **Large numbers of files:** Like TIFF, JPEG is a good choice if you'll be generating large numbers of files and intend to do little or no post-processing. JPEG files are great for display on Web pages, like the one shown in Figure 8-4. Or, if you want to distribute pictures in digital albums on CDs, in online albums, or as prints no larger than 11 x 14 inches, the least-compressed JPEG option your dSLR offers should produce files that are easily up to these tasks.

✔ **Good enough quality:** If you do end up editing JPEG files, you'll find the quality is good enough as long as you remember to save your final version as a TIFF or Photoshop PSD file. That helps you avoid the quality loss that can result from repeatedly opening and editing JPEG files. If you still need a JPEG file, say, for display on a Web page, create one and retain your new TIFF or PSD versions in case the image requires more editing later on.

✔ **More compatible with software:** JPEG can be more compatible with some image management/albuming software than other formats. The ancient application I've been using for ten years doesn't handle RAW files at all, so I always catalog a JPEG version of the file that's produced at the same time as the RAW file. (See the section "JPEG+RAW" later in this chapter.)

✔ **Writes to memory faster:** Your digital SLR probably can write JPEG files to your memory card faster than any other type of file. This speed might not matter if you're taking only a couple pictures at a time; the photos first go into the camera's high-speed memory buffer, which sucks up JPEG, TIFF, and RAW at similar speeds. However, writing these images to the memory card takes longer, and after the buffer fills, you can't take any more photos until some shots make their way out of the camera's internal memory onto the card. I've used dSLRs that are so fast at writing JPEG files to a high-speed CompactFlash card that I can take sequence photos almost continuously for a dozen shots or more.

✔ **Take less room on cards:** You can fit a lot more JPEG files on a memory card of a particular size. A 1GB card can store about 300 photos snapped with a 6-megapixel camera with the typical JPEG Fine setting, nearly 600 photos at a representative medium-quality setting, and as many as 1,100 shots at the highest compression setting. Only 180 RAW shots from the same camera might fill a 1GB card.

I don't usually recommend using card storage space as a criterion for choosing which file format to use. I'd rather you purchase enough memory cards, instead. However, in some situations (such as vacations) storage is limited, and using the JPEG format, particularly the highest-quality setting, makes a good compromise.

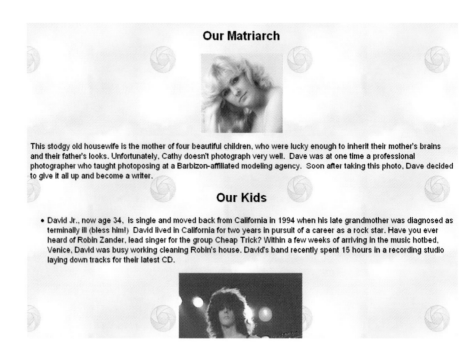

Figure 8-4: JPEG files are good for Web display as-is.

JPEG+RAW

Most digital SLRs include an option to save a pair of files every time a picture is taken: one as a JPEG file and a second in the RAW format. A few cameras, usually the high-end pro models, let you select the quality level for the JPEG version, so you choose between a high-quality JPEG and one that's more compressed and lower in quality. Other cameras have a fixed JPEG quality level for the supplemental file, often the version that has the highest compression ratio.

The ability to save JPEG+RAW is a valuable capability. It lets you shoot JPEGs for cataloging, reviewing, and using in less-demanding applications, such as small prints, online auctions, and Web display, while retaining RAW versions as digital negatives in case you need to do more extensive tweaking. Generally, the image pairs share filenames (only the file extension is different), so it's easy to match them up.

The storage card space penalty is very low. My dSLR can save 180 RAW shots per 1GB card, and 160 JPEG+RAW image pairs. It's truly a case of getting the best of both worlds. This is the mode I use by default.

RAW in the raw

People often describe RAW files as "unprocessed" image files that contain all the information captured by the sensor. That's nonsense!

As I explain in Chapter 2, the sensor catches photons in little analog buckets (setting aside the wave/particle duality of light, as well I should!). The data collected is manipulated by your camera's digital signal processor, a special chip that converts the analog information into digital format. At the same time, the Bayer-filtered image data that mimics separate red-, green-, and blue-sensitive pixels is interpolated to create three different color channels of 12 to 16 bits. That's a lot of processing right there!

All that preprocessing can have a significant impact on the quality of your image, and that's *before* your camera settings are applied. You can't do a whole lot to RAW files to reverse the changes that have been made. What RAW does for you is let you apply *after taking the photo* those settings you normally make in the camera, such as white balance, sharpness improvements, color saturation, and to an extent, exposure. If your shutter speed was too slow and you have a blurry photo, you can't fix that. If your f-stop was too large and your depth-of-field is inadequate, you can't fix that either. You can apply a little sharpening, which might help somewhat in either case, but you have no way to undo serious errors you made when you snapped the photo.

Working RAW

Saving in RAW format is the best option if you frequently need to fine-tune your images. RAW lets you make changes to settings that normally you apply in the camera, either to individual files or batches of them. For example, if you take a whole series of shots under a particular lighting setup and later decide on a single group of settings to apply to all of them, you can do that quickly with one batch process. Also, you can manipulate individual photos to your heart's content.

Using RAW Files as Digital Negatives

The more you shoot, the more you realize that it's always a good idea to have that (relatively) unprocessed image as a sort of digital negative you can go back to at any time to work with anew. These files can be a treasure trove of images that will prove invaluable at a later time, whether or not you think so now.

Salvaging images from RAW files

Your image-editing skills will improve, and with an image saved in RAW format, you can salvage images that weren't usable before you gained new capabilities. Pictures that you didn't think you had any use for might turn out to be worthwhile with the passage of time.

For example, take the photo shown in Figure 8-5, which I originally used in Chapter 6 as an example of how you can take photos in dim light without a tripod if you have a lens with a large maximum aperture. It's true that the original photo *was* taken at dusk, and the camera *wasn't* mounted on a tripod. It was taken with a fast lens, too, exactly as described. However, as they say, here is the rest of the story. (You'll see that you don't need to have the patience of Ansel Adams to take landscape photos.)

Figure 8-5: This picture wasn't carefully composed. It was a grab shot produced from a RAW file shot on the spur of the moment.

I took the picture one evening when I was out scouting locations for future shoots. I was driving across a causeway that crossed a lake a few miles from my home, and I decided the view was interesting. While driving at 45 miles per hour, I picked up my camera and shot the image shown in Figure 8-6 *through the open window of my minivan.* (Don't try this at home!) The ISO sensitivity was at 1250, the camera was in Shutter Priority mode with a shutter speed of $\frac{1}{1,250}$ of a second preselected, and an aperture of f2 — chosen by the metering system — let me capture a relatively unblurred image despite my relatively high motoring speed. I know all this information because it was recorded in the EXIF data that accompanied the RAW file.

This was a grab shot in every sense of the word. Yet, when I needed a photo taken in dim light with a large f-stop, this throw-away proved useful. Because I'd saved in RAW, I was able to manipulate the photo a bit to make it a little more interesting by cropping out the guardrail and portions of my vehicle.

Archiving RAW files

If you want to use RAW files as your digital negatives, you need to have a way to store them, because they're sure to eat up your hard drive space quickly. I have virtually every image I've shot in RAW archived on my computer's hard drives as well as on DVD. That includes shots of my feet taken when I tested an electronic flash, semi-blank frames that are seriously underexposed, and all manner of out-of-focus and poorly composed pictures. As my example in the preceding section shows, you never know when you might find some use for a garbage shot.

Blank DVDs are so inexpensive these days that you have no excuse for not saving *all* of your digital negatives. (Just don't forget to copy them to whatever format replaces the current DVD format in ten, or five, or two years.) With most operating systems, all you need to do to archive files to a DVD is drag and drop them to the DVD drive.

Finding RAW image-editing applications

Remember, to work with RAW files, you need an application that can read them. A variety of RAW converters are at your disposal. Some of these are provided by your camera's vendor and, as you might expect, work only with the RAW files for that line of camera. Unless you own several different digital cameras from different manufacturers that can produce RAW files, these proprietary converters might be all you need. Or, you can check out third-party RAW applications if you prefer. The following sections introduce some of the more popular proprietary and third-party applications.

Figure 8-6: Here's the original RAW file before image editing.

Nikon Capture

Nikon offers the eponymous Nikon Capture, an extra-cost ($99) program that handles both older and the latest versions of RAW files created by Nikon cameras. Besides offering control over settings you could have made in the camera, this utility provides some interesting additional capabilities. For example, it can defish images taken with Nikon fish-eye lenses, producing non-distorted photos with straight lines where straight lines ought to be. This is one way to get super-wide-angle photos from your trusty fish-eye lens.

Nikon Capture, shown in Figure 8-7, has a separate lightness/chroma/hue palette for modifying these image attributes directly, along with post-shot noise reduction features and vignette control to remove (or add) darkening/lightening to the corners of photos. Also handy is an image-dust-off feature that compares your shots with a dust reference photo and removes spots caused by dust on the sensor. You can use this utility to control a tethered camera for remote shooting or time-lapse photography.

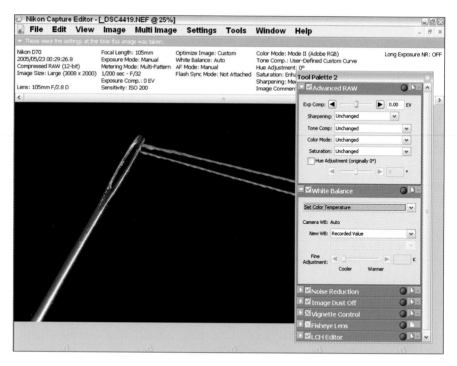

Figure 8-7: Nikon charges $99 extra for Nikon Capture, but the extra features it offers are worth the cost.

Canon EOS File Viewer and Digital Photo Professional

Canon supplies owners of its dSLRs with the simple Canon EOS File Viewer, a basic file utility, as well as the more upscale Digital Photo Professional tool (see Figure 8-8). Like Nikon Capture, Digital Photo Professional can convert batches of files unattended by using parameters you specify. It works with both the original Canon CRW format as well as the newer CR2 RAW format, plus TIFF and JPEG. I like its ability to compare the original RAW image with the edited version, so you can see exactly how the changes you have made affect the manipulated photo.

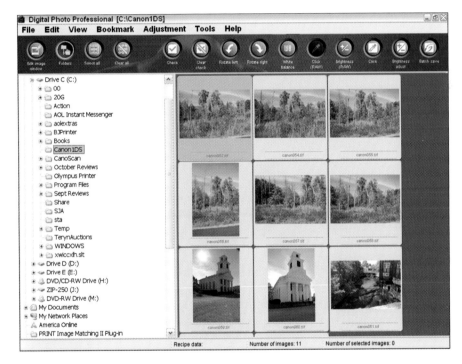

Figure 8-8: Digital Photo Professional is an advanced RAW file utility for Canon dSLRs.

Third-party applications

Third-party RAW converters range from the very inexpensive to the paycheck chompers, as shown in Table 8-1.

Table 8-1	Some Third-Party RAW Applications		
Application	*Cost*	*Platform*	*Web Site*
IrfanView	Free	Windows	www.irfanview.com
GraphicConverter	$30	Mac	www.lemkesoft.com
Bibble Pro	$129	Windows, Mac OS X, and Linux	www.bibblelabs.com
Capture One PRO (shown in Figure 8-9)	$499	Windows, Mac	www.phaseone.com
Adobe Camera RAW (see Figure 8-10)	Comes with Photoshop or Elements	Windows, Mac	www.adobe.com

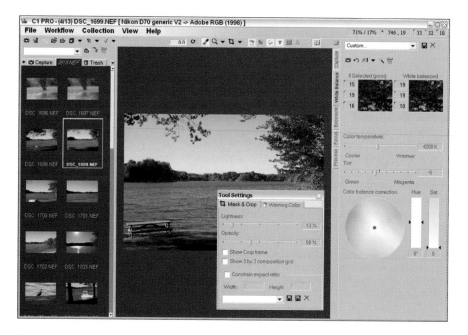

Figure 8-9: Capture One PRO from Phase One is a pro-quality RAW utility.

Figure 8-10: Adobe Camera RAW supports a wide range of RAW formats.

At this time, the most popular and widely used third-party RAW converter is probably Adobe Camera RAW (or, commonly, ACR), which is supplied with Photoshop Elements and Photoshop CS 2.0. It works with a long list of RAW formats from vendors including Canon, Nikon, Sony, Fuji, Olympus, Pentax, and Sigma. It does most of the general-purpose RAW conversion tasks that the vendors' own utilities handle, and it has the advantage of working transparently with lots of different RAW formats, plus Adobe's new DNG format.

9

Action, Flash, and Other Challenges

The difference between a novice digital photographer and one with some solid experience is often apparent in how that shooter handles more challenging photographic situations. Action photography, electronic flash photography, and situations that combine both electronic flash and available light seem to be the trickiest for photographers making the transition from neophyte to grizzled veteran. (Nobody really looks forward to being grizzled, but remaining a neophyte forever isn't a pleasant prospect, either.) These types of photography all offer challenges on both the technical and creative levels. If you can handle them, you can tackle anything.

This chapter looks at some of the technical stuff you need to understand to make the transition, while taking top-notch action, flash, and sequence photos. Although you find a bit of nuts and bolts here, stay calm and stick it out — my intent isn't to make you go nuts and bolt!

Kind of a Lag

Shutter lag, first-shot times, and those annoying pauses between photos do more than interrupt your photographic momentum — they can cause you to miss photos. Fortunately, of all digital cameras, dSLRs do the best job of reducing those awkward moments to a minimum. In the following sections, you find out what causes this lag and what you can do about it.

Comparing point-and-shoot cameras to dSLRs

Users of non-dSLRs feel the pain of shutter lag the worst. Of the dozens of point-and-shoot and electronic viewfinder cameras I test each year, most of them average lag from 0.6 to 0.9 seconds when shooting photos under high-contrast lighting (which makes it easy for the camera's autofocus system to lock in). In challenging low-contrast light, the best cameras average 0.9 seconds, most can take up to 1.9 seconds, and a few pause for an interminable 2.5 seconds before squeezing off the shot. When the lag is bad enough, you end up with photos like the one shown in Figure 9-1, in which I pressed the shutter release as the flume ride started down the slope, but camera didn't take the picture until the subjects had passed out of the ideal position.

Figure 9-1: The flume ride was a little higher up the slope than this when I pressed the shutter release!

Digital SLRs operate on a different plane of existence, fortunately. Most of the time such a camera seems to take the picture as soon as you press the shutter button. The actual elapsed time might be 0.2 seconds, or at least three times faster than what you get with a typical point-and-shoot digital camera.

Shutter lag of any length can cause you to miss a photo, particularly if you're engaged in action photography, where the difference between capturing the decisive moment and capturing the not-interesting moment *after* the decisive one can be measured in milliseconds. Shutter lag can be a problem with portraits, too. You say, "Smile!" and your subject smiles, but then she frowns when nothing happens. Guess which expression you're most likely to capture?

Understanding the sources of lag

Shutter lag is primarily caused by the delay in locking in autofocus between the time when you press down the shutter release halfway and when you fully depress it to take the picture. But this isn't the only factor you want to be aware of.

There's a secondary kind of lag that can't be blamed on a camera's pokey auto-focus system. If you're taking a lot of photos in a row and your camera takes a long time to write them to the memory card (or your memory card is a slow one that can't accept data as quickly as your camera provides it), you can run into unfortunate delays. Your camera's buffer fills up, you press the shutter release, and nothing happens.

But wait! There's more! A third kind of delay can occur when you're shooting with electronic flash. It might take a second or two (or three, or four) for your flash to recharge after you've taken a flash photo, and you're either unable to take a picture until the flash is ready, or your camera goes ahead and takes the shot and provides incorrect exposure.

Fortunately, you can do things to counter all these shot-to-shot delays. Read on to find out how.

Minimizing shutter lag

As I said, even the best-performing dSLR might not take a picture at the exact instant you'd like the shot to be captured. Hey, a 90-mph fastball travels 132 feet per second, so during a 0.2 second delay the ball moves 26 feet. That's almost half the distance between the pitcher's mound and home plate!

Here are some ways to improve your results:

- ✔ **Anticipate the action.** It takes practice, but you can press the shutter release a fraction of a second before the action peaks. It helps if you understand the activity so you know approximately when, say, a skier is about to leap over a mogul, or you can tell the difference between a pump fake and an actual forward pass. By shooting just prior to the decisive moment, as I did for Figure 9-2, you can improve your timing.

- ✔ **Take lots of photos.** Hand-in-hand with the previous tip is the proviso that you'll end up missing that crucial moment quite a few times. If you take lots of photos, you're bound to get some good ones, and the practice helps you improve your timing. The day before I sat down to write this chapter, I photographed a professional women's softball game and took nearly 400 pictures over six innings. This wasn't a scattershot approach, attempting to get a good picture through dumb luck. I was trying to take *lots* of good pictures in an attempt to get a few *great* ones.

- ✔ **Use your sequence capabilities.** Your dSLR's continuous shooting mode can boost your odds by grabbing quick bursts of two or three shots per second. However, it's also likely that all the pictures in a sequence will be taken just before, just after, or between the best moments.

✔ **Switch to manual modes.** Although digital SLR autofocus systems are remarkably speedy, they can be thrown off by rapidly moving subjects or shift between the background and the foreground as you frame your image. You might have better luck turning off the autofocus and manually pre-focusing on a particular point, such as first base, the goal line, or the position where an ice skater is expected to leap into a triple-axel. If you don't expect lighting conditions to change much, use manual exposure, too. Fewer automatic features can lead to quicker response from your camera.

✔ **Lock and load.** When using auto modes, follow the action and then lock in exposure and focus by using the lock control provided by your digital camera. When your camera is locked in for both exposure and focus (usually by pressing the shutter release down halfway), pressing the shutter release the rest of the way should take your picture a bit more quickly.

Figure 9-2: Shoot just before the decisive moment to catch the action at the right time.

Minimizing first-shot delays

Some digital SLRs take awhile to "warm up" before you can take a photo. The original Canon Digital Rebel was notorious for this, requiring up to three seconds from the time you turned it on until it reported for duty. Worse, the Digital Rebel tended to go to sleep as a power-saving measure while it was turned on, resulting in multiple 3-second delays during a shooting session.

This delay was largely eliminated in the Digital Rebel XT, which turns on in less than half a second, a figure matched by most other digital SLRs on the market today.

You can virtually eliminate first-shot delays with a simple technique: Don't turn off your dSLR! Point-and-shoot cameras typically go to sleep after a few minutes because their LCDs drain so much juice. Digital SLRs use very little battery power when turned on, so you can safely leave them activated for hours (or days) at a time.

Digital SLRs are more power-efficient because the LCD is switched on only when reviewing pictures or navigating menus. The autofocus and exposure systems turn themselves off after a few seconds if you aren't actively taking a picture, but both revive almost instantly when you tap the shutter button. A few cameras, like some Pentax *ist models, switch off the top-panel monochrome LCD status panel, which is annoying, but doesn't contribute to much delay. Only the built-in electronic flash uses a significant amount of power, and it, too, goes into standby automatically.

If you get in the habit of turning on your camera at the beginning of a shooting session and not turning it off again until you're ready to pack the camera up and put it away, you avoid nearly all first-shot delays. Your flash needs to recharge from time to time, but that won't impact most of your photography.

Minimizing shot-to-shot delays

All cameras have an interval between shots that limits your ability to take a new photo immediately after taking the last one. Most of the time, this delay is negligible. That's because digital SLRs typically have a good complement of built-in super-fast memory called a *buffer,* which accepts photos as quickly as you take them, freeing the camera to take another picture. As long as the buffer retains enough room to accept new shots, you can take pictures as fast as you can press the shutter release.

Unfortunately, not all dSLRs have sufficient buffer memory for all the shots you might want to take, particularly if you're using the continuous sequence modes. When that happens, delays can set in. Here are some of the things you can do to minimize them:

  ✓ **Monitor the buffer.** Keep an eye on the buffer indicator in your viewfinder. It might be a bar readout or numbers that show how many frames remain. If you think a moment that might be more important than the one you're shooting now is imminent, back off and let your buffer drain to make room.

✔ **Get a faster memory card.** As I note in Chapter 4, some memory cards are faster than others. With some digital cameras, a better-performing card can reduce shot-to-shot delays. When a camera feeds photos to the memory card faster than the card can accept the images, a bottleneck takes place and the buffer can fill. A faster card just might eliminate the problem. Note that this won't work with every dSLR. Some have very large buffers and can often write even to standard memory cards at roughly the same speed as new images are captured. You might be able to shoot photos all day and not notice any delay, except, perhaps, when shooting long bursts. A faster card is of most benefit for dSLRs that have smaller buffers.

✔ **Shoot at a lower resolution.** I don't advocate shooting smaller image files (you never know when you can use the full resolution), but in a pinch you can switch to a lower resolution to increase the number of shots you can take in a row. If rapid-fire is more important than image quality, go for it!

✔ **Enlarge your buffer.** This is an unlikely option, but I'm mentioning it for the sake of being complete. Some digital SLRs can be upgraded with additional buffer memory by the factory for a reasonable cost. The affected models are generally older, higher-priced professional cameras. Your digital SLR is unlikely to have this option.

Minimizing flash delays

Your camera's built-in electronic flash can cause delays when you're forced to wait for it to build up a full charge between shots. Some cameras have a useful option of locking the camera to prevent taking a photo before the flash is recharged, which blocks spoiled photos but, obviously, doesn't eliminate the annoying delays. Others let you fire away, risking an underexposed photo if the flash doesn't have enough charge.

Keep these tips in mind when you want to keep shooting flash pictures without pausing:

✔ **Close-up shots use less power.** If you're taking close-up photos, you can probably shoot quicker and with fewer delays than if you're using up your flash's maximum power with every shot.

✔ **Reduce flash power.** A related technique you can use for photos taken at lesser distances is to reduce the power setting of your flash. Many built-in speedlights and external units can be set to ½, ¼, or ⅛ power. If that's all you need, use it and enjoy faster operation.

✔ **Use an external flash.** The flash built into your camera sucks juice from your camera's main battery and so has been designed to use the minimum amount of power necessary to do the job. This conservative approach can mean slower recycling. External flash units that fit on your camera's hot shoe or use a connecting cable usually have beefier batteries and recycle much more quickly.

✏ **Use an add-on battery pack.** You might be able to connect your external flash to an add-on battery pack that offers *really* fast recycling, on the order of a second or less.

Shooting in Sequences

In the consumer marketplace, very cool features tend to filter down from higher-end products to the gear that we peons can afford. Power seats and power windows once were found only in pricey luxury cars, and now you'd have a hard time finding a vehicle without them. Speedy motor drives on cameras, once the province of professional photographers, eventually made their way into the lowliest point-and-shoot film cameras. And now, because *burst mode, continuous advance,* or *sequence shooting* are found on every digital camera, you can also produce a series of shots like that of a speeding train, as shown in Figure 9-3.

The chief differences between the continuous shooting mode found in $149 point-and-shoot cameras and your digital SLR are the speed, flexibility, and number of shots that can be captured in a sequence. Where a basic digicam owner is lucky to grab 2 frames per second (fps) for a half dozen shots, digital SLRs typically can snap off from 6 to 24 pictures at 3 to 8 fps without breaking a sweat. Your results will vary depending on the camera and format you use.

Figure 9-3: Continuous shooting lets you capture a sequence of shots.

As I mention earlier in this chapter, sequence photography is no substitute for good timing. You still get better results by taking a picture at precisely the best moment than by capturing random frames in great bursts of exposures.

Your camera might have several different continuous modes, ranging from a basic mode at 3 to 5 fps to a high-speed continuous advance of up to 8 fps. Nikon's flagship D2X model achieves that high speed only by cropping the image from its 12.4-megapixel 4,288-x-2,848-pixel mode down to a 3,216-x-2,136-pixel frame that yields a measly 6.8 megapixels.

Nikon's solution is interesting in that it crops a cropped frame further, so the D2X's 1.5X crop factor becomes a 2X crop factor in high-speed mode. The extra cropping is theoretically an advantage for digital photographers who imagine that a highly cropped image multiplies the focal length of their lenses, as I expound at length in Chapter 6. Figure 9-4 shows the view through the DX2's viewfinder in cropped high-speed mode. The inner bracket represents the area of the cropped image.

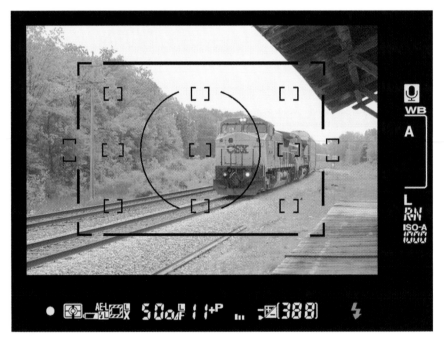

Figure 9-4: Some cameras crop the field of view when shooting at the highest frame rates.

To use your digital camera's burst mode, all you need to do is activate it and then fire away, taking into account the need for good timing, the capacity of your camera's buffer, and all the other tips for minimizing delays, which I discuss in the earlier section, "Kind of a Lag."

Stopping Action in Its Tracks

Freezing action isn't all it's cracked up to be. My recent foray into pro softball shooting had some strange results, as you can see from Figure 9-5. I was testing a long lens to see whether I could successfully hand-hold it, and I bumped up the shutter speed of my dSLR to $\frac{1}{2,500}$ of a second. That lofty speed did nullify any camera shake, but it had the additional effect of freezing a hard-thrown softball in midair.

Without the added dimension of a little motion blur, you can't tell whether the ball is headed toward the player or away from her (she's actually just thrown it), and it really appears as if the ball isn't moving at all but, rather, it seems to be suspended from overhead by a string. This shot wasn't destined to be a prize-winner anyway, but now, at best, it looks a little weird.

Figure 9-5: It looks like this softball is hanging from a string, not flying through the air.

The lesson here is that stopping action completely might not be the best idea, unless the image contains all the other elements of a good action shot so that it looks like a frozen moment rather than a staged setup. Instead of completely stopping all movement, you might want to incorporate at least a little blur into your shot to give it more of a sense of excitement.

The key to stopping action successfully (and believably) is to choose the correct shutter speed. Your shutter slices off little moments in time; the briefer the exposure, the smaller the slice and the less blur-causing subject movement. To make things interesting, your shutter sees motion at the same speed in different ways, depending on which way the subject is moving:

- **Across the frame:** Motion parallel to the width or height of the frame seems to move fastest to the sensor, and the subject blurs more easily. Higher shutter speeds, from ⅟₅₀₀ to ½,₀₀₀ of a second in many cases, are required to stop this motion, compared to movement in other directions.

- **Toward the camera:** Motion moving toward you appears to have a much slower rate of speed, and such subjects blur the least. You can use a much slower shutter speed to freeze this kind of motion. For some kinds of subjects, shutter speeds of ⅟₆₀ to ⅟₂₅₀ of a second might work.

- **Diagonal motion:** This type of movement falls in between the first two. An automobile going from the upper left to the lower right is crossing the frame at the same time it's coming towards you, so you'll need an intermediate shutter speed, on the order of ⅟₁₂₅ to ⅟₅₀₀ of a second.

- **Close up/distant:** Subjects closer to the camera cross the frame more quickly than those farther away, and so require a higher shutter speed.

- **Relative speed:** If you move the camera in the same direction as the subject's motion, a technique called *panning,* the relative speed difference is less, so a lower shutter speed may be used. The next section has some tips on panning.

Going with the flow (or, panning)

The term *panning* comes from the word *panorama,* or "whole sight" if you happen to speak Ancient Greek in the home. It refers to an unbroken view of an area, like the view a motion picture camera produces when rotated smoothly from side to side. Panning is always horizontal; the "vertical" equivalent is called *tilting.*

In either case, because the swiveling motion of the camera (usually) follows the direction the subject is moving, the subject appears to the camera to be moving at a slower rate of speed and can be captured at a slower shutter speed, as shown in Figure 9-6. Instead, a static background, which isn't moving at all, might appear to be blurry.

You can pan with a handheld camera or with a camera mounted on a tripod that has a swiveling panorama (pan) head. Here are some tricks to getting good panned shots:

- **Have the right attitude.** To pan without using a tripod, position your body so you're facing in the direction at the end of the pan. Then twist to the start position and untwist as you follow the action smoothly, triggering the shutter when you want to snap a picture.

- **Level your platform.** To pan with a tripod, make sure the tripod and pan head are level with the direction of the movement so that as you rotate the camera, it follows the action smoothly.

- **Practice, practice.** Try out your pan a few times before you actually take a picture. As you practice, your technique will improve.

- **Move smoothly.** Don't use jerky movements. Follow the movement of your subject closely.

Figure 9-6: A shutter speed of 1/60 of a second was fast enough to capture this baserunner.

Catching peak action

Many kinds of action culminate in a peak, where the motion stops for a moment before resuming. A basketball player at the top of his or her leap before uncorking a jump shot, a ski jumper at the apex of a soaring flight down a slope, or a roller coaster poised at the top of a hill can all be captured at relatively slow shutter speeds.

You can find lots of action peaks that don't involve sports, too. Your child on a swing can be frozen for an instant at each end of the swing's arc. Birds in flight stop pumping their wings and ease into a lazy glide to ride thermal currents.

The magic bullet for catching peak action is patience and perseverance. Figure out just when the crucial moment is likely to occur, and then time your shot accordingly.

Zapping action with flash

Electronic flash units are still sometimes called *strobes* after the stroboscopes used by Dr. Harold Edgerton at MIT to freeze shattering light bulbs and to stop bullets in flight. When flash is used as the only source of illumination in a photo, it can be very effective at stopping action because of its very brief duration.

Indeed, most electronic flashes built into digital SLRs have a *maximum* duration of about $\frac{1}{1,000}$ of a second, and might last only $\frac{1}{50,000}$ of a second or less when used for close-up photography. That's because the most effective way of controlling the exact output of a flash is to limit the length of time that the energy stored in the unit's electrical capacitors is emitted. To produce a small blip of light, the flash releases only a tiny amount of energy in a very short time. To produce more light, give the blip a longer duration.

If the shutter speed and f-stop you use to capture an image with the flash is such that the continuous or *ambient* illumination isn't strong enough to register, the image will be produced by the flash alone, so your camera's actual shutter speed is irrelevant. That is, you might be shooting at $\frac{1}{250}$ of a second at f8, but action will be stopped by the electronic flash's $\frac{1}{2,000}$ of a second duration.

You find out more about flash in the next section.

Flash in the Pan: Other Keys to Good Flash Photography

Actually, you *can* use flash while panning (or when your subject is moving) to produce an interesting effect, but I save that for a bit later in this section.

First, it helps to understand a few concepts about using flash, whether you're applying this tool to action photography or other types. In the following sections, I help you understand how flash works at different distances, how to sync flash and shutter to get the effect you want, as well as other techniques that can help you improve your flash photography in less than 1/500 of a second.

Understanding flash at different distances

The most important flash fact to remember is that electronic flash differs from the continuous illumination you know as daylight in one important respect: Daylight appears to be relatively even at most working distances, but the brightness of flash diminishes rather quickly as the distance between the subject and the flash increases. You can step 10 or 20 feet away from your subject in daylight, and the exposure does not change. Move the same distance from your subject when using flash, and the illumination decreases dramatically.

That's because electronic flash, like all illumination, obeys something called the *inverse-square* law. Light diminishes relative to the inverse of the square of the distance. So, if you're photographing a subject that's 4 feet from your flash, you need four times as much light when the distance is doubled to 8 feet, not twice as much. That also means that if you photograph two subjects, one 4 feet from the camera and one 8 feet from the camera, the more distant subject will be underexposed by 4X (two f-stops) if the closer subject is properly exposed. Figure 9-7 shows a high school quarterback who's properly illuminated by electronic flash, but the figures in the background are much darker.

Figure 9-7: Electronic flash tends to illuminate only one plane properly.

This pesky law applies to daylight, as well, but the distance between the light source and subject is so much greater that you can ignore the consequences — unless you plan on stepping back 93 million miles between shots.

In practice, your camera's built-in flash probably won't do a good job illuminating anything 24 feet from the camera (say, a quarterback stepping back to unleash a pass) unless you use a high ISO setting. Your flash has probably been optimized to shoot subjects around 12 feet from the camera at around f8 or so, and it will produce poor results at 24 feet, for which f5.6 might be required. Those kinds of situations call for more powerful, external flash units.

In addition to the sharp fall-off in illumination, using flash has some other disadvantages:

- Flash photos can look harsh, with bright foregrounds and very dark backgrounds, thanks to that inverse-square nonsense.

- Flash photos can produce a ghost effect when there is enough ambient light to produce a blurry secondary image along with the flash exposure.

- Electronic flash uses your camera's internal battery at a tidy clip.

You can see why proper use of flash is one of the more interesting challenges facing dSLR users.

That sync-ing feeling: Coordinating flash and shutter

Many new SLR owners become confused over the options for synchronizing electronic flash with their camera's shutters. This section clears up that confusion.

As you might know, digital SLRs can use a combination of electronic and mechanical shutters to control the length of time the sensor is exposed. An electronic shutter is just that: The sensor is controlled electronically to allow it to capture photons for a fixed period of time. The electronic shutter is used for very brief exposures.

The mechanical shutter physically opens and closes to expose the sensor, and is used for longer exposures, from 30 seconds (or whatever your camera's maximum exposure happens to be) to a length of time that is known as the camera's *flash sync speed*. It's called that because it is the shortest shutter speed that can ordinarily be used to take a picture with the electronic flash.

The reason for that is easy to understand. The mechanical shutter used in dSLRs travels in front of the sensor, just above the plane of sharp focus (and is called a *focal plane* shutter for that reason). The shutter consists of two curtains. The *front curtain* opens first, moving across the plane of the sensor until it is fully open. Then, after the sensor has been left exposed for the desired amount of time, the *rear curtain* begins to follow it, gradually covering the sensor until it is completely concealed. Because of the brief duration of the flash, the flash must be fired only when the sensor is entirely uncovered. Otherwise, your picture will consist of a partial frame, showing only the portion of the sensor that happened to be uncovered when the flash went off.

Exposure way back when

In ancient times, use of electronic flash involved arcane practices that are almost too unpleasant to put into words. It was often necessary to calculate flash exposure *manually,* which meant you had to measure or estimate the distance between your flash and the subject and divide a mysterious figure called a guide number by that distance to determine the right aperture to use. And the guide number (GN) was different for every ISO setting and varied depending on whether you were using meters or feet to measure the distance!

So, if your flash had a GN (in feet) of 80 with ISO 100 film and your subject was 10 feet from the camera, you'd have used an f-stop of f8 to take your picture, cross your fingers, and hope it worked out. Of course, you rarely got to work with nice round numbers. More often, you'd have a GN of 120, a distance of, say, 8.2 feet, and a recommended f-stop of f14.6. What's with *that?* Such electronic flash units had little dials on the back that you could use to calculate exposures.

If you were smart, you'd use an electronic flash meter which could read the actual flash illumination falling on the subject and provide a reasonably exact exposure recommendation. Of course, you had to walk over to the subject, trigger the flash, and read the result. Flash meters have always been more practical in the studio than out in the field.

Eventually, electronic flashes were given little electronic sensors that could measure the light bouncing back from the subject and turn themselves off when the correct exposure was made. There wasn't a good way of informing the flash whether that light was bouncing back from a very bright subject or a very dark subject, so the exposures weren't necessarily accurate, but modern flash units might still retain this sensor and offer that kind of exposure calculation as an option.

You can synchronize the flash in two ways, each producing a slightly different effect:

- **Front-curtain sync:** This is the default mode used by cameras. The electronic flash is triggered as soon as the front current has reached the opposite side. This records a flash exposure of the subject. Then, the shutter is allowed to remain open for the rest of the exposure. If there is sufficient ambient light and the subject is moving, you end up with a streak in the direction of the subject movement, as if your subject were preceded by a ghost. Most often, you don't want to see that.

- **Rear-curtain sync:** In this mode, the flash doesn't fire until the rear curtain begins to move at the *end* of the exposure. The ghost image, if any, registers first and terminates with a sharp image at your subject's end position. In this case, the ghost image trails the subject, like the cool streak that follows the Human Torch everywhere, as you can see in Figure 9-8. If you must have a ghost image (or want one), this is the way to go.

Figure 9-8: With rear-curtain-sync flash, the ghost image trails the sharp image of the subject.

What if you want no streak at all? In that case, try to use a shutter speed that's high enough that the ambient light doesn't register an image. The higher your camera's flash sync speed, the better your opportunity for using a shutter speed that's so brief that you won't get a ghost image. Less is more: A $\frac{1}{500}$ of a second sync speed, like the one found on certain Nikon dSLRs, works better in that regard than slower speeds, such as the $\frac{1}{200}$ of a second sync speed of the Canon Digital Rebel XT or the $\frac{1}{180}$ of a second of the Pentax *ist DS.

Don't confuse front- and rear-curtain sync with *slow-sync,* which is a digital SLR option in automated modes that sets the camera to choose slow shutter speeds to *deliberately* add exposures from ambient light to the flash image. Slow-sync doesn't work well with moving subjects; use it with the camera mounted on a tripod so the background can be recorded along with the flash exposure.

Another flash sync option found on some dSLRs is *high-speed sync,* which uses longer (but weaker) flash exposures to synchronize the flash at even higher shutter speeds than the camera's nominal flash sync speed. This option is best applied to close-up photography, where the diminished flash output is sufficient for a good exposure.

Getting the right exposure

Your dSLR most likely uses a *dedicated* flash unit designed specifically for your camera, and it is built right into the camera, mounted on top in the hot shoe, or connected to the camera with a cable or wireless triggering mechanism.

Dedicated flash units are commanded by the camera itself, which measures the amount of flash that reaches the sensor and tells the flash when to shut itself off. This is called TTL, or through-the-lens metering, and is generally the most accurate type of flash exposure calculation. Communication between the flash and camera might also include information about which zoom setting is being used on the lens (so the flash can change its coverage to match) and what color temperature the flash emits (so the camera can compensate).

Flash exposure systems can also work with a preflash that's used to calculate the right exposure or integrate the distance data supplied by your camera's focus system to adjust flash output. There's also good old manual flash exposure, in which the flash pops at whatever power setting you specify (such as full, half, or quarter power), and you set the f-stop yourself by using a flash meter, guide number estimates (see the nearby sidebar "Exposure way back when"), or good old-fashioned guessing.

Yo, Trigger! Setting Off an External Flash

The mechanism used to set off your flash involves some considerations, too. Perhaps you want to separate an external flash from your camera by a distance that's too long for a connecting cable. In that case, you have a couple options:

✏ **Slave device:** This activates the remote flash when its sensor detects the light from your main flash.

Slave units work well when you plan to use several electronic flash units together. You can end up with brighter overall illumination or use the position of the different flash units to provide specific lighting effects.

✏ **Wireless trigger:** This more sophisticated approach sets off your flash without the need for a main flash at all. The camera or a device attached to the camera provides the signal that trips the remote flash unit(s). These often have a selection of four or more channels, which let you control flash units individually and also avoid conflicts with other photographers who happen to be using similar wireless devices at the same. Wireless sync can operate by radio signals or preflashes from the main camera that themselves don't contribute to the exposure.

In addition to the type of trigger you can use for your external flash, I have one more slightly important topic to discuss: how to avoid frying the electronics of your camera when using an external flash! Sounds like a good idea, right?

All digital SLRs that allow connecting an external flash use a triggering circuit that closes a switch that fires the flash. The triggering voltage from the flash that passes through this switch in your camera might vary from a few volts to 250 volts or more.

Modern digital cameras might not respond well to voltages of more than 10–15 volts, and some very bad things can happen to the camera's circuitry if more juice goes through than recommended.

Flash units built specifically for your camera or for digital camera in general will rarely cause difficulties. The problem seems to reside with older flash units and newer cameras. One solution is to determine from your flash vendor the exact triggering voltage. You can often find this figure on the Internet, and the information is usually as reliable as any guidelines you find on the Internet. (Not very.) My preference is to use a voltage isolation device like the Wein Safe-Sync, which separates your camera from the actual voltage used by the electronic flash.

The Safe-Sync, shown in Figure 9-9, receives the signal from your camera and passes the information along to your electronic flash. The flash fires, your camera isn't fried, and everybody is happy. You can mount the device in your camera's hot shoe and then slide the flash into the shoe on top of the Safe-Sync. Or, you can link a flash with a PC cord by using the connector on the side of the gadget.

Figure 9-9: A voltage isolation device can safely connect your dSLR with any flash unit.

10

Composition and dSLRs

S ome would say that good composition is exactly the same whether you're using a digital SLR or the least-expensive point-and-shoot camera. Others would say that those folks need to spend more time using a dSLR. Some significant differences exist between composing photos with a snap-shooting camera and a digital single lens reflex, the primary one being that you can do it.

Your basic non-SLR camera might rely on a tiny LCD that's 3.0 inches diagonally at the max (but likely much smaller). This LCD is easily washed out in bright light, might be too dim to view under reduced illumination, and is grainy and subject to ghost images if the camera or subject moves. It might display only 85 percent or less of the actual subject matter, and it probably turns itself off after a minute or two because it hogs so much power. And that's the good news.

The bad news is that these cameras often have an alternate viewfinder that's even worse than the LCD. That's a tiny optical window that not only shows just part of the actual image, it shows you the view uncentered. Depending on the location of the optical viewfinder, it will probably seduce you into cutting off the top of your subjects and maybe a little on the right side, as well. This paragon of technology doesn't show depth-of-field even as poorly as the LCD.

Your dSLR's viewfinder probably shows 95 percent of the actual photo at a magnification of 0.75X to 0.95X life size at a normal focal length (roughly the equivalent of 45–50mm). You have a good picture of the depth-of-field by default, and you can usually press a depth-of-field preview button to get a better idea of what's in focus and what isn't. A digital SLR's viewfinder is live all the time — even when the camera is turned off, and the view winks out for just a split second during exposure. There is no ghosting. You're never in danger of cutting off your subjects' heads.

So, coming up with a good composition when shooting with a point-and-shoot camera is more than problematic — it's an outright challenge. Given that a dSLR makes it easy for you to compose images in the first place, be sure to consider applying some of the tips listed in this chapter.

Composing a Photo: The Basics

Good composition is a little like good art. Even when people aren't consciously aware of all the components that go into great compositions, they still know what they like. That's because the very essence of composition is to arrange subject matter in a way that is both pleasing and which communicates the message the photographer is trying to get across.

That communication can be very subtle. Once, I was watching one of my favorite films by Japanese master Akira Kurosawa with the DVD commentary turned on. The film scholar/commentator pointed out that when Kurosawa wanted to express tension in a scene, he frequently arranged the actors and their surroundings in triangular compositions. During calmer scenes, the composition was more open and square-like.

When I knew what to look for, the late director's compositional legerdemain leapt off the screen, as obvious now as they were unnoticed before. I realized that good composition can strongly affect my feelings about an image, even if I wasn't consciously aware of the techniques being used.

I help you understand some of the rules for composing images — and understand when they can be bent or broken. Composition is all about communicating messages in a pleasing way or, conversely, in a disturbing way if that's your intent.

Composing for message and intent

Before you can frame your image in the composition you desire, you need to know what your messages and intent are. You don't need to spend hours contemplating your photo before you shoot. Simply keep the following questions in mind as you bring your dSLR to your eye and compose your picture:

✔ **What do I want to say here?** Am I simply trying to portray my subject in a thoughtful or playful mood, or is my intent to show the anguish and hard life of a typical migrant mother? Am I looking to create a peaceful shot of a forest scene, or do I want to show the ravages humankind has wrought on the environment? Or, is my goal to make my client's widget look tempting so someone will buy it? Some good photos make statements; others convey images of quality or affordability. A few more attempt to evoke humor. If you know in advance what kind of message you want to convey, and who your audience is, you'll be way ahead in the compositional game.

✔ **What's my main subject?** Wow! What a great lot of classic automobiles all lined up at the drive-in. Wouldn't that make a great picture? An array of these cars might make a memorable shot — but it might not make a good composition. Instead of trying to cram a half-dozen autos into one shot, choose one and let the others create an interesting background. Your photo should always have one main subject, even if that main subject is a group of people posing for a portrait.

✔ **Where's the center of interest?** Your main subject is generally your center of interest, and it probably shouldn't reside in the center of the photograph. But it *should* be in a place that attracts the eye and encourages examination of the rest of the image.

✔ **Do I want a vertical or horizontal composition?** Digital SLR shooters are much less likely to fall into the trap that the point-and-shoot set is subject to: composing all photos horizontally, simply because that's the way the camera was designed to be held. A dSLR easily pivots between vertical and horizontal orientations, so you can choose vertical compositions for tall buildings and NBA players, and you can use horizontal layouts for ranch homes and NFL quarterbacks who've just been flattened by a linebacker. Of course, you can always crop your image from one orientation to the other within your image editor, but that wastes pixels. Figure 10-1 shows an image that quite logically falls into the vertical composition mold.

Figure 10-1: Some subjects are best suited for vertical compositions.

✔ **Do I want to print this image in black and white?** In that case, textures and contrasts can become a more important part of the composition.

✔ **How should I arrange the subjects in my photo?** Placement of the subjects within the frame is a key part of good composition. You might be able to move some objects or change your shooting angle to alter the composition. The arrangement of your subjects will determine how the viewer's eye roams around in the frame. There should be a smooth path to follow, starting with your main subject and progressing to the other interesting elements in the photo.

✔ **Where should I stand?** The distance from you to your subject and your angle can have a dramatic impact on your composition. A high angle provides a much different view than a low angle, and shooting at eye level is likely to be boring. Getting close emphasizes a subject in the foreground while potentially minimizing the importance of the background. Backing away can make the foreground appear to be more expansive. You have to change your shooting angle by physically moving, but you can achieve a specific distance by zooming, switching to a prime lens of a particular focal length, or simply taking some steps forward or back. And in a pinch, you can crop your photo in an image editor.

✔ **What's in the background?** Backgrounds can make or break a photo. Sometimes you want a plain background to draw emphasis on the center of interest. Other times the background will be part of the composition and add interest. Take a careful look at what's in the background before you shoot. If you re-examine Figure 10-1, you'll see that the bush in the background could be a little distracting or, worse, form a merger with the lion statue. You find out more about mergers later in this chapter.

Applying the Rule of Thirds

Every book on photography you'll ever read will include a blurb describing the infamous Rule of Thirds, which posits that the ideal locations for objects in a composition reside one-third of the way from the top or bottom margins and one third of the distance from either side. For example, in Figure 10-2, the castle is located at one node, the sun at another, and the "horizons" line up roughly one third of the way from the top and bottom of the picture. Most of the books won't tell you exactly *why* dividing an image into thirds is such a good idea. After all, couldn't you follow the Rule of Quarters, the Rule of Fifths, or even the Rule of Six and Seven-Eighths?

The origins of the Rule of Thirds

In reality, the Rule of Thirds wasn't created by some all-knowing artist back in the dawn of time, nor was it created arbitrarily. The Rule of Thirds was created by Mother Nature herself. The ancient Greeks studied many of the most pleasing works of nature and discovered that most of them adhered to a specific proportion that could be described in a particularly harmonious mathematical way.

Figure 10-2: The Rule of Thirds offers guidelines for placing the horizon and other significant parts of an image within the frame.

They deemed this particular proportion golden and used it to construct a Golden Rectangle, which, if its long side is defined as 1, the short side is 0.618 as long. Bisecting this Golden Rectangle produces Golden Triangles, and if you do it enough times you end up with four points that divide the original rectangle into thirds. Zazaam! With all that math and natural beauty driving it, the Rule of Thirds *has* to provide pleasing proportions. Of course, the typical digital film frame isn't necessarily a Golden Rectangle, but the Thirds rule can be applied nevertheless.

Putting the Rule of Thirds to work

To use the Rule of Thirds, simply try to locate your subjects at one of the imaginary intersection points in the viewfinder. Remember that if your dSLR has optional grid lines, they probably *aren't* arranged to follow this rule. Also know when to ignore the guideline. It's okay to center your subject or locate it at the far right, top, or bottom if you have good reasons for doing so. Most close-up photos and many portraits, for example, place the subjects right in the middle of the frame, usually because there are no other compositional elements in the photo that need to be arranged to provide balance.

Posers and Poseurs

People photography is one of the most enjoyable types of picture-taking, and digital SLRs are especially adept at it. Whether you're posing friends, family, and colleagues for casual or more formal portraits, or attempting to catch, say, the next rock star wannabe onstage, your dSLR has the features you need to excel.

Compared to point-and-shoot digital cameras, digital SLRs provide more flexibility in choice of lenses, more control over depth-of-field (so you can throw a distracting background out of focus), and better image quality with the longer exposures sometimes necessary for people shots at night. Despite all you've got going for you, be sure to keep the compositional tips in this section in mind as you snap away.

You can use thousands of good poses for individuals or groups, but you don't need to memorize dozens of options to get good portraits. If you're a beginner at people pictures you might want to look at some poses that work in magazines and books. However, a few simple rules can help you build workable subject arrangements from scratch. Read on for details.

Shooting individual portraits

Portraits of individuals are theoretically easier than pictures of groups because you have only one subject to worry about. Of course, you have to please that subject with your results. Everyone wants to be portrayed in a flattering way, and it's the photographer's job to see that a subject *looks* the way he or she imagines himself or herself — or better!

Here are some tips:

- Make sure your subject is relaxed and comfortable. Seated is better than standing for anything short of a full-length portrait, and a stool is often the best seat because there is no back or arms to intrude into the photo, and a perch on a stool discourages slouching. However, a picnic bench, handy rock, fence, or even the kitchen table can provide a place for your subjects to relax while you capture them for posterity.

- If your victim isn't facing the camera, have him or her look into the frame, rather than out of it. Otherwise, the viewer is going to be wondering what is going on outside the picture area that is so interesting.

✔ As I learned from my days photographing models, even the most attractive people can have hands and feet that are positively grotesque when photographed from their worst angles, which are the backs and palms of the hands and bottoms of the feet. Most of the time, bare feet won't be a prominent element in your portraits, but if you photograph the edges of hands, they can become an expressive part of your photo. Exception: baby hands and baby feet can be cute from any angle, particularly to the parents and close relatives. But be aware that some childless adults and a few other types are powerfully sick of adorable pictures of somebody else's kids, so this charm isn't necessarily universal.

✔ Bald heads aren't necessarily as problematic as they once were, because athletes, musicians, and those who aspire to coolness often shave their heads specifically to get the bare pate look. If your subject is sensitive about involuntary baldness, just lower your camera slightly and elevate your subject's chin. If you're using external lights, avoid adding glare to the top of the head.

✔ Long, large, or angular noses might be a badge of honor and personality for some, and perhaps a plus for thespians seeking character roles for their distinctive faces. For everyone else, try having subjects face directly into the camera.

✔ Alfred E. Neuman, Dumbo, and H. Ross Perot just wouldn't look the same without their distinguishing ears. Less-famous folk sometimes appreciate it if you minimize their prominent ears in photographs or, at the very least, avoid making them the center of interest. Try shooting your subject in profile, or arrange the lighting so that the ear nearest the camera is in shadow.

✔ To minimize wrinkles or facial defects such as scars or bad complexions, use softer, more diffuse lighting. Shooting in the shade or bouncing light off a reflector (which can be something as simple as a white shirt worn by an assistant or passerby) can provide a more flattering rendition. A diffusing filter on your lens or diffusion added in your image editor can help, too. Or, zoom out or take a step back to shoot your subject from the waist up, as shown in Figure 10-3. That reduces the relative size of the face in the final picture.

✔ Avoid reflections off eyeglasses. Have your subject raise or lower the chin a bit so the glasses aren't bouncing light directly into the lens. If using flash, position the flash at an angle. You can see many reflections through your SLR viewfinder, but for flash shots, review your picture and reshoot if reflections are a problem.

Figure 10-3: Teenagers are often best pictured with soft lighting in full-length or waist-up poses.

Shooting group photos

Group photography has all the potential pitfalls of individual portraits, multiplied by the number of people in the shot. However, the following special considerations are unique to photographing groups:

 ✔ **Remember that each group shot is also a portrait of all the individuals in the shot.** The guidelines for creating flattering portrayals remain basically the same. (I list the guidelines in the preceding section.) Unfortunately, optimizing everyone's visage in a single shot can be tricky because you can't have one person in profile, another from a low angle, and a third with special lighting to minimize yet another kind of defect. Fortunately, though, because individual faces in a group shot are relatively small, these problems can take care of themselves as long as you keep everyone relaxed and smiling.

✐ **Watch the eyes!** Make sure everyone in the photo is looking in the same direction, which should generally be in the same direction their noses are pointing. Check for blinkers and nodders, too. Try to take at least one photo for every person who is in the photo (that is, at least six for a six-person pose) just to get one in which everyone's eyes are open. Then double that number to be safe.

✐ **Arrange your subjects into interesting patterns.** Make sure that all the heads aren't in a single horizontal or vertical line, although it's possible to make exceptions for special poses, like the one shown in Figure 10-4.

Figure 10-4: This shot works best in a nontraditional pose, with the mother and daughter facing each other.

✓ **Triangular and diamond shapes work best for groups of three or four people.** If you have more than that in a shot, break them up into multiple triangles and diamonds. Copyright restrictions dating back to the year 1662 prevent me from including in this book Rembrandt's portrait we know as *The Dutch Masters,* but if you google this picture (or just buy yourself a box of cigars), you see that it contains a cunning arrangement of *three* triangles to represent just six people. The trio on the left make up one triangle, the three on the right make up a second, inverted triangle, and the same figures produce a third triangle if you look only at the three gentlemen in the center.

Tips for Publicity and PR Photography

I made my living taking publicity and public relations (PR) photographs for more years than I care to count, so you'd think I'd be competent at it by now. I have learned enough that I can summarize the difference between the two in a single sentence:

Publicity photography is intended to make someone or something famous; PR photography is designed to make someone or something likeable.

A typical publicity photo might be one showing a rising 28-year-old TV/movie star out on a date with a 45-year-old thespian whose career has seen better days. If the picture captures the public interest, it's likely to boost the careers of both, regardless of whether it portrays the pair in a favorable light, and regardless of whether it was taken by a paparazzo or supplied by a publicist.

A publicity photo can also picture an object, rather than a person. Perhaps a giant blow-up figure promoting a new movie has been stolen from the roof of a fast-food restaurant and now resides on the front lawn of a college fraternity. Everybody wins here: the restaurant, the movie producers, and the college students who gain 15 minutes of fame.

Photos intended to improve public relations are almost always provided by the PR agency or publicist of the person or product that benefits. If the 28-year-old and 45-year-old stars happen to be arrested after crashing a sports car through the window of a jewelry store, you can bet that some PR photos will soon appear picturing those same personalities doling out dinner at a soup kitchen or entertaining the troops in some foreign country.

Of course, the approach isn't quite that cynical in the real world, and both publicity and PR photos can be used for quite serious and laudable purposes, I'm told.

Your job, if you choose to accept it, is to create pictures that will do their intended job. As such, you must realize that publicity and PR photos don't revolve as much around a particular subject as they do a particular purpose. Portraits, sports photos, landscape pictures, and even travel photography all can be included in this category, so you'll want to follow the guidelines for each. But, in particular, keep these things in mind:

- **These photos all have a particular message or two to convey,** and your composition should revolve around that message, whether you hope to portray a particular person as a fine upstanding citizen, or represent a product as a good value, premium-priced luxury item, a or technological breakthrough that will save the world. Keep your message in mind at all times.

- **Keep It Simple, Silly (KISS).** Exclude everything that doesn't help convey the message out of the photo. You don't want viewers of the picture to become interested in something else that they find more compelling.

- **Look for unusual angles.** Your historical society just purchased an old steam engine. Ho hum! If you want newspapers in your area to run your PR shot of the classic, shoot an eye-catching picture that makes the editor sit up and take notice, like the one shown in Figure 10-5.

- **If you're shooting a PR picture, you must represent the person or product accurately, within reason.** If you don't do that, your image loses credibility, and reputable news media will decline to run it. No adding marbles to a bowl of soup to make the vegetables rise to the top. Don't show your company's CEO running a marathon when the most exercise she gets in real life is pounding on the boardroom table. That doesn't mean you're obligated to picture every defect and problem, only that you shouldn't deliberately use your photographs to mislead the audience.

Figure 10-5: Unusual angles can add interest to your PR photos.

   ✔ **If you're shooting a photo for publicity, go ahead and ignore all the advice in the preceding paragraph.** Nobody takes your efforts seriously, anyway. Your photos are desirable only if they're a bit over the top and perhaps more than a little sensational. A photo showing an Academy Award winner punching out one of his mates in a bar is a lot more salable than one of him mending a fence on his ranch. The latter is more likely to be a PR photo released when he's released out on bail, and a much tougher sell.

Capturing Architecture

Architectural photographs frequently call for wide-angle lenses, which let you take in large expanses of a building and its surroundings without having to step back a mile or two. Indoors, the same wide-angle lens makes it possible to photograph interiors without having to step outside and shoot through an open window. Wide-angle lenses also allow you to include foreground detail, such as landscaping, which can be an important part of an architectural photo.

On the plus side, the interchangeable lenses available for digital SLRs generally have a much wider view than you can get with even the wide-zoom model point-and-shoot digitals. Several non-SLR cameras from Nikon, Olympus, and others have wide-angle lenses that are the equivalent of a 24mm lens on a 35mm film camera or a full-frame digital SLR. Frequently, that isn't nearly enough; only digital SLRs allow you to fit lenses as wide as 15mm for a true ultra-wide view.

Of course, the wide-angle perspective comes at a price, especially if you're using a digital SLR with the crop factor that comes with the territory in cameras that have smaller than full-frame sensors. On a camera with a 1.5X crop factor, a 20mm extra-wide lens becomes an ordinary 30mm wide-angle lens, and 16mm ultra-wide optic has a 24mm view. Although you can readily buy true ultra-wide lenses for your digital SLR — including zooms that take in the equivalent of an 18mm full-frame lens at the wide end, and 15mm fisheyes — these lenses can be expensive. Even so, if you want to shoot architecture frequently, you'll spring for the lenses you need.

The next sections outline some of the details you need to consider when shooting architecture, indoors or out.

Reeg, your perspective is out of control!

Whether or not it's a good thing, most people take photographs with the camera at eye-level and the back of the camera parallel to the plane of the subject, and at right angles to the ground. I'm always harping about using interesting angles, both high and low, but, most of the time photos are taken straight-on with little or no tilting in any direction.

Wouldn't you know it? Camera tilts commonly come into play when the shooter is taking architectural photos. Outdoors, tilting the camera up is often necessary to photograph tall structures, which seems like a good idea until you see that the building appears to be falling back in the final picture. That little bit of tilt can make the picture look somewhat bizarre, as you can see in Figure 10-6, thanks to a syndrome called *perspective distortion*. Fortunately, unless you're inside a cathedral or domed stadium, you probably won't need to tilt the camera upward, and you can avoid the most common kinds of perspective distortion when shooting interiors.

The most logical solutions for this distortion outdoors don't always work well. You can take a few steps back so you won't need to tilt the camera (or tilt it as much), but that often means that intervening trees, fruit carts in the plaza, and other obstacles now intrude on your photo. A wider lens sometimes helps, although you'll end up wasting a lot of pixels on foreground subjects that you'll end up cropping out of the picture.

Figure 10-6: Tilt your camera back, and a tall structure appears to be falling away from you.

If a handy building stands across the street, you might be able to ascend about halfway up, shoot out a window, and take in both the base and top of your target structure without tilting the camera at all, but you'll rarely be that lucky.

Your digital SLR might be compatible with any of the available *perspective control* lenses, which can move their optics off-center enough to take in more of a subject in any one direction without the need to tilt. However, perspective control lenses can cost a bundle, might not be available for your camera, and are tricky to use.

Your best bet might be to do the best you can and then use your image editor to correct the perspective distortion. Photoshop CS2 has a handy Lens Correction tool, found in the Filters➪Distort menu, shown in Figure 10-7.

Figure 10-7: Photoshop's Lens Correction tool can help fix perspective distortion.

The Lens Correction tool can fix perspective distortion, plus correct chromatic aberrations and mend pincushion and barrel distortion (the tendency to bow vertical and horizontal lines inward or outward, respectively). Apply this corrective filter, and you can end up with an image like the one shown in Figure 10-8.

Charge of the lighting brigade

Architectural photos, indoors or out, can also suffer from lighting problems. As with other types of photography, one of the main challenges to you, the photographer, is to make sure the lighting helps render your subject in the most suitable way for the particular type of photograph you'll be taking.

Figure 10-8: The corrected tower looks like this.

In Figure 10-9, for instance, I decided to let uneven lighting work for me. The shadows of the upper rafters of the railroad station were dark, and the highlight areas of the surrounding area washed out, concentrating attention on the platform area. In most cases, though, you're not so lucky, but you can turn to Table 10-1 for solutions to many common lighting problems.

Figure 10-9: Sometimes uneven lighting can work for you, concentrating attention on one part of the image.

Table 10-1	Handling Common Lighting Problems
Problem	**What to Do?**
Too little light. If you're shooting outdoors at night, or indoors, it's very likely that you won't have enough light to make a proper exposure with the camera hand-held.	Provide extra lighting (with flash, perhaps), mount your camera on a tripod to allow a longer exposure, or use a technique like *painting with light,* in which the shutter of a tripod-mounted camera is left open in a time exposure while the photographer or an assistant illuminates the subject with repeated electronic flash bursts, a flashlight, or other light source.

(continued)

Table 10-1 *(continued)*

Problem	What to Do?
Too much light. Having too much light is rarely a problem. Architectural photography usually is friendly towards bright (but not harshly lit) environments that allow using short shutter speeds and/or small apertures that provide lots of depth-of-field.	Although rare, in very bright situations, you may need to use a neutral density filter to cut back on the amount of light.
Harsh lighting. You might find yourself in a situation where the light is glaring, contrasty, and harsh.	You may need to soften the lighting by intercepting direct illumination so that it bounces off reflectors.
Uneven lighting. Harsh lighting can be uneven, but uneven lighting isn't necessarily harsh. You simply might find yourself with plenty of suitable illumination in part of your frame, and not enough light in other parts.	Break out the electronic flash or reflectors to cast a little light in the gloomy portions of your subject.
Mixed lighting. Indoors, it's common to have multiple light sources illuminating your room. Space located near windows might be lit by outdoor light that is quite bluish compared to the warm interior light. These mixed light sources can be fairly ugly if left unmodified.	Pros do things like draping orange filter-like material over windows to give it the same color as the interior light or filtering their electronic flash so it will match the room illumination. Your best bet might be to draw the blinds or turn off the interior lights and stick with the window light and perhaps a few supplemental electronic flash units with the same white balance.

You've been framed!

Most kinds of photography benefit from building a visual frame around your subject, but architectural photos benefit more than most. If possible, frame your main subject by using doorways, windows, arches, the space between buildings, or the enveloping branches of trees as a pseudo border. Usually, these frames are in the foreground, which creates a feeling of depth, but if you're creative, you can find ways to use background objects to frame a composition.

Designing Your Landscape Photos

Landscape photography is another photographic pursuit that benefits from the dSLR's ability to use wide-angle lenses. Landscapes also happen to be, after portraits, one type of photography that is most likely to be blown up to huge sizes and displayed on the wall. As much as people love their loved ones, they are also fond of Mother Earth, and enjoy sharing photographs of each.

Like architectural photography, landscapes lend themselves to contemplative shooting. Scenery changes slowly over long periods of time, so Ansel Adams-esque quests for the perfect angle, idyllic weather, and ideal conjunction of the stars and planets are understandable and not at all unreasonable. Given enough time to work with, you can use all the compositional suggestions that I mention in this chapter.

Use curves, lines, and shapes, like those shown in Figure 10-10, to guide the viewer's eye. In this case, the lines draw the eye to the center rock formation. Fences, gracefully curving seashores, meandering roads, railroad tracks, and receding tree lines all can lead the viewer through your carefully crafted composition. Curved lines are gentle; straight lines and rigid geometric shapes are more forceful. Although you can't plan on moving things around helter-skelter to improve your composition (rocks, mountains, and streams pretty much must remain where you found them), you're free to change angles and viewpoints until your picture elements all fall into place.

Figure 10-10: Lines and shapes can guide your viewer through your photograph.

Landscape photography also happens to be one of the more happily gadget-prone photographic pursuits. Gradient neutral density filters — dark on top and clear on the bottom — can balance a brilliant sky with the less-bright foreground. Gradient color filters, which I describe in more detail in Chapter 15, can blend a warm orange color on one half with a rich blue on the other, producing an interesting split effect between sky and foreground.

Tripods are a valuable tool for landscape photos because they steady the camera to help you take razor-sharp images that you can blow up to mammoth size. They're also handy as a camera stand that keeps your lens pointed in the right direction while you spend lots and lots of time thinking about your shot. Panorama heads work in conjunction with your tripod to allow leveling your camera as you crank off overlapping shots at the correct intervals.

When you're ready to shoot, keep some of these tips in mind:

- **Avoid splitting your photo in half with the horizon.** Remember that Rule of Thirds! Place the horizon one-third down from the top if you want to emphasize the foreground, or one-third up from the bottom if the background and sky are your most favored subjects.

- **You don't have to compose landscapes in landscape mode.** Try shooting some verticals. If you incorporate strong vertical lines, such as trees off to one side of the shot, your landscape photo can be naturally converted to a vertical orientation.

- **Shoot lots of sunsets (or sunrises if you're *that* kind of person).** Sunsets and sunrises always look good because the light has a marvelous golden quality, and they're different each time — even if you shoot from the same location. Remember that the sun rises and sets in a slightly different place on the horizon each day of the year.

- **Manually focus if you must.** Autofocus systems sometimes have difficulty finding enough contrast for focusing automatically, especially if there is lots of sky in the photo. Most landscapes will be focused at infinity, anyway.

Compositional Ideas That Travel Well

Travel shots are often a combination of architectural photography and landscape photography. As you roam around on vacation, you're bound to find interesting things to photograph within cities, as well as in the countryside. The chief difference between travel photography and architectural or landscape pictorials is that the travel shots will invariably have one or more members of your party standing smack in the middle of the picture waving or pointing.

It doesn't have to be so. Oh, of course you want to prove you've been to the Eiffel Tower or Grand Canyon, so go ahead and take a few shots with you or your companions mugging for the camera. But then shoo everybody out of the way and take a few well-composed photos you can be proud of. After all, 20 years from now most of your family members in the photos will be old and wrinkly. But the Eiffel Tower and Grand Canyon will be an unaging part of your vacation memories if you take the time to capture some memorable photos while you're there.

Vacation photos are your chance to apply some of the basic compositional techniques I discuss throughout this chapter. A few new principles to consider include:

- **Try to balance your compositions.** Place interesting subject matter on both sides of the frame. I don't mean that you need to have two centers of interest, only that your photo shouldn't be lopsided. If you pose a person on one side of the frame, include a building or some foliage on the other side to create a balanced look. This trick encourages viewers to explore the image, rather than feel uneasy because they're wondering why all that empty space is on the other half of the photo.

- **Avoid mergers.** *Mergers* are the (usually) unintentional combinations of unrelated subjects spliced together in disturbing ways. The classic merger is usually a tree growing out of the top of someone's head (but you can do the same thing with the Eiffel Tower if you're careful and have tired of having your subjects just stand in front of it and wave).

  Mergers can also happen when subjects seem to grow out of the edges of the picture. For example, if you have a tree branch drooping down into your image but there is no tree anywhere to be seen in the rest of the photo, the branch appears to have sprung from the edge of your picture. Examine your compositions carefully to spot and eliminate mergers before you capture them in pixel form.

- **Don't be afraid to try some new subjects.** Certain travel photos are almost obligatory. Return from Spain without a picture of a flamenco dance, or come back from Philadelphia lacking a shot of Independence Hall or the Liberty Bell, and your acquaintances might doubt you've actually been where you claim. But don't let those expectations limit you.

  I like to photograph what I call the Gettysburgs of each location I visit — the places many people have heard of, but have rarely seen pictured. In the United States, that might be a view of the St. Louis arch taken from underneath the arch itself, rather than from the other side of the Mississippi River, or a close-up of a sign at a nostalgic old drive-in restaurant, like the one shown in Figure 10-11. In Europe, you might want to photograph El Toboso, a village in Spain where Don Quixote's Dulcinea lived, rather than snap only the same-old-same-old photos at the Alhambra or the Costa del Sol.

With a little imagination, you can return from your trip with well-composed, interesting photos that will capture the spirit of your vacation, but not look like they were cribbed from post cards.

Figure 10-11: Look for unusual subjects, especially nostalgic Americana like this drive-in restaurant sign.

Part IV
Fine-Tuning Your Output

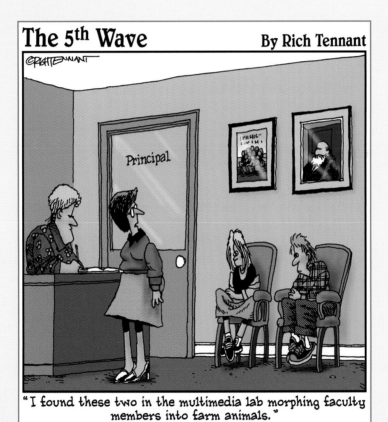

The 5th Wave — By Rich Tennant

Principal

"I found these two in the multimedia lab morphing faculty members into farm animals."

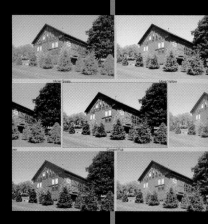

In this part . . .

*Y*ou aren't done yet! Pressing the shutter simply takes the photo. Then, you might want to *make* the photo by using the creative tools available with image-editing software. This part shows you some of the things you can do with your image, including the joys of distributing them as hard copy prints.

Chapter 11 helps you do basic retouching with the image editor of your choice, salvaging murky photos, correcting unacceptable colors, and removing annoying spots. Chapter 12 shows you simple techniques for combining one or more photos, removing backgrounds, and getting creative with selective modifications. Chapter 13 proves that making good hard copies doesn't have to be hard.

11

Fixing Up Your Images

One of the best things about digital photography is that your images are digital all the way. You don't need to scan film or a print or do any conversion. What you shot is what you got — a digital image full of pixels just waiting to be tweaked, fine-tuned, shifted around, and optimized. You can do a lot of that in your camera, but for even greater image enhancement you need an editor such as Adobe Photoshop Elements, Paint Shop Pro, or even the granddaddy itself, Photoshop CS2.

If you're really, really good at digital SLR photography, your images might not need any fixing at all, right? *Nobody* is that good; even the most sharp-eyed shooter will still want to use image editing. You can take that perfect composition and create an entirely new picture by judicious cropping. Perhaps you can modify your perfect exposure to produce a special high-contrast effect, or a low-contrast moody look. You can creatively twist great color balance with oddball colors. You might even find that the perfect shot of the Eiffel Tower would look even better if you transplanted the structure to a cornfield in Kansas.

These are all things you can do with an image editor. This chapter and Chapter 12 show you what you can do to fix up images or transform existing shots into entirely new ones.

Editor-ial Comments: Choosing an Image Editor

Which image editor should you use? It could be argued that Adobe Photoshop is the best image-editing software on the planet. It could also be argued that owning your own private jet is the best way to travel around the country. Not everyone can afford private jets or Photoshop, and not everyone wants to spend time learning how to pilot them. That's why so many alternatives to Adobe's flagship image editor have flourished.

Some image editors have every imaginable feature, but others take a bare-bones approach. Do you need to be able to edit CMYK (cyan/magenta/yellow/black) image files and make color separations, or are you just looking to correct red-eye problems? Do you want absolute control over every parameter, or would you prefer that your image editor handle simple tasks with a wizard-like interface? Image editors differ both in the features they have and the approaches they take to image editing. The trick is to figure out which editor has the features you need and an approach that is compatible with your working style.

Because you're working with a digital SLR, I assume that your editing requirements are — potentially — a little on the ambitious side. Certainly, you want to adjust tones, fix color, or sharpen things up a little. But you also might have a hankering to drop out backgrounds, remove an extra head from your brother-in-law from another planet, or combine several of your best shots into one. So, in this chapter, I assume that you want to go beyond the basics with your image editor and your image-editing activities. (In Chapter 12, I explain how to do so.)

For an ambitious soul like you, the image-editing choices are numerous.

Adobe Photoshop

Photoshop is a verb? With apologies to R. Buckminster "I Seem to Be a Verb" Fuller, Adobe Photoshop is well on the way to joining our language as a process rather than just a product. The average person who has never used an image editor, when confronted with an obviously manipulated photograph, is likely to say, "That looks photoshopped!" Common misusage of its trademark might pain Adobe, but the company has to be pleased at how widely known and used the product is.

Since it appeared on the market in the early 1990s, Photoshop, including its latest incarnation, Photoshop CS2, has gained its number-one position over the years by virtue of a complex set of circumstances, many of which relate to how cool the product really is. Consider these points:

✔ **Photoshop does everything any sane digital photographer or graphics worker would want to accomplish.** Recent releases have filled a lot of holes, including long-requested ability to curve text along a path. If you can't do it with Photoshop, you probably don't need to do it.

✔ **Photoshop does *not* include (unlike, say, a certain Office suite) feature bloat in the form of capabilities that nobody wants or uses.** You might not need every single Photoshop feature now, but someday you might. Photoshop has no equivalent of a dancing paper clip.

✔ **Photoshop works identically with both PCs and Macintoshes.** With some minor interface differences, Photoshop works the same with both PCs and Macs.

✔ **Understanding how to use Photoshop is a marketable skill.** Certainly, it takes months to become a Photoshop master, but the knowledge you gain won't help you only with your current job, but, potentially, your next one, as well. Employers won't take notice if you're a Paint Shop Pro guru (unless the company happens to use that program), but might place a premium on Photoshop expertise.

Despite its cost and learning curve, Photoshop, shown in Figure 11-1, is certainly not out of the reach of the average dSLR owner. Most computers built in the last couple years are certainly powerful enough to run it, especially if you upgrade to 2GB of RAM, which shouldn't cost more than $200. Anyone serious about photography will be willing to spend the time to master it, and it's available for both PCs and the Mac.

Figure 11-1: Photoshop CS2 in action.

Attractive upgrade offers let you purchase a full copy of Photoshop for a fraction of its original $600 list price. Thereafter, you can upgrade when Adobe comes out with a new release (on roughly an 18-month schedule) for about $150. You can even skip a release (upgrading, say, from Photoshop 7 to Photoshop CS2) if you don't need the very latest features.

The good news

Photoshop's strength is its complete feature set, with tools for doing retouching, compositing, complex color correction, and even Web design. If you specialize in one type of image processing over another, you'll find that Photoshop has everything you need in its well-organized tool set.

Photoshop is a nimble, cross-platform, cross-application tool. It can read, write, and manipulate all the industry-standard file formats as well as many nonstandard file types. You can resample images to change the image size, resolution, and color depth. Photoshop excels at providing images that are optimized for specialized uses, such as commercial printing and Web graphics. As part of the Adobe Creative Suite, Photoshop also is well-integrated with several leading page-layout programs and Web-development programs, such as Illustrator, PageMaker, InDesign, and GoLive. Now that Adobe has acquired Macromedia, you can expect some integration with that subsidiary's products, as well.

Photoshop provides a rich set of tools for everything from simple image manipulation (cropping and color balance adjustments, to name two) to selecting complex shapes from an image and applying sophisticated filters and effects to the selected area. Photoshop also includes a full set of painting tools that you can use to retouch your images or to create original artwork.

Adobe designed Photoshop to accept filters and plug-in program extensions provided by third-party suppliers, such as Andromeda, Applied Science Fiction, Alien Skin, Auto FX, and Extensis. A robust aftermarket has evolved to supply a wide assortment of plug-ins that let you quickly and easily apply all manner of textures, edge treatments, special effects, and other image manipulations to the images you edit in Photoshop.

The latest Photoshop version has a whole new way to review images on your disk called Bridge, a standalone application that you can open without powering up Photoshop.

The bad news

Photoshop doesn't do natural media well; that is, it has trouble mimicking various types and styles of brushes, charcoal, pens, and other tools needed to paint original images. For that, you need Corel Painter. In fact, many graphics pros own both, using Photoshop for color correcting and retouching and using Painter for creative brushwork.

Photoshop's $600 list price has to go into the bad news column. Photoshop can also develop into a money pit. Serious Photoshop users have a thirst for plug-ins, which can each cost as much as, say, Paint Shop Pro. Although Photoshop comes with more than 100 plug-ins, you can never be too rich, too thin, or have too many filters for your image editor.

Don't downplay your investment in time required to figure out how to use Photoshop. Although you can pick up the basics in a few weeks, if you really want to master every nuance and trick, be prepared to spend even more time. There's a good reason why a search for Photoshop books on Amazon.com returns more than a thousand results. Hundreds of authors who had to learn to use this application are eager to share their knowledge with you. You probably need to buy two or three of the best books and read them thoroughly to master the basics and most common shortcuts.

One of the most comprehensive books on the market is *Photoshop CS2 All-in-One Desk Reference For Dummies,* by Barbara Obermeier (Wiley).

Finally, Photoshop is definitely not a program you can use once a month. You can invest all that time learning to use it and then forget half of what you learned if you don't work with the application on a weekly basis. Photoshop is a commitment.

Adobe Photoshop Elements

Adobe Photoshop Elements is a powerful junior version of the full Photoshop program. Elements has most of the functionality, but it lacks some of the features that the average photographer might be able to get along without. At about $100, it's more affordable, too.

Elements, shown in Figure 11-2, shares much of the same user interface with Photoshop. Although it's missing a few features that Adobe deems professional, such as Layer Masks and CMYK editing, Elements includes most of the basic image-editing tools that the typical digital photographer needs on a regular basis. That includes image-selection tools, retouching tools, painting tools, a generous assortment of filters, and the ability to expand those filters by accepting the same Photoshop plug-ins as its sibling program.

The good news

A price tag of $100 puts Elements within the reach of anyone, and its reduced feature set is a good match for the needs of the typical digital photographer. Most of the standard selection, retouching, and painting tools from Photoshop are available in Elements. If your image-editing needs revolve around retouching and manipulating individual pictures one at a time, you'll probably never miss the more advanced Photoshop features.

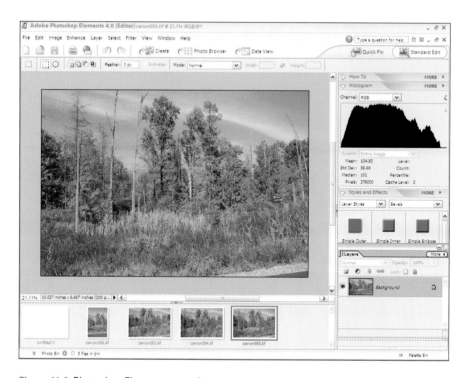

Figure 11-2: Photoshop Elements at work.

TIP

The automated commands on the Enhance menu make quick work of common image-editing tasks, such as adjusting backlighting or color cast. As a result, an occasional user working with Elements can complete those tasks faster and more accurately than a seasoned graphics pro working with Photoshop.

Elements also makes a good introduction to Photoshop for people who plan to upgrade someday. After you master this program, you can transfer much of what you learned directly to Photoshop. You make filters, most kinds of selections, and basic tonal and color corrections in much the same way in both applications.

The bad news

Compared to the most basic non-Adobe image editors, Elements can be a bit daunting. The similarity to Photoshop works against you if you're a total image-editing neophyte, because the menus and palettes bear more similarity to Photoshop than they do to, say, Roxio PhotoSuite. Even so, dSLR photographers probably wouldn't be happy with the simplest image editors, anyway, so the "easy, but not *that* easy" interface of Elements won't offer much of a downside.

The other downside is Adobe's tendency to introduce new features for Elements in its Windows version first, with the Macintosh upgrade following months later. Some features are available only in the Windows edition. For example, the Elements file browser is available only in the Windows version; Adobe expects Mac owners to depend on iPhoto and other Mac-specific tools.

Corel PhotoPaint

Corel PhotoPaint, one of three image editors available from graphics giant Corel, is the image-editing program that is included in the popular CorelDRAW Graphics Suite. Various versions of this program are available for both PCs and the Mac, although the Mac version is several releases behind and might be difficult to locate.

PhotoPaint, shown in Figure 11-3, is a reasonably full-featured photo-retouching and image-editing program. Although its feature set cannot match the full version of Photoshop, PhotoPaint stands solidly among a second tier of products that deliver a large portion of Photoshop's functionality for a relatively small portion of that program's price.

Figure 11-3: Corel PhotoPaint comes with the CorelDRAW graphics suite.

PhotoPaint offers a full set of selection, retouching, and painting tools for manual image manipulations. It also includes convenient automated commands for a few common tasks, such as red-eye removal. PhotoPaint accepts Photoshop plug-ins to expand its assortment of filters and special effects.

The good news

Corel PhotoPaint is a respectable product as a standalone image editor. However, its greatest strength is its integration with CorelDRAW and the rest of the Corel graphics suite. If you use CorelDRAW to create and edit graphics, you've probably got PhotoPaint installed on your computer, and you'll feel right at home using the product. All the PhotoPaint menus, dialog boxes, and palettes behave just as they do in CorelDRAW.

The bad news

PhotoPaint is available only as part of the CorelDRAW Graphics Suite. At $400, CorelDRAW Graphics Suite is a good value, provided you need the main CorelDRAW program and any of the other components of the suite. However, $400 is a lot to pay for PhotoPaint alone, especially because other image editors are available for around $100.

Paint Shop Pro

Paint Shop Pro (PSP) is the latest image-editing program to join the Corel fold. The company that originated it, Jasc, is no more. PSP is a general-purpose image editor that has gained a reputation as the "poor man's Photoshop" for providing a substantial portion of Photoshop's capabilities at a fraction of the cost. The program lists for about $100, but you can often find it for sale at a substantial discount.

This Windows-only program features a fairly complete tool kit that includes selection, painting, and retouching tools for direct manipulation of your images. It also offers a sizable collection of wizard-like commands that automate common tasks, such as removing red eye and scratches. Paint Shop Pro, shown in Figure 11-4, includes a nice assortment of filters and effects, and you can expand that assortment by adding almost any of the Photoshop plug-ins.

The good news

Paint Shop Pro originated as a shareware program, but was so good that it eventually became a thriving retail product. It's been around for more than a decade and has had plenty of time to evolve and mature into a robust, easy-to-use product. Indeed, many people rate Paint Shop Pro as the easiest to use of the general-purpose image editors, and it's among the lowest priced programs in its class.

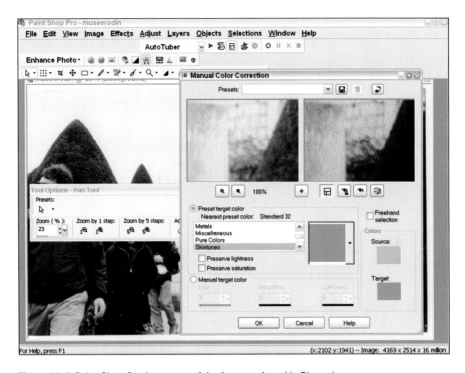

Figure 11-4: Paint Shop Pro has many of the features found in Photoshop.

Paint Shop Pro supports layers, which enable you to achieve some fairly sophisticated editing effects. This is a surprising capability in such a low-cost image editor.

The bad news

The breadth and depth of the Paint Shop Pro feature set is a little uneven. The program shows surprising depth in some areas, such as the availability of layers, and shallowness in others, such as the limited choice of selection and paint tools. Also, some tools (such as the Histogram Adjustment command) require more knowledge and experience to use effectively than do the corresponding tools in some of the other editors.

Evaluate the program carefully to determine whether its particular strengths and weaknesses are a good match for the mix of work you need to do.

Corel Painter

Corel's third image-editing program is Painter, which continues to be popular among photographers and artists because of its ability to create content from scratch. As such, it might not be your favorite application for retouching your digital pictures, but if you need to paint something on an existing image with a fuzzy brush soaked in oil paints, this is your baby, and this baby works for both PCs and Macs.

Painter, shown in Figure 11-5, is adept at re-creating in digital form a wide range of traditional artist media, such as charcoal, pastels, and various kinds of paint. Painter includes a basic assortment of tools that you can use to edit existing images, but the program is really designed for artists to use in creating original illustrations.

The good news

Painter's natural media effects are incredible. Some other programs allow you to select different paintbrush tools and adjust their color, size, edge softness, and a few other attributes. But Painter takes the concept of brush effects to a whole new level.

Figure 11-5: An image being edited in Painter.

In Painter, you can define not only the characteristics of the brush, but the texture of the paper or canvas; the thickness of the paint on the brush; and how the paint, brush, and paper interact. As a result, the program can realistically simulate the very different effects of a watercolor wash on hot-press paper, oil on canvas, pastels on a sanded board, or any of a huge assortment of other media/material combinations. Painter comes with a large inventory of predefined brushes and art materials, which you can use or modify to suit your artistic impulse. With the right settings, you can even watch the digital paint drip and run.

A pressure-sensitive graphics tablet is almost a must with this program.

The bad news

Expect to be confused the first time you work with Painter. Its bewildering array of palettes have options that allow you to exercise precise control over each brush stroke. Just finding where each feature or palette is located can be a challenge, and working your way through the various options each time you want to do something can be tedious. As you gain experience with the program, it becomes easier to use, but figuring out how to use Painter effectively takes no small amount of time and commitment. This isn't a program that lends itself to occasional, casual use.

Painter's image-editing capabilities are more attuned to the needs of an artist who wants to incorporate part of an existing image in a new composite than they are to routine image enhancements and corrections. If you're looking for a digital darkroom where you can crop, correct color, and repair your digital photographs before printing, you need to look elsewhere.

At about $300 (for the downloadable version), Painter is somewhat expensive. You probably wouldn't want to buy it just to fool around with it. If you need this program's capabilities, though, $300 can be a bargain.

Macromedia Fireworks

At the time of this writing, no one knows what will happen to Macromedia Fireworks now that the company has been acquired by Adobe. Fireworks is a dual-platform image-editing program developed by the same company that developed market-leading Web-development software and Web animation software — Dreamweaver and Flash, respectively. Although Adobe probably purchased Macromedia to gain access to Dreamweaver and Flash, Fireworks and other applications included in the purchase might continue to be offered.

I hope so, because Fireworks, shown in Figure 11-6, has all the features needed to handle most any routine image-editing chore. The basic selection, retouching, painting, text, and drawing tools are all present and accounted for, and the program supports layers and Photoshop plug-ins to expand its basic filters. However, Fireworks doesn't try to be the most versatile, general-purpose image editor on the market. Instead, the program excels in the more specialized job of preparing images for use on the Web.

The good news

Fireworks competes head-to-head with the Adobe program ImageReady, which, it has been announced, is being completely folded into Photoshop and will no longer be a standalone application. So, Fireworks will be Adobe's only standalone program that specializes in Web-related image editing.

The application is excellent for creating Web graphics, such as banners, image maps, and rollover buttons. Fireworks also provides an excellent set of tools for working with text and with shapes, and the program can automatically generate the HTML and JavaScript code needed for rollover effects and image maps.

Fireworks does a great job of optimizing images for use on the Web (another ImageReady specialty). The Preview tab of each document window in Fireworks allows you to instantly preview different image-optimization settings as you edit your image. The Image Optimization dialog box pulls all the various file format, color depth, size, and resolution settings together into one place where you can experiment with various settings and observe their effects on file size and image quality.

Figure 11-6: An image being edited in Fireworks.

This program's chance for continued existence might hinge on its close integration with Dreamweaver, which will certainly remain in the Adobe product line. If you're building a Web page in Dreamweaver and need to optimize an image on that page, all it takes is a couple mouse clicks to open the image in the Fireworks Image Optimizer dialog box. With a few more mouse clicks, you can optimize and save the image and then return to Dreamweaver, where the newly optimized image appears automatically on the Web page you're editing. You have to see this feature in operation to appreciate just how slick it is and how much time it saves.

The bad news

Fireworks doesn't have the comprehensive image-retouching and painting tools found in other image editors, and it supports fewer file formats than other Adobe products.

Ulead PhotoImpact

Ulead PhotoImpact, shown in Figure 11-7, is unique in that it is just about the only general-purpose image-editing program that hasn't been acquired by another company. For more than a decade, PhotoImpact has been on the market as a Windows-only program, and it has a particularly strong palette of features.

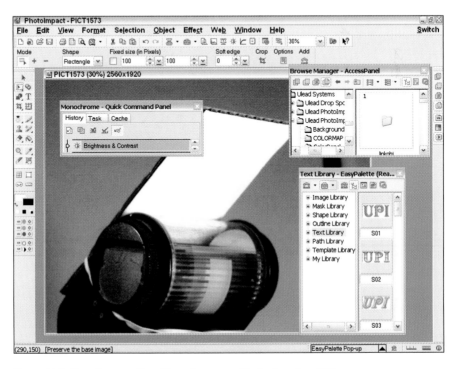

Figure 11-7: PhotoImpact offers Photoshop versatility for less than $100.

PhotoImpact includes a full assortment of brushes for painting, retouching, and cloning in addition to the expected selection, cropping, and fill tools. It also offers tools for text and vector shapes, as well as tools for creating slices and image maps for use on the Web. PhotoImpact supports layers and includes a generous collection of effects filters, which you can expand with Photoshop plug-ins. Auto-process commands are available to automate many of the most common image-correction and -enhancement tasks.

The good news

Price! Like Paint Shop Pro, PhotoImpact offers a lot of what you get in Photoshop, but for less than $100. It's also a good tool for repetitive operations, although the PhotoImpact batch and auto-process tools are no match for the Photoshop Actions. Still, you can select multiple image files and then apply any one of a long list of filters, enhancements, or auto-process commands to all the selected files.

PhotoImpact also includes some specialized features for creating Web graphics, including wizards that lead you through creating Web backgrounds, banners, and buttons. Its image-optimization features are good for people who would otherwise use ImageReady or Fireworks.

The bad news

I've found the PhotoImpact user interface odd and inconsistent, and some features feel more like add-on modules than built-in components.

Fixing Your Photos

You can manipulate your photos in two different ways: by fixing anything seen as a defect without really changing the content extensively, and by combining and reorganizing images in more drastic ways. I show you the basics of combining and reorganizing (which includes *compositing,* or melding several different images or parts of images) in Chapter 12. In the following sections, I stick with the techniques for making repairs and fixes.

The most common fixes for digital photos fall into five categories:

- **Cropping:** As you discover in Chapter 10, you can often improve a photo just by removing items that don't belong or that distract from the composition. *Cropping* — adjusting the borders of an image — is the easiest way to do this.

- **Tonal adjustments:** Your images might be too bright or too dark, or worse, include some parts that are too dark and others that are too light. Although your dSLR includes features that let you make some adjustments for tone (including specialized tonal settings called *custom curves*), frequently these adjustments are easier to make with an image editor.

✔ **Color correction:** If your colors are off, you can usually fix them in your image editor. If your colors are accurate, you might want to *make* them seem off as a creative effect. You can do both with your editor.

✔ **Spot removal:** Your dSLR shots might have a variety of different spots and artifacts that need to be removed. A dirty sensor can produce dust spots on pristine images. Perhaps birds in the sky off in the distance are too small to look like anything other than blotches. Your subject might have a small scratch or defect. You need an image editor to touch up these spots.

✔ **Sharpening/blurring:** You can change the emphasis within your composition by selectively sharpening or blurring parts of the picture. You can also salvage a shot that isn't quite sharp enough with a little sharpening, or smooth out rough texture with blurring.

The following tips apply specifically to Photoshop; your image editor can perform the same tasks, but it might use different commands.

Cropping

If you know anything about composition, you know that images can often be vastly improved with some judicious trimming. Figure 11-8 shows you what I mean. At first glance, it appears to be a photo of a powerful jet fighter climbing into the sky at dusk, possibly preparing to attack an enemy in a dogfight. When I show people this photo, they often ask whether I took it from the air, or perhaps from the ground with a very long telephoto lens.

Figure 11-8: Cropping tightens a composition and adds drama.

The answer lies in the uncropped version of the photo, shown in Figure 11-9. (Please don't feel cheated by the mundane origins of this picture!) As you can see, it's a photo of an old jet mounted on concrete pylons on the front lawn of a high school in my area (nickname: Aviators). I loved the plane, but I found that it was difficult to get a good angle. So, I shot a picture anyway, darkened it a little to make the image look more dramatic, then cropped the image tightly, and trimmed out some utility wires to produce a much more exciting view.

Figure 11-9: The original shot is slightly less inspiring!

Photoshop gives you several ways to crop a picture. Here are some of the fastest and most versatile:

- Create a rectangular marquee around the part you want to crop to, and then choose Image⇨Crop. Photoshop trims off everything outside the selection marquee.

- Draw around the area you want to crop with *any* line-oriented selection tool, including the Lasso, Polygonal Lasso, and Magnetic Lasso. The area specified doesn't even have to be remotely rectangular in shape. However, a cropped rectangle *is* what you'll end up with. Photoshop crops to the smallest rectangle that includes all of the image within your selection, as you can see in Figure 11-10. For details on using these Lasso tools, see Chapter 12.

TIP

✔ If the image you want to preserve is included inside a border that's roughly the same tone, such as a picture frame surrounding a photo hanging on a wall, you might be able to select that border with the Magic Wand and then reverse the selection with Ctrl+Shift+I (⌘+Shift+I on the Mac) and crop to the image that's now selected.

✔ Use the Crop tool, which is probably the best choice because it allows you to adjust the borders of the selection individually before making the crop.

Figure 11-10: I made a selection with the Lasso tool, and Photoshop kindly cropped to the selection for me.

To use the Crop tool, follow these instructions:

1. **Select the Crop tool (press C to make it active or select it from the Tool Palette).**

2. **Drag a selection that roughly includes the area in the cropped image.**

3. **Grab the handles on the top, bottom, or side selection borders and move in or out to adjust the cropping exactly the way you want.**

   Notice that the area outside the crop selection darkens, making it easier for you to visualize the final picture, as shown in Figure 11-11.

4. **Press Enter (Return on the Mac) to apply the crop to your image.**

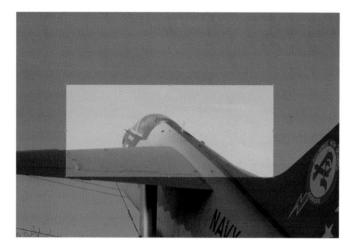

Figure 11-11: The Crop tool allows you to precisely specify the crop borders.

Fixing murky or contrasty photos

Tonal adjustments are another fix that you'll frequently want to make. Digital SLRs have the ability to capture a broad range of tones, called a *dynamic range*. That lets you capture detail in dark shadows as well as bright highlights. Unfortunately, many scenes have a dynamic range that's too long for even the best digital sensors. When that happens, you might end up with pictures that have lots of detail in the shadow areas, but the highlights are washed out (or *blown* in digital parlance).

If an exposure captures highlight detail, your shadows might be murky. Indeed, some dSLRs are programmed to deliberately produce this murky effect, on the theory that it's easier to retrieve underexposed information in shadows that are dark, but not completely black, than it is to regain detail in highlights that have gone completely white.

Some images might have a very limited range of tones, including whites, some intermediate grays and colors, and blacks, but lacking the other in-between tones. These images are said to be *high contrast*. Others are rather bland-looking, with lots of individual tones spread throughout the image, but few true blacks or whites. Such images are said to be *low contrast*. The problem doesn't always lie with your camera: The lighting in your scene might be too contrasty or too low in contrast to render the scene attractively.

If your images are high or low in contrast, or are simply too dark or too light, you might be able to fix the problem in Photoshop or another image editor.

As you might expect, Photoshop has several tools that can help you. Some work well, but others are atrocious or intended only for beginners. In the following list, I run through all the tools, so you'll know which traps to avoid:

- ✔ **The "auto" tools:** Photoshop includes two tools, Auto Levels and Auto Contrast, located in the Image⇨Adjust menu. They can analyze your photo and correct the brightness, contrast, and tonal values for you. These tools have no idea of what kind of effect you're going for, so the results might or might not please you.

- ✔ **The Brightness/Contrast controls:** Also on the Image menu is a deceptively simple set of sliders that allow you to brighten or darken everything in an image or change the contrast of the entire image. The problem is that you very seldom want to apply that sort of adjustment uniformly to every pixel in an image. Lighten the shadows with the Brightness slider, and you probably make the highlights *too* light. Slide the control to the left, and your too-light highlights probably turn an ugly gray while your shadows turn black. Expect the same poor over-all results with the Contrast slider. Use the Brightness and Contrast sliders *only* when you need to make an entire image brighter, darker, or different in contrast.

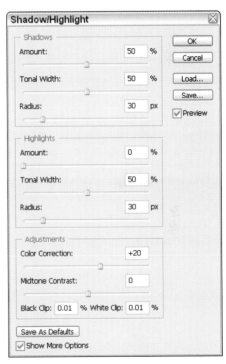

Figure 11-12: The Shadow/Highlight controls allow you to adjust tonal areas individually.

- ✔ **The Shadow/Highlight controls:** These controls do what the Brightness slider should have done. They let you adjust the brightness of the shadows and highlights individually, using a dialog box like the one shown in Figure 11-12. This one's a keeper, and I explain it in more detail in the next section.

- ✔ **Levels:** The Levels dialog box lets you specify how tones are distributed in your image. I explain this one later in the chapter, too.

- ✔ **Curves:** The Curves dialog box gives you full control over the tones in your image. Stay tuned for more on this.

Working with the Shadow/Highlight controls

When you activate this dialog box, it defaults to settings suitable for fixing images that have been backlit, with the shadows much too dark. The Shadow slider will be at 50 percent, and the Highlight slider at 0 percent. If you've selected the Show More Options check box, you see the full dialog box shown in Figure 11-12.

Note that the full dialog box has three areas: one for shadows, one for highlights, and one for adjustments. The Shadow and Highlights areas have the same three sliders. Here's how you can use each one to fix contrast in an image:

- **Amount:** This is the degree of change to be applied. A higher number equals a more drastic application of the tonal change.

- **Tonal Width:** This represents the number of tones, from the 256 different tonal levels in the image, that are affected. For example, if you set Tonal Width to 25 percent, one quarter of the 256 tones (64 tones) are modified. A value of 50 percent affects 128 tones and produces a more pronounced change.

    The best way to decide what value to use is to watch your image as you move the slider. Use a small value to brighten only the very darkest shadow areas or to darken only the lightest highlight areas. Increase the value to brighten more of the dark areas or darken more of the highlights. Don't use very large values or you'll end up with glowing haloes at the boundaries between the shadows and highlights.

- **Radius:** The Radius slider helps Photoshop determine what should be considered a highlight pixel and what should be considered a shadow pixel. Ordinarily, the control examines each pixel's neighbor to make this determination. Increasing the Radius value enlarges the size of the neighborhood so that more pixels are counted as highlight or shadow pixels rather than middle-tone pixels (which are *not* affected by the Shadow/Highlight control). Monitor your preview image to see whether you're getting the effect you want.

The third area of the dialog box, the Adjustments area, controls other parameters. These include:

- **Color Correction:** This isn't a color-correction tool as much as it is a way of compensating for color shifts that occur when you're fiddling with the tonal controls. Use it to remove these casts.

- **Midtone Contrast:** Although the shadow and highlight controls adjust only the darkest and lightest areas, this slider lets you apply some fine-tuning to the middle tones.

✔ **Black and White Clipping:** Use these controls to increase contrast intentionally by dropping (or *clipping*) a desired percentage of black or white tones from your image.

Working with levels

The Photoshop Levels dialog box allows you to control the tonal values of an image much more precisely than you can with the Shadow/Highlight controls. Most good Photoshop books have a whole chapter on using levels, but I can provide a good introduction.

The Levels dialog box shows a graph called a *histogram,* which is very similar to the histogram you can view on the LCD of your dSLR after you've taken a shot. Your camera histogram shows you only whether all the tones are being captured, and you can do little other than adjust exposure up or down or perhaps make a tonal setting change in your camera's menus. The one in the Levels dialog box (Image➪Adjustments➪Levels) actually lets you change the tonal values.

As you might know, a histogram is a graph that shows the relative number of pixels at each of 256 brightness levels. The more pixels at a particular brightness, the higher the bar at that level. Histograms provide a mountain-range-type curve, like the one shown in Figure 11-13, with most of the tones usually distributed in the middle, and fewer trailing off towards the dark tones (left side of the graph) and light tones (right side).

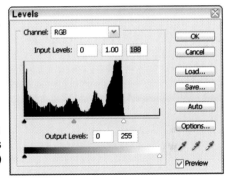

Figure 11-13: The Levels dialog box provides more precise tonal control.

The objective of the Levels command is to avoid wasting any of the 256 possible tones that can be represented. You do that by moving a trio of triangular sliders at the bottom of the graph:

✔ Move the black triangle to the right until it touches the edge of the black tones actually present in the image, as shown in the graph.

✔ Move the white triangle to the left until it touches the edge of the actual white tones.

✔ You can move the middle gray triangle to lighten or darken the overall image by adjusting the midtone position.

If you remember these basics, you can improve your images significantly without learning the additional fine-tuning capabilities of the Levels dialog box. Should you want to spread your wings and discover more, I recommend *Photoshop CS2 All-in-One Desk Reference For Dummies* (Wiley).

Working with curves

If the Levels dialog box is worth a chapter or two, the Curves dialog box, shown in Figure 11-14, is worth an entire book! Curves are a way of changing the highlights, midtones, and shadows entirely independently. It allows you to change the values of pixels at any point along the brightness-level continuum, giving you, in effect, 256 locations at which you can make corrections.

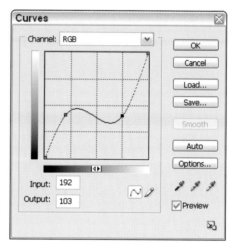

Figure 11-14: Curves allow controlling tonal values at 256 different brightness points in your image.

The Curves dialog box includes a two-dimensional graph, with the horizontal axis mapping the brightness values as they are before you make image corrections. The vertical axis maps the brightness values after correction. By default, the lower-left corner of the graph represents pure black (0,0), and the upper-right corner represents pure white (255,255). When you open the dialog box, the graph begins as a straight line because, unless changes are made, the input will be exactly the same as the output, forming a direct 1:1 correlation. As you change the shape of the curve, you change the values in the image at each point within the curve.

The best way to see what this tool can do is to play with it. After you've been using Photoshop for a while, you'll begin to see how curves can provide the precise control you need over tonal values.

Correcting those colors

Sometimes, despite the best intentions and competent technique, you end up with pictures that have bad color. Perhaps the picture has a green color cast caused by fluorescent lights, or it has too much red because you took it late in the day. Fortunately, image editors such as Photoshop let you fix these. Lots of tools are at your disposal. Some are easy to use, but others take a little practice.

Before you get started, keep in mind that you can't add color that isn't there in the first place. If your image is way too red, you can't compensate by adding its opposite color (cyan). Image editors work by *subtracting* hues. So, if your picture is dominated by red and has very little green or blue, when you remove the excess red, you don't end up with a correctly balanced image. You wind up with a picture that is grayish because a little bit of red, blue, and green are all that's left.

Photoshop's color-correcting tools include the following:

- ✔ **Auto Color:** This is another one of those pesky "auto" controls that uses Photoshop's guesswork to provide a possible correction to your color problems, but most likely, the correction isn't what you want.

- ✔ **Color Balance:** The Color Balance sliders let you seemingly add red, green, or blue while subtracting their complements (cyan, magenta, and yellow). You can use the sliders while viewing your image to make color corrections. Of course, as I note earlier, you can't really add a color to an image; the dialog box's operation is just an easier-to-understand representation of

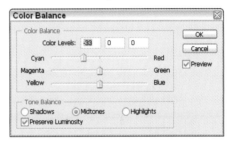

Figure 11-15: Change color by subtracting red, green, blue, cyan, magenta, or yellow.

  what's really going on. That is, when you move the Red/Cyan slider to the right, Photoshop actually is subtracting cyan. Move it to the left (to "add" cyan) and you're really subtracting red. If you understand what's going on, you aren't really fooled, but you don't mind, either. The same thing takes place when you adjust the Magenta/Green and Yellow/Blue sliders. The Color Balance dialog box, shown in Figure 11-15, allows you to apply these color changes to the highlights, midtones, and shadows.

- ✔ **Hue/Saturation:** This control changes color by using different components than the standard color balance tools use. Instead of modifying the primary colors of light, it adjusts the overall color of the image (hue), how pure or rich the colors are (saturation), and the lightness or brightness of the color. Moving the Hue slider rotates the color clockwise or counterclockwise around the edges of the color wheel shown in Figure 11-16. The Saturation slider adds richness, turning a muted pink into a deep rose or dark red, for example. The Brightness slider controls the overall luminosity of the image and is generally less used.

✔ **Variations:** The Variations dialog box gives you a way to compare different color and darkness alternatives for an image. You get to choose the one that looks best, as you can see in Figure 11-17.

✔ **Curves:** I've come full-circle to the Curves tool again. You can use this complex tool for more than adjusting basic (grayscale) tonal values. You can actually control the tonal rendition of each of the primary colors in an image. Using the Curves tool in this way usually requires a lot of experience, unless you're very adventuresome.

Use whichever combination of color-correction tools works for you. They all have particular advantages and disadvantages.

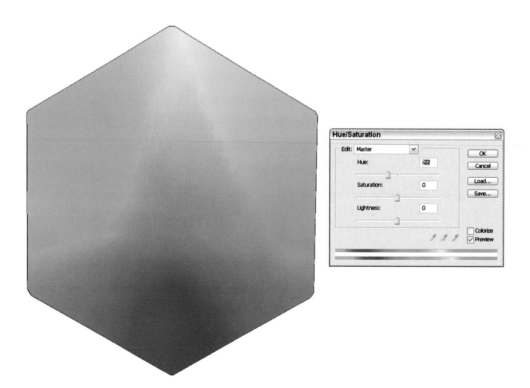

Figure 11-16: Hue, saturation, and brightness can be controlled separately with this dialog box.

Figure 11-17: The Variations dialog box lets you choose the best rendition from a selection of versions.

Spot removers

Unwanted artifacts in your image might not be arty, but they are facts. Your job, should you choose to accept it, is to remove them. There are several different causes of spots, speckles, and other naughty bits (and bytes) in your images, and Photoshop has the tools to remove them. In the following sections, I offer an overview of how to use these tools.

Reducing noise

A little noise in your image can be a good thing. Noise can add an artsy, grainy effect and serve to add some texture to an annoyingly smooth surface. Indeed, detractors of one particular brand of digital SLR say that the remarkably noise-free results produced by that camera look plasticky. I'm not going to mention the particular camera model, because the rebels who prefer that brand see this lack of noise as a definite advantage.

This little tidbit isn't widely known among digital photographers who don't have a graphics-production background: One advantage of noise is that a little noise actually makes smooth gradients reproduce better because of the way press equipment and the halftoning process operate. Now you know.

However, for most folks, noise is unwanted. You can often prevent it by using your dSLR's noise reduction feature. But what do you do if noise turns up in your captured image?

You're in luck! Photoshop CS2 introduced a Reduce Noise plug-in, found in the Filters⇨Noise menu. The dialog box, shown in Figure 11-18, has four main sliders. You can specify the strength of the noise reduction, whether noise reduction should be done at the expense of image detail, how much to tone down the colored speckles that are endemic in most noisy images, and whether the remaining details should be sharpened after the noise has been removed. You can also have the tool search for and remove defects caused by JPEG compression. In Advanced mode, you can access a second tab that allows you to specify the noise reduction by color channel, which is useful because some channels, such as green, might be more prone to noise than others.

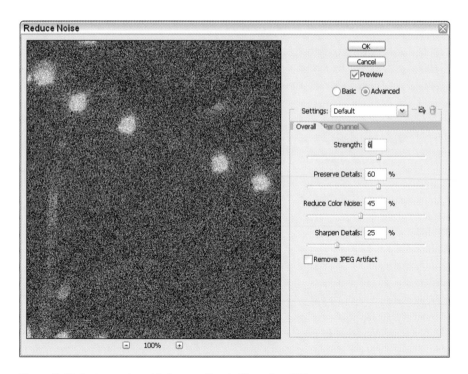

Figure 11-18: Reduce noise with the new filter in Photoshop CS2.

Spotsylmania

Photoshop gives you several ways of eliminating other kinds of spots, scratches, and so forth. These include filters like:

- **Despeckle:** This filter looks for areas of great contrast in your image because such areas are likely to be edges. Then, it blurs the non-edges, making any spots and speckles less obvious. Because the edges are still sharp, your image still might look relatively sharp. This filter works best with images that are sharp in the first place but plagued with artifacts, and it's less effective with images that are already somewhat blurry. It's a good tool for eliminating halftone dots, too.

- **Dust & Scratches:** This filter actively hunts through your image for spots. It includes two sliders: a Radius slider that lets you specify the size of the area around a potential spot to be searched, and a Threshold slider that determines how distinct a spot must be before it is considered a defect.

Send in the Clone Stamp

The Clone Stamp tool is useful for removing spots and other defects by copying a portion of the surrounding pixels, which should have a similar color and texture, over the ailing portion of your image.

To use the Clone tool, follow these steps:

1. **Choose the Clone tool from the Tool Palette or press S to make it active.**

2. **In the Option bar, select a brush of an appropriate size from the Brush drop-down menu.**

   A soft-edged brush is usually best.

3. **If you want to gently copy over the area to be fixed and blend the pixels more evenly, set the Opacity slider on the Option bar to less than 100 percent.**

   Anything from 25 percent to 90 percent works well.

4. **Make sure the Aligned check box is selected in the Option bar.**

   This lets you stop and start the cloning process while retaining the same positional relationship with the origin point you choose in the next step. When Aligned isn't selected, each time you begin cloning again, the origin point goes back to the original location.

5. **Place the cursor in an area near the portion you want to copy over. Hold down the Alt key (Option key on the Mac) and click in that area to select the origin point.**

6. **Move the cursor to the area you want to copy over, hold down the mouse button, and paint.**

   Figure 11-19 shows you an example of what you can do with the Clone Stamp.

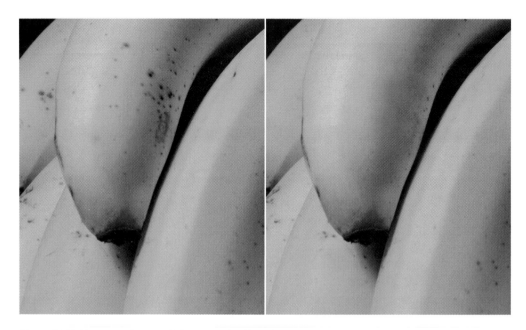

Figure 11-19: If your results are a little spotty, the Clone Stamp can help you out.

Healer, heal thyself

The Healing Brush, Spot Healing Brush (new to Photoshop CS2), and Patch tools let you copy pixels from one place in an image to another, similarly to the Clone Stamp tool, but while taking into account the lighting, texture, and other aspects of the image. That makes for smoother, less obvious touch-ups. Here's how each one works:

- **The Healing Brush** works like a brush in much the way the Clone Stamp tool does. It copies pixels from a sample origin point you specify.

- **The Patch tool** operates like a tire patch, pasting an area of pixels you choose on top of the part of the image you want to fix.

- **The Spot Healing Brush** works like the Healing Brush, but you don't have to specify an origin point; it automatically samples pixels around the area being healed and uses them to copy over the defective spots.

Look sharp, be sharp

If you have an image that isn't sharp enough, or if you want to increase the contrast between one area and another by sharpening one part, Photoshop's varied sharpening tools can do the job for you. Keep in mind that sharpening works by increasing the contrast between transitions in tone of an image. So, while you're adding sharpness, you're also increasing contrast. It's easy to end up with too much of a good thing.

If you want to sharpen the entire image, use the various sharpening filters. In the Filters➪Sharpen menu, you'll find a selection of choices. These include

- ✔ **Sharpen:** Applies a fixed amount of sharpening to the entire image or selection.
- ✔ **Sharpen More:** Applies a stronger fixed effect.

   You should use either of these filters, Sharpen or Sharpen More, only when you need a touch of sharpening and don't need to be precise.

- ✔ **Sharpen Edges:** This filter seeks out the areas of transition in an image (the edges) and sharpens only those areas, preserving the smoothness in the rest of the image. As with the first two filters, you can't specify the amount of sharpening to be applied.

- ✔ **Unsharp Mask:** This filter does let you control the degree of sharpening, especially as it's applied to the edges of images. This should be your tool of choice for most image sharpening because it applies sharpening more intelligently and flexibly.
- ✔ **Smart Sharpen:** This filter includes three tabs that let you specify sharpening parameters, as with Unsharp Mask, but you can also control sharpening separately in shadow and highlight areas.

If you want to add some sharpness in specific areas quickly (say, to sharpen the eyes in a portrait), Photoshop has a Sharpen tool in the Tool Palette that lets you "paint" contrast. It's easy to overdo this tool, so be careful.

Blurring for effect

Blurring is the exact opposite of sharpening: Instead of heightening the contrast difference between adjoining pixels, the color and brightness differences are reduced so that pixels are much closer to each other in terms of their color levels, brightness, and contrast. Your eyes see this as a low-contrast blur effect.

Selective blurring can reduce the effect of noise or spots or even make some areas seem sharper in contrast. You can blur one area while sharpening another to create an especially dramatic look, as shown in Figure 11-20. Of course, you can also go too far with blurring and end up with something that isn't even recognizable, or you can fail to blur enough, leaving the content as distracting as ever. The key is to find a happy medium where objects are still recognizable, but nobody will spend much time looking at them.

Figure 11-20: An apparent contrast in sharp and blurred areas of an image can be dramatic.

Photoshop has blur effects to match those in the sharpen category, including the Blur tool and filters such as Blur, Blur More, Gaussian Blur (the equivalent of Unsharp Masking, but in reverse, in many ways), and Smart Blur. Photoshop also has more specialized blur effects, including:

- The kind of blur you get from subject or camera motion at relatively slow shutter speeds

- Blur produced by lens effects

- Radial blur, as if you were photographing a record player turntable from above as it spun

- Box blur, which blurs by using mosaic-like boxes

- Shape blur, which uses your choice of oddball shapes to blur your image

- And much more

Combining and Reorganizing Your Images

*Y*ou gotta love those eye-catching magazine covers. *National Geographic Magazine* moved the Great Pyramid to create an improved composition. *TV Guide* gifted Oprah Winfrey with Ann-Margret's figure — literally. More recently, *Newsweek* featured a full-length photo of Martha Stewart based on a head shot of the home economics queen grafted onto the body of a model. It's been estimated that someone creates a new fake image in Photoshop every 30 seconds. I want to find that guy and ask him when he finds time to sleep!

Perhaps you don't want to fool anyone into thinking that Mao Zedong is swimming in the Yangtze River. Your motives for doing some heavy-duty image manipulation are much purer. Maybe you'd like to add an extra wing onto your house to show around at your high school class reunion. Or, it's time to remove Madge from the group shot of your organization's Regional Sales Managers, because Madge has been reassigned to the mail room.

Worse, you have an unsightly photo showing your mother-in-law with a tree apparently growing out of her head, and you'd be happier if the image showed just the tree. That's the sort of thing you can do with an image editor, such as Photoshop. The simple editing and retouching tasks I detail in Chapter 11 are cool enough on their own, but in this chapter, you get serious performing *real* imaging magic to add or subtract objects, move them around, or combine photos.

This chapter focuses on image editing with Photoshop. Your favorite image editor might work similarly or have cool features of its own.

Making Selective Modifications

A wag once said that time is what keeps everything from happening at once. The same can be said of selections in Photoshop: The ability to select one portion of an image makes it possible to modify only that selection while leaving everything else in the photo untouched. Selections are the basis for just about every variety of image manipulation I describe in this chapter. You'll see this is true the first time you use the Sharpen filter to enhance the sharpness of everything in an image, because along with sharpening that face in the foreground, the Sharpen filter will make some unwanted details in the background more visible, too.

What is a selection?

In Photoshop, a selection is all the stuff inside the crawling *selection border,* which is sometimes called "marching ants." Selections can consist of image area within straight or irregular outlines; include multiple disconnected areas in one selection; and have relatively solid edges or fuzzy, fading edges, as shown in Figure 12-1.

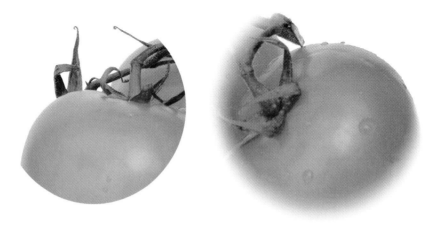

Figure 12-1: Selection edges can be sharp (left) or fuzzy (right).

A selection defines an area in which modifications can take place. You can create selections with three kinds of edges: antialiased (smoothed), feathered (fading out gradually), and non-antialiased (jagged edged). Selections can be totally opaque, semitransparent, or graduated in transparency.

Performing everyday changes with selections

After you successfully select part of your image, you can do lots of things with the selection. These include:

- **Copying** the selected area to an area of memory called the Clipboard, where it sort of sits around waiting (until you copy something new to replace it) so you can paste it down into a new layer of its own. The copied portion is surrounded by transparency, so it floats over the image area in the layers below it. Press Ctrl+C (or ⌘+C on the Mac) to copy a selected area.

- **Cutting** the selected area so it is removed from your image. The cut portion ends up on the Clipboard, just as if it were copied, and is available for pasting until you replace it on the Clipboard with something else. Press Ctrl+X (or ⌘+X on the Mac) to cut a selected area.

- **Changing** the selection. After you make a selection, you can change its boundaries, making them larger, smaller, more or less feathered or irregular. You can also add other selections to your original selection, transform the size and shape of the selection, and invert it. Use the Select menu to adjust a selection.

- **Filling** with the contents of other selected areas or images you've copied to the Clipboard, thereby pasting one image into another. Press Ctrl+V (⌘+V on the Mac) to paste down an image that has been copied to the Clipboard.

- **Painting, filling, or modifying** the selected areas by using any of the brush-like and painting tools, while rendering the rest of the image (the nonselected area) immune to your fiddling. You can paint with color or fill the area with a color or pattern. To apply changes, you can use the Clone Stamp, Gradient tool, Dodge and Burn tools, Blur/Sharpen tools, and many more utensils.

- **Applying** a filter only to a selected area.

- **Masking** selected areas to prevent them from being modified accidentally. Use masking when you want to do a little brushwork on the background of an image but *don't* want to mess with a face in the foreground. Select the face as a protected mask (Photoshop lets you use selections as either an active or a protected image area) and go to town.

- **Transforming** the selected area by changing its size, shape, or perspective; by flipping it horizontally or vertically (or both); and by rotating it. Use Select⇨Transform Selection to apply these changes.

✔ **Saving** selections to use later when you want to reselect the same portion of an image. Use the Selection⇨Save Selection command, and store the selection as a file under a name you choose.

✔ **Converting** selections into vector-oriented paths that you can manipulate with the Pen tool. You go the other way, too, converting paths to selections. Use the Make Work Path and Make Selection options, respectively, in the Paths palette.

Making Basic Selections

Photoshop has three main selection tools: the Marquee tool, the Lasso tool, and the Magic Wand. Each tool has multiple variations. For example, the Marquee tool includes Rectangular, Oval, and Single Row/Column versions. The Lasso tool includes Polygonal and Magnetic varieties. The Magic Wand is pretty much the Magic Wand (it's magic, it's a wand, and that's about it), but it has options that dramatically modify the way it works.

The tool you use depends on the shape of the image you want to select. In the following sections, I offer the simple steps for using each tool.

Making rectangles, squares, ovals, and circles

Normally, you draw a Marquee selection by clicking and dragging to the correct size:

1. **Simply select one of the Marquee tools from the Tool Palette (the tools are all nested within the same icon), or press M to select the Marquee.**

2. **Then click and drag in your image, releasing the mouse button when the selection is the size you want.**

    Cancel your selection by clicking outside the selection border when using a selection tool, or by pressing Ctrl+D (⌘+D on the Mac). Make its borders visible/invisible by pressing Ctrl+H (⌘+H on the Mac).

You can view all the nested tools hidden in a Photoshop Tool palette icon by clicking on the small triangle in the lower-right corner of the icon. To display all the tools, right-click (Ctrl+click on the Mac) the icon.

To radiate a selection outward with the clicked point as the center of the selection, hold down the Alt key (Option key on the Mac) while dragging. Hold down the Shift key while dragging to create a perfect circle or square, as you can see in Figure 12-2.

Selection Marquee

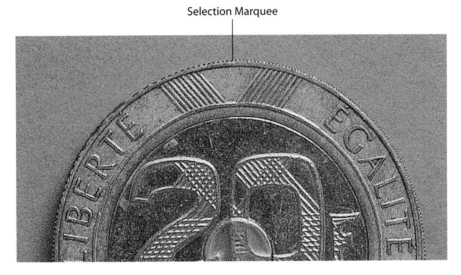

Figure 12-2: Round things lend themselves to selecting with the Elliptical Marquee.

The Option bar gives you increased control over your Marquee selection:

- ✔ **To create a selection with particular proportions** (say 5:7 if you want to crop to the shape of a 5-x-7-inch print), select Fixed Aspect Ratio in the Style drop-down list.

- ✔ **If you want a selection with specific pixel dimensions,** such as 640 x 480 pixels, select Fixed Size in the Style drop-down list.

- ✔ **To feather the edges of your Marquee selection,** which creates a fading border effect, type a pixel value into the Feather box.

Selecting odd shapes

You can use the Lasso tool to make freehand selections of a part of an image:

1. **Just select the Lasso tool from the Tool palette (or press L).**

   You can choose from three types of Lasso:

   - The default lasso sketches in a selection as if you were drawing with a pencil.
   - Click multiple times with the Polygonal Lasso to create odd-shape selections with straight lines.

- The Magnetic Lasso, at work in Figure 12-3, looks for edges as you drag, and it hugs those edges by using Option bar options such as width; edge contrast; frequency (number of magnetized points to lay down); and (with a pressure-sensitive tablet) pen pressure, or line thickness.

2. Drag around the outline of the area to be selected.

Figure 12-3: The Magnetic Lasso clings tightly to outlines.

Selecting pixels

The Magic Wand tool, as used in Figure 12-4, selects pixels that are similar in hue and value to the pixel you first clicked on. The Magic Wand is a good tool for selecting plain areas with few contrasting details, such as the sky, blank walls, or solid colors. After you select this tool, use the Option bar to set how the tools should work:

✔ You can set the Magic Wand tool to select only pixels that touch each other (contiguous) or similar pixels anywhere in the image (noncontiguous). Select either mode from the Option bar.

✔ Decide how fussy you want the wand to be by choosing a Tolerance setting from 0 (*really* fussy) to 255 (will accept just about anything).

A default value of 32 usually works best, but you can increase or reduce this number to select more or fewer pixels.

✔ Selecting the Use All Layers box tells the wand to select pixels based on information in all the layers of your image rather than just the currently active layer.

Figure 12-4: The Magic Wand is good for selecting evenly toned, evenly colored subjects, like the sky in this picture.

Painting selections

Photoshop's Quick Mask mode is a great way to create your selections by painting them with any size and shape brush that you want. While in Quick Mask mode, you can also use other selection tools, such as the Lasso tool or Magic Wand, to select areas that you then fill with the mask color. Here's how:

1. **To enter Quick Mask mode, just click the Quick Mask icon in the Tool palette or simply press Q.**

2. **If you double-click the Quick Mask icon, you can set several options, such as the opacity and color of the tone used to represent the painted mask.**

   If you're working with a subject that contains a lot of red, you might want to use a mask painting color other than red. You can also select whether the painted area represents a selection (an area that can be worked on) or a mask (a protected area).

3. **Using the Brush, paint the area you want to mask.**

   For the image shown in Figure 12-5, I wanted to blur part of the background, so I painted a selection that included the parts to be blurred.

Figure 12-5: Paint your selections by using Quick Mask mode.

4. **Apply whatever changes you want to make to the selected area.**

   In my example, shown in Figure 12-6, I applied the Blur filter.

5. **Press Q again to exit Quick Mask mode.**

Figure 12-6: The painted areas become blurred.

Fiddling with your selections

After you select part of an image, you can apply all sorts of effects to your selections, including marking the Anti-Aliased box in the Option bar to smooth the edges of freehand or elliptical selections. (Rectangles don't need smoothing.) Type a value into the Feather box to create a selection that fades out over the range of pixels you specify. Add to a selection by holding down the Shift key while you drag with any selection tool to create additional selected area. Subtract from a selection by holding down the Alt key (Option on the Mac), while dragging the area you want removed. If you want the selection tool to default to normal, add, or subtract mode, you can also click the Normal, Add, or Subtract icons (natch) on the Option bar. Another handy tool is the Intersect button, which lets you create a selection that consists only of the portion that *overlaps* both the new and original selection.

You can also modify selections by using the Select menu. There you find options for selecting everything in the image (usually it's easier to press Ctrl+A to select all, or ⌘+A on the Mac) or to select nothing (press Ctrl+D, or ⌘+D on the Mac). You might also choose to select based on a range of colors that you specify; to feather the current selection; to modify the selection border width, size, and smoothness; to grow the selection to adjacent pixels meeting the current tolerance parameters; or to select pixels anywhere in the image that are similar to those already chosen.

The Transform Selection option can be useful for sizing, rotating, or skewing a selection.

Adding to and Subtracting from Your Pictures

Instead of tearing all your wedding photos in half, you can replace your ex-spouse with a potted plant, which might be more appropriate than you think. Did your brother-in-law end up mugging in *every single* group photo taken at your last family reunion? Does that 1977 Pinto parked in the driveway otherwise detract from the beautiful landscaping in the photo of your stately manor home? Sure, you could have been smarter when you snapped the original photo, but at least you have the opportunity to redeem yourself by removing the offending person or object in Photoshop.

Evicting your ex-brother-in-law

Okay, your sister has untied the knot, and her former spouse has left the state. Why is he still haunting all the family photos? Your best move might be to take him out (unless you live in the kind of family where that phrase has a different context). Photoshop can do the job. Figure 12-7 shows a typical "problem" picture. The guy on the left is the one I want to get rid of. I can copy portions of the background over the parts of him that overlap areas I want to keep, and then crop the image so the rest of him is excluded from the final photo.

Figure 12-7: How can I get rid of the guy on the left?

The steps to follow are fairly easy:

1. **Use a selection tool to grab parts of the background to either side of the person you want to delete, and then copy the selections to a new layer.**

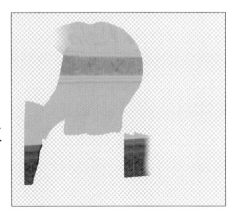

Figure 12-8: Copied background pieces look like this.

A new layer is created automatically when you paste down your copied selection. The resulting layer looks like Figure 12-8.

You can make the initial selection by using the Lasso tool or in Quick Mask mode. Then press Ctrl+J (or ⌘+J on the Mac) to copy the selection directly to a new layer. This is usually a lot faster than pressing Ctrl/⌘+C (copy) followed by Ctrl/⌘+V (paste).

2. **Move the background pieces so they cover the unwanted ex-relative.**

After they're pasted down, the copied pieces reside in their own layer, so you can move them around as you want within that layer.

3. **Pressing E to select the Eraser, use an eraser brush (I selected a soft-edged eraser brush) to remove the edges of the background pieces so they blend in with the original background, as shown in Figure 12-9.**

Figure 12-9: Blend in the background pieces.

4. **Flatten the image (choose Layer⇨Flatten) to merge all the layers.**

5. **With the Crop tool, trim the image so it includes only the two main subjects and some of the background around them, as you see in Figure 12-10.**

Figure 12-10: The photo without the evicted guy looks like this.

Bringing a family closer together

In some situations, you'll want to bring two subjects who are separated closer together. Perhaps you deleted a person in the middle, leaving a huge gap. Other times, the problem stems from a series of unfortunate seating events. You can use the same techniques from the preceding section to bring family members (or any other subjects) closer together.

I started with the photo shown in Figure 12-10 and brought the people closer together by following these steps. Although every picture is unique, you can likely follow similar steps in your own photos:

1. I copied the fellow on the right and pasted him down into his own layer.

2. Then, I copied some of the background that surrounded him, because that makes it easier to blend him in later on.

3. I clicked the Eyeball icon in the left column of the Layers palette to make the new layer invisible temporarily.

4. Going back to the original layer (click it to reactivate), I copied portions of the background surrounding his original location and pasted them down in a new layer to cover up the original figure.

5. I blended in the new background so it looked natural.

With your own photo, you might need to lighten or darken the background (choose Image⇨Adjustments⇨Brightness/Contrast). Or, copy some of the pixels from one area to the overlapping area by using the Clone Stamp to blend the transition.

6. I clicked the Eyeball icon in the hidden layer with the guy to make him visible again.

7. I used the Eraser to remove some of the edges so the guy blended in with the two layers underneath.

8. I flattened the image (Layer⇨Flatten) and cropped to produce the final photo shown in Figure 12-11.

Figure 12-11: Photoshop brought these brothers closer together.

Adding New Backgrounds

You can't always count on having a background that's as interesting as your main subject. If you catch Renée Zellweger or Hugh Grant sneaking out the back door of a restaurant and the background is a pile of garbage cans, you end up with a photo that isn't worth a mention in Bridget Jones' diary. Go to work in Photoshop and replace those cans with, say, Central Park, and you might have something.

Adding a new background is easy, particularly if the existing background can be easily selected with the tools I describe in the section "Understanding selection basics," earlier in this chapter. Figure 12-12 shows a shot taken on an overcast fall day, when the foliage was at its most colorful and the clouds in the sky were dull and lifeless. I shot the photo anyway and let Photoshop come to the rescue.

Figure 12-12: A dull sky needn't ruin a perfectly good fall photo.

I used the following steps to improve the original background. You can use the same steps for any background you want to replace:

1. **Find some suitable background in another photo and paste it into a new layer in the photo that needs the facelift.**

Select the new background, and then press Ctrl/⌘+C, followed by Ctrl/⌘+V in the document that needs the new background.

The new cloudy sky for my picture looked like Figure 12-13.

Figure 12-13: Along come some beautiful clouds just when we need them!

2. **Switching to the original layer, use the Magic Wand to select the background that you want to replace and set a Tolerance level.**

   I selected the main, dull-looking sky area and used a Tolerance level of 32.

3. **If you have lots of separate little bits of background (like the little bits of sky that peeped through the leaves in my picture), choose Select⇨ Similar to expand the selection.**

   The selection now includes all the niggly little bits of background that would have been a pain to select individually.

4. **Invert the selection by choosing Select⇨Invert (or just press Ctrl+Shift+I in Windows or ⌘+Shift+I on the Mac), so that everything *except* the sky and gaps in the leaves is selected.**

5. **Switch to the layer that contains the new background, and then press Delete to remove the replacement sky area that isn't needed.**

   After I pressed Delete, I was left with only one broad patch of clouds, plus many smaller slivers, as shown in Figure 12-14.

Figure 12-14: Every cloud has a sliver lining.

6. **Flatten that image like a pancake (Layer⇨Flatten) to end up with your final, one-layer image.**

I ended up with the photo shown in Figure 12-15.

Figure 12-15: Nothing brightens a dull day more than a background check.

Combining Several dSLR Photos into One

About the most entertaining thing you can do with a mouse (assuming you're not a cat) is combining photographs to create a new image (also called *compositing*). One of my favorite tricks involves taking an everyday object, such as my car, and placing it in exotic locales. Dropping a new object into an existing photo is no more difficult than replacing a background, and in some respects it's a lot easier.

Figure 12-16 shows the automobile in question parked in a grungy gravel driveway.

Figure 12-16: You can take this vehicle for a drive without even leaving Photoshop!

The steps are fairly simple: Just select the object and copy it to a new layer on an image that contains a suitable background. The only hard part is blending in the object so it looks like it belongs there. I show you how I did both:

1. **Use the Lasso tool to select the object, including lots of the background, and pressed Ctrl+J (⌘+J if you're using a Mac) to copy the selection to a new layer in the current document.**

2. **Click the Eyeball icon in the layer with the background to make it invisible, and then switch back to the copied layer and use the Eraser tool to remove everything that isn't part of the object (in my case, my car).**

Using the Eraser makes it easier to remove the surroundings carefully, a bit at a time. Make a mistake, and you just need to press Ctrl+Z (⌘+Z on the Mac) to reverse your last step. If you don't catch a goof in time, work your way through the History palette one step at a time until you get back to the point where you want to resume erasing.

A hard-edged eraser makes a good tool for working on straight edges (like the top of the automobile), and a soft-edged eraser brush comes in handy for areas where you don't have to be precise (like the undercarriage). It wasn't necessary for me to be too precise around the underside of the car because I planned to blend that portion in with the road in the new background.

You want to end up with an image that looks like Figure 12-17.

Figure 12-17: Extract the object carefully so you can blend it in with its new background.

3. Copy the extracted object and paste it in a second image.

I selected an image of a rural roadway in southern Spain.

4. Sprinkle in special touches as needed.

The auto didn't look like it belonged in this setting, so I added a few special touches:

- I darkened the underside of the car (especially in front) to make it look as if the car were casting shadows on the ground around it.

- Shadows from the surrounding trees were cast on the road, so I used Quick Mask mode to select some areas on the side (just beneath the side mirror), and darkened those areas to match the road shadows. I selected an area above the front wheel well, extending across the hood, and another on the back deck and *lightened* them as if the bright ray of sunlight were striking those surfaces.

- I used the Photoshop Lens Flare plug-in (Filters⇨Render⇨Lens Flare) to add a bright glare to the rear quarter-window.

5. **When all is satisfactory, flatten the image (Layer⇨Flatten).**

   I ended up with the version shown in Figure 12-18.

Figure 12-18: A successful composite is a lot of work, but it's worth it.

The pitfalls of compositing images

You can see that a lot of work might be necessary to make the merger of two images look realistic. The pasted-in objects must have similar texture, lighting, and be shown from the proper angle and perspective. You can't take a photo from a low angle on a cloudy day and paste an object from that image into a background taken from a higher angle on an overcast day. If you do, you get a less-successful result, like the atrocity shown in Figure 12-19.

In this case, I started with the same automobile picture but decided to jazz it up a little. I copied the original car layer and painted the duplicate with various colors, including red for the body and brown for the convertible top.

Then, I merged the colored layer with the original layer by changing the Blending Mode options in the Layers palette from Normal to Overlay. That combines the colors in the top layer with the detail in the layer underneath.

Figure 12-19: Something is wrong here. This looks like a cutout pasted onto a poster.

The car certainly looks sportier, but the scale is all wrong for the plaza it's now set in. The angle of view is too high, and the lighting is wrong because the background image was taken on an overcast day. Not my best effort!

Getting creative with compositing

Don't be afraid to experiment when combining images. You can create realistic composites, like the one shown on the right in Figure 12-20, or completely preposterous fantasies, like the one in Figure 12-21.

For the castle/moat photo, I added some clouds, and then reversed the upper half of the photo to create a more vivid reflection in the moat. The Eiffel Tower on the shore of the Mediterranean Sea demonstrates what can be done if you have Photoshop and don't know much about geography.

Figure 12-20: From so-so to postcard-worthy with a few minutes of compositing effort.

Figure 12-21: It seems like everyone in France takes off for the Mediterranean Sea in August, so why not *La Tour Eiffel, aussi?*

Hard Copies Aren't Hard

In This Chapter

▷ Some day your prints will come
▷ Output options
▷ Choosing your printer

*Y*ears ago, some wise futurists predicted that digital photography would spell the end of photographic prints, just as the advent of word processing, fax machines, text messaging, and e-mail would cause the postal service to close its doors, overnight delivery services to go bankrupt, and manufacturers of file cabinets to switch to more profitable products, like personal aeroplanes. If you believed these folks, the paperless office would be followed by the printless home, and everyone would be reading and viewing photos on computer monitors, TV sets, and cell phones.

Of course, these seers are the grandchildren of the prognosticators who foresaw the invention of the automobile, but had no clue about smog, traffic jams, or road rage. If anything, we're creating *more* prints today than a decade ago because we can make them at home or in the office, upload digital files to our local megamarts for one-hour printing, or stop by a retailer's handy kiosk to custom-print hard copies for about the same cost as those automated machine prints we got from film back in the dark ages.

Technology has helped create brand-new uses for images, including e-mail and desktop presentations, without reducing the original need for hard copy prints. Electronic distribution of images has blossomed, but not at the expense of traditional applications for prints.

This chapter outlines some of your options and shows you that hard copies really don't have to be hard.

Prints? What Prints?

As I explain in Chapter 16, some photo-sharing sites are geared for serious photographers. They display your prize images in sharp-looking galleries rather than the more amateur-oriented "albums" provided by consumer photo-sharing services. You can also display your images on your own Web pages, e-mail them to friends and colleagues, exchange them over instant messaging services, and array them into PowerPoint presentations. A photographic image can easily begin and end its life as bits and bytes, created by a digital camera and viewed only on a display screen.

But you probably won't want to go that route for all your photos. Passing prints around and displaying framed photos on the wall or grand piano is one of the greatest joys of photography. Digital photography makes printing copies for distribution or festooning your furniture with frames easier than ever. Here are some very good reasons for making prints:

- **Share with friends and family.** This is the traditional application for prints. Do you want to drag a computer along to the next family reunion — or do you want to have a stack of prints to pass around?

- **Display your work.** Some companies do make LCD photo frames you can set on the piano to show off a picture or two, but making an 8-x-10-inch or bigger enlargement to frame and hang on the wall is much more satisfying (and, possibly, ostentatious, as you can see by the ornate frame in Figure 13-1).

- **Sell yourself and your work.** Many photographers are turning to digital portfolios, but when you want to have images available for viewing by prospective employers or clients, a print is still the best way to show off your work.

- **Submit for approval.** You've got the job — now you need to secure the approval of your boss or client. You could e-mail a low-resolution copy to the person passing judgment, assuming that person can view the image on a computer. Or, you can print a fine-tuned proof that's an accurate representation of your image and use that.

- **Restore or re-create an existing photo.** Not all digital prints need to originate from your digital camera. You'll often need to create a restored or enlarged copy of an existing print, with all the wrinkles and tears removed, and perhaps make improvements in your subject matter through judicious image editing (which I cover in Part IV). A scanner, inkjet printer, and Photoshop might be all you need.

- **Create camera-ready or for-position-only art.** Most professional printers today can work from digital files. However, it's often helpful to have a print to paste up into a layout, either for reproduction or to create a dummy that can be used for approval purposes.

✔ **Make a teaser.** My local newspaper prefers to receive submissions as high-resolution TIFF files on a CD. Even so, I always include a print or two of the shots I want the editor to look at. A compelling print can bring my CD up to the top of the editor's to-do pile.

Figure 13-1: You can hang a print on the wall, but it's hard to frame a computer!

You Pays Your Money, You Takes Your Choice

When it comes time to make a print, you need to choose whether to make it yourself, use an online service, or work with a local retailer or print lab. Oddly enough, with today's technology, you can sometimes end up using all three methods with a single print order. You can, for example, upload digital images online to your local retailer, and then trot down and pick prints while making a few yourself with the lab's kiosk.

Indeed, your choice of method for printing images is not so much an economic decision as it is one of convenience, flexibility, and control. Some options are easier than others. Some let you do more things with your image before printing. Others give you absolute control over how your image looks. All of them end up costing roughly the same on a per-print basis, which is why many serious photographers use a mixture of methods.

Making prints yourself

If a photographer is serious enough about photography to be using a dSLR, that photographer probably wants a photo-quality printer close at hand to run off prints as needed. Here are some considerations to take into account for the do-it-yourself approach:

- ✒ **Equipment:** You need to invest in a printer. Good photo printers can cost $100 to $300 or more, which isn't a lot when amortized over the two or three years (or longer) that you'll be using the device. Better printers are always coming along, of course, so you might want to upgrade sooner.

    You need to factor in the price of the printer, as well as consumables like paper and ink, when calculating the per-print cost of your hard copies.

- ✒ **Speed:** Doing your own printing is the fastest way to get a hard copy in your hands when you're in a hurry.

- ✒ **Quality:** As you become familiar with your printer's operation, you can often tweak your images to look their best with your particular setup. You might do the fine-tuning in your image editor or by using the printer's own controls.

- ✒ **Flexibility:** If you print your own images, you can use a larger variety of paper stocks than your local retailer might have available. You can make prints in odd-ball sizes or print on *both* sides of a sheet (which you can do with some photo-quality printers with duplexing capabilities, such as certain Canon Pixma models).

- ✒ **Reliability:** Unless you have more than one color printer, your rush projects will always be dependent on the continued health of your mainstay. Fortunately, should your printer fail, you can use one of the other printing options or run down to the local Quik-E-Mart and buy a new printer for $50 or so. Remember to have extra ink on hand!

Online output outsourcing options

The universe seems to be moving online. I'm sure someday remote digital cameras will be set up at key tourist spots, like the Taj Mahal, allowing you to take your vacation pictures without ever leaving home. About the only thing you won't be able to do through the Internet is walk your dog.

Meanwhile, you can order and distribute prints right from your computer. Yahoo!, AOL, Shutterfly, Kodak, and others have Web-based picture services you can use to share and print your best efforts. Technically, you don't even need a computer or digital camera. Nokia has an agreement with the Kodak Picture Center that allows cell phone users to phone in images they've snapped and place orders for prints.

If you're using the more typical method of uploading pictures from a computer to a Web service, you definitely want a broadband connection. Your digital SLR photos are likely to be megabytes in size, even if you're shooting in JPEG format. Although most digital photographers have broadband at home and work, you won't always be able to upload photos quickly (such as when you're traveling).

Here are some advantages of uploading prints over the Web:

- **Get honest-to-gosh photo prints.** When you order digital prints online, you can receive hard copies made the old-fashioned way with conventional photographic paper and chemicals. If you value the quality and potentially extended longevity of traditional photo prints, online ordering is one way to get them. (You can also get real prints locally, as I explain in the next section.)

- **Have prints delivered to your home . . . or elsewhere.** The online services will make prints and mail them back to you, or even mail them to a third party. That makes a Web-print service especially useful for sharing prints with folks back home when, say, you're touring Paris and you get a few minutes at *un café de cyber*. (The City of Light has dozens of cyber cafes, by the way, ranging from Jardin de l'Internet to Station Internet Rive Gauche.)

- **Drop off prints virtually and pick them up in person.** Retailers like Wal-Mart let you upload images to their Web sites and pick them up at your local store. The prints usually are ready by the time you get there.

- **Save time and money.** If you don't plan to edit your photos much (or the chore is already out of the way), you can't beat the ease and economy of ordering prints online. Just upload, specify print sizes and other details, and pay only 29 cents or even less per print. What could be easier?

Live and in person!

If you like, you can also trot down to your local retailer or professional photo lab and get your prints directly. This approach combines some of the advantages of making prints yourself and using an online service. For example, you can use a kiosk and perform cropping and some image editing just as you would at home — even if you're on vacation hundreds of miles from your own computer. Also, you enjoy the speed and economy of using a lab geared up to produce quantity prints.

Photo labs produce quantity prints. If you need a whole bunch of hard copies, you'll almost always find that a quick trip to your retailer will save you money and time.

Your in-person options range from using a standalone kiosk, like the one shown in Figure 13-2, to view and print photos using the kiosk's printer, working with a kiosk that's connected to the retailer's digital photo lab, or handing your digital memory cards (or a CD you've burned) to a technician and leaving everything up to her. You might find these services at a retail store or avail yourself of a lab geared to serious amateur and professional photographers. Either way, you walk in, get your prints made, and walk out (or, sometimes, return to pick up your pictures later).

Figure 13-2: Walk up to the kiosk and make your prints live and in person.

Keep in mind that not all photo labs are made the same. Before you plunk down your cash, ask whether the photo lab can accommodate the type of media you use and whether it offers choices for printing:

- **Media compatibility:** You don't need to worry about having a broadband connection because retail locations will accept your memory cards, CDs, and other media. Or will they? Some older kiosks and facilities might not be compatible with every odd-ball memory card, mini-CD, or Sony media-of-the-month. Fortunately, digital SLRs generally use the universally accepted CompactFlash or Secure Digital cards, but if you happen to have some photos on a mini-xD or Sony Memory Stick Duo, you'll want to ascertain in advance that your chosen retailer can work with it.

- **Choice of photo-quality or printer-quality output:** Some retailers give you a choice of the type of output you receive. You can have a print made by a kiosk's built-in printer or by the store's digital photo lab that uses conventional photographic paper and chemicals.

Choosing a Printer

Digital SLR owners have only one special consideration when choosing a personal printer for their hard copy needs: As serious photographers, they're likely to want really, really good prints to match the stunning images they create with their sophisticated cameras. As a result, just any old printer probably won't do. You'll want a printer that's especially good for outputting photographs, such as the snapshot photo printer shown in Figure 13-3.

Figure 13-3: Some printers do one thing — snapshots — and do it very well.

Fortunately, printer quality and flexibility have improved dramatically in the past few years. This section helps you choose the perfect printer.

If you read all the general tips here but would still like reviews of a specific model before you buy, you'll likely find the reviews at CNET helpful. Go to http://reviews.cnet.com, and you'll find the printer reviews in Peripherals section.

Today, you can choose between inkjet and dye-sublimation printers. Output devices such as thermal wax or laser printers have become niche options for some specialized applications or, in the case of the color lasers, for mass-production uses where image quality isn't paramount.

Inkjet printers

Most of the photo printers sold now are inkjet models. These models produce images by squirting tiny droplets of ink onto paper, using various methods to control the size and placement of the drops. For example, Epson uses piezoelectric crystals sandwiched between two electrodes to vibrate the ink cartridge, with different levels of voltage causing the crystals to vibrate in ways that adjust the colors and the amount of color sprayed through a nozzle onto the paper. Other inkjet printing systems use heat or other properties to control the flow of ink. With resolutions ranging from about 300 dpi to 1,440 dpi and higher, inkjets can easily produce photo-quality images, assuming you use good-quality photo paper.

Current models run the gamut of features and prices, with many excellent models available from $100 to $300. If you're willing to spend more than that, you can buy a wide-carriage printer capable of handling paper wider than 8.5 inches. As a photographer, you might indeed want to make 11-x-14 or larger prints.

If you're shopping for an inkjet printer, look for the following features :

- **Size and design:** Some printers hog your desk space or feature clumsy paper paths that require lots of space behind or in front of the printer for the paper trays. A few printers weigh a ton, too. If a printer is so unwieldy that you can't locate it near your computer, you'll end up doing a lot of walking or reaching to retrieve your printouts.

- **Speed:** Output speed is likely to be important to you only if you make lots of prints and don't like to wait. Some printers can be two or three times faster than others, so if speed is crucial (say, you and your printer are at an event where you need to output prints for customers on demand), check your intended printer's specification carefully. Be sure to make a test print, too, because vendors use best-case figures even though you'll probably be printing under worst-case conditions.

- **Number of inks:** Most photo printers today use six colors of ink: black, cyan, magenta, yellow, photo cyan, and photo magenta. Some add several more colors of various hues. The two latter inks are "weak" versions that can be used to provide more subtle gradations of tone. A few printers add red and green tanks (see Figure 13-4), allowing them to print richer reds, additional orange tones, and more realistic greens. Some have both a photo black and text black ink.

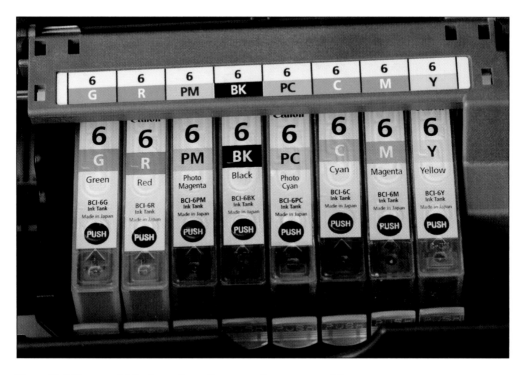

Figure 13-4: The more ink tanks you have, the more colors you can print.

Generally, in terms of quality, the more ink tanks the better. But, you have to keep those inks replenished at a cost of $11 or so per tank. If your quality needs are slightly lower, you might be able to get away with a printer that has fewer colors. I have both a four-color inkjet (for quick and dirty printouts) and an eight-color model (for slow and exquisite output).

✏ **Resolution:** More resolution is usually better (some models provide 1,200 x 4,800 dpi resolution), but there are some trade-offs, such as the traditional gamut versus dot-size dilemma. More inks produce a larger range of colors, but printers offering this increased number of colors often use larger ink droplets and correspondingly lower resolution. So, a printer with only six colors but which outputs higher resolution 1-picoliter droplets can produce more detail, but fewer colors, than a printer that has eight tanks and coarser 2-picoliter droplets. Higher-resolution printers with tinier nozzles often suffer from clogging issues, too, and the special inks they require might not have the same longevity in the final prints.

- **Paper handling:** Some inkjet printers produce *only* 4-x-6-inch prints. They're designed to output snapshots only, quickly and economically. Others let you print 5-x-7- or 8.5-x-11-inch prints as well as other sizes. You'll want to investigate your printer's ability to handle various paper stocks and thicknesses, too.

- **Memory card access or PictBridge capabilities:** A printer that has built-in memory card slots or a PictBridge-compatible camera-to-printer USB cable connection (shown in Figures 13-5 and 13-6, respectively) is especially convenient. Your digital SLR might allow you to specify images for printing right in the camera. Then, you insert your memory card in the printer's slot or connect the camera to the printer with a cable, and start the printing process.

- **Duplex printing:** The ability to print on both sides of a sheet automatically is useful not only for creating text documents. If you're preparing an album or portfolio you can print on both sides of the sheet using special dual-sided photo paper and printers that have duplexing capability.

Figure 13-5: A memory card can go directly from your camera to the printer . . .

✔ **Input/Output trays:** The input tray(s) hold the paper you'll be printing on; the output trays catch the finished prints as they come out. The higher the capacity of each, the better for you. One of my favorite printers has a vertical 150-sheet input tray that doesn't take up any space behind the printer, and a second 150-sheet cassette that fits underneath the printer. I can put different types and sizes of stock in each, alternating between, say, 8.5-x-11- and 4-x-6-inch sheets, or fill up both with the same paper and print 300 sheets in a row. Your output tray should be large enough to catch all the prints you make in a session without spilling any on the floor.

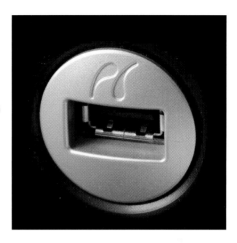

Figure 13-6: . . . or you can link your camera to the printer with a PictBridge cable.

✔ **Controls:** You'll find printers with a plethora of controls to adjust every function, perhaps an LCD to use to preview images, and a keypad to navigate menus and options. Others might have a power switch, a paper tray select button, and little more, requiring you to control every parameter from your computer by using the printer driver.

Each approach has its advantages: You can use printers with lots of controls, if they have memory card slots, in portable or standalone mode without any computer attached. Printers that rely heavily on the printer driver are usually faster to operate, and they allow you to store groups of settings on your computer for re-use at any time.

Dye-sublimation printers

The dye-sublimation printer has been enjoying a rebirth of sorts now that vendors have managed to bring down the costs for the equipment and the prints. You can find excellent snapshot-size dye-sub printers for $150 or less, and pay about $0.29 a print, the same as you would for an inkjet print or one from your local photo lab.

The advantage of dye-sublimation printers is that even the most modest of them produces prints that are superior to run-of-the-mill inkjet output. The best can generate prints that are exquisite indeed. Most of the dye-sub printers you'll encounter will be 4-x-6-inch photo printers, but I've enjoyed using 8.5-x-11-inch models from Olympus and other vendors, too.

Despite the cryptic name, dye-sublimation printers work in a relatively straightforward way. A strip of plastic film, called a *transfer ribbon,* is coated with cyan, magenta, and yellow dye. When a print job is sent to the printer, a thermal print head heats up the page-sized panel of plastic transfer ribbon. Variations in temperature control the colors and the amount of color that are applied to the paper. Because the paper has a special coating on it, the dye sticks to the paper. Often, a final clear protective layer is applied after the color has been laid on. A dye-sub ribbon cartridge is shown in Figure 13-7.

Dye-sub printers can apply color with a vast range of tones because each of the hues can be added over a range of 256 colors, for a possible 16.8 million different colors. These printers don't need the high resolution that inkjet printers require to mimic millions of colors by combining teensy dots of ink. So, a 300 dpi dye-sublimation printer can achieve photo output that's as good or better than a 1,440 dpi inkjet.

Figure 13-7: Individual color panels apply one hue at a time to your print.

That means that dye-sub printers are useful almost exclusively for photographs; text quality is generally quite poor at the 300 dpi or lower resolution. Still, the subtle results they produce are great for professional designers, artists, and photographers. The high cost of the special paper and ribbons in larger sizes might be prohibitive for small businesses and home users, but the 4-x-6-inch models are economical enough for anyone.

In terms of considerations to look for, some of them are the same as for inkjet printers. Size and design, speed, paper-handling options, availability of memory cards, and the placement and use of controls all are important factors for dye-sub printers, too. Others, such as the number of inks, resolution, duplexing capabilities, and paper handling, don't apply.

Part V
The Part of Tens

In this part . . .

This Part of Tens gives you 30 very cool ways to get more enjoyment from your digital SLR photography.

Chapter 14 offers the ten easiest ways to improve your photography immediately with better lighting, improved perspectives, and clever use of interchangeable lenses. Chapter 15 serves up ten things you might not have thought of doing with your digital SLR, or if you have, you might not have explored fully. No single book contains all the answers, so Chapter 16 showcases ten online resources that can help you improve your images, gather the latest information about new products and techniques, and display your work for the world to see.

Digital Photography on the Net

Ten Ways to Improve Your dSLR Photography

*E*ach chapter in this book is chock-full of tips that help you improve the quality of your dSLR photos. Add all of them to your shooting repertoire, and you'll be well on the way to technical excellence and photo perfection. However, if you're looking for the top ten techniques to provide instant results, you can't beat the collection of quality-enhancing approaches that I outline in this chapter.

Does Lighting Ever Strike Twice?

Yes, good lighting can be repeatable if you know what you're doing. And nothing can destroy a photo faster than bad lighting. You can make lots of improvements to a challenging subject simply by using good lighting techniques.

Your uncle's bald head, a teenager's less-than-perfect complexion, a harshly lit beach scene, a drop of falling water — you can portray all these attractively with effective lighting techniques. In your uncle's case, throwing the top of his head in shadow and avoiding shiny lights on his upper hemisphere can minimize the glare from his bare pate. The teenager might benefit from diffuse lighting that softens the texture of his or her face. You can fix up that glaring direct sunlight on the beach by using a reflector to bounce light into the shadows. And you can freeze a drop of water in midair with a halo of light added by an electronic flash.

To use light effectively and take your photography to the next level, here are some tricks you'll want to master:

- ✓ **Managing the quality of light:** Light can be highly directional or soft and diffuse. It can cast sharp shadows and dot your subjects with specular highlights. Light comes in different colors, too. Figure 14-1 shows the kind of effect you can get with diffuse light.

- ✓ **Using multiple lights:** Photographers create some of the best pictures by using two, three, four, or more lights. One source can be used to illuminate the main part of your subject, and others can outline its edges, fill in the shadows, or call attention to a particular area. Some lighting arrangements are used often enough that they have their own names: broad lighting, rim lighting, Paramount lighting, and so forth. Other arrangements are setups you create yourself.

    If you can master applying multiple lights to model and shape the appearance of your subjects, you'll have a powerful tool at your disposal.

- ✓ **Making best use of a light source's duration:** Generally, electronic flash units are the main noncontinuous light source photographers put to work. Using the duration of the flash creatively requires practice and experience. Some techniques are simple. For example, you can use your flash's brief duration (particularly when shooting up close) to freeze even the fastest action. More complex is the use of repeating flashes to trace movement, or balancing flash output with ambient light to create combination exposures. Entire books have been written on these topics, so you have lots to discover.

- ✓ **Subtracting light:** Sometimes, you don't want to *add* light to a scene as much as you want to *remove* it, to create a particular lighting effect or look. *Barndoors* are little flaps that look like a horse's blinders, and fit over an electronic flash or other light source to block the light or feather it onto a subject. Opaque sheets can block light coming from a particular direction, functioning as a sort of reverse reflector. Gadgets that stage lighting directors call *cookies* or *gobos* can change the size and shape of a beam of light. With lighting effects, sometimes less *is* more.

Figure 14-1: Use diffuse light to soften an image.

Choosing a Righteous Resolution and Other Settings

Strictly speaking, the resolution of your digital SLR is the number of pixels captured — say 3,008 x 2,000 pixels for the typical 6-megapixel model. Most of the time, the top resolution is the one you want to select. However, as I discuss in Chapter 8, the file format you choose can affect the sharpness and file size of a digital image, too. It's the overall sharpness — which is affected by resolution — that you want to work with.

Some digital SLRs offer a choice of both compressed and uncompressed RAW files, perhaps a TIFF option, and several levels of JPEG compression. You can always select the highest resolution, least compressed, least processed image format. But if you answer "no" to any of the following questions, you'll want to put some thought into your resolution/format/settings decisions:

- Do you have unlimited memory card and hard drive space?
- Do you mind waiting while your pictures transfer to your computer?
- Do you want the ultimate in quality?
- Are you willing to spend at least some time with each shot in an image editor?

Even if you're one of the rare folks who answer "yes" to these questions, you still have some things to think about. In the following sections, I explain some situations that call for special considerations.

Changing environments

You're taking candid photos under conditions that vary abruptly and unexpectedly, say, at a concert or party in a night club with frequent lighting changes. Or, you're outdoors at sunset and both the quantity and color of the illumination changes over the course of 10 or 15 minutes.

Although the high resolution afforded by your camera's RAW option has its value, in rapidly changing environments, you should place a higher premium on the RAW format's ability to

- ✔ Adjust white balance and exposure after the fact.
- ✔ Apply noise reduction.
- ✔ Apply tonal curves.

Particularly when it comes to white balance, you'll find that the manual changes you make when the file is imported into your image editor are likely to be more accurate and more easily customized than the default or automatic settings that your camera applies. For details on how to correct these problems in an image editor, flip to Chapter 11.

Living with limited memory card space

You're leaving for a two-week vacation, and you have three 1GB memory cards, want to leave your laptop at home, and don't own one of those portable CD/DVD burners. None of the other options — such as uploading your shots to the Internet at a cyber café — seem attractive. You likely need to explore a resolution other than the highest RAW resolution. For example, the following list illustrates one possible scenario out of dozens, given a particular camera (the numbers you can expect vary, depending on what camera you use):

- ✔ At the highest RAW setting, say this particular camera gets 182 shots per 1GB card, or 13 shots per day over two weeks. You'd need to arm yourself with many, many memory cards and spend a good part of your vacation time swapping out used cards for empty ones.

- ✔ At the highest JPEG setting, that same camera gets 333 shots per 1GB card, or 24 shots per day over two weeks. So at this setting, the camera gives you a more reasonable number of photos for a very slight loss of quality. But this still might not be enough pictures per day for your two-week vacation, even if you have three 1GB cards.

- ✔ At the second best JPEG quality, say the 1GB card will get you 600 shots with this particular camera, or 42 shots per day. This is a more reasonable number of pictures, but on this camera, this quality limits prints to sizes no bigger than 5 x 7 inches.

Your best solutions might be to pick up a fourth or even a fifth 1GB memory card (for about $60 each). Or use your digital SLR's "second best" JPEG quality level for general shots, but switch to the highest JPEG quality level for any shots or sequences that might be suitable for enlargements beyond 5 x 7 inches. That way, you can grab hundreds of snapshots for smaller prints, but still come home with a good selection of higher-resolution photos for those special blow-ups.

Shooting for a low-resolution destination

You're shooting a bunch of pictures for your eBay auctions or for display on a Web page, and the largest final image size will be about 640 x 480 pixels. Most of the time, having pixels and image quality to spare is good because you can crop and edit to your heart's content before shrinking the original shot down to its finished size.

Auction or Web pictures sometimes are captured with fixed setups on a sort of photo assembly line with the same background and settings, and there really isn't any need for the maximum in resolution and sharpness for your main shots. In fact, all those extra pixels can slow you down. You might be better off shooting at a lower resolution, such as 1,600 x 1,200 pixels, to speed things up. If you're *really* careful in your choice of composition and lighting, you might even be able to get away with taking photos at something very close to their finished size, say 640 x 480 pixels, eliminating most post-processing altogether.

Hurrying along

The highest resolution/lowest compression settings take longer to store on your memory card and require extra time to transfer to your computer. The huge size of the best images can affect your shooting in several ways:

- ✔ **When shooting bursts of continuous shots:** Some digital SLRs slow down their continuous shooting mode when saving images in RAW, TIFF, or RAW+JPEG modes. Instead of 3 or 4 frames per second (fps), you might be able to grab only 2 fps at the highest resolution. A camera with a larger internal buffer or a memory card with a faster write speed might help, but simply reducing the resolution or boosting compression might give you speedier bursts with little loss of quality. The Nikon D2X camera actually takes advantage of this phenomenon, cropping its default 12 megapixel images down to 6.8 megapixels to increase its top continuous shooting rate to 8 fps.

- ✔ **When you transfer photos:** Memory card readers are usually the fastest way to transfer photos from your camera to your computer. Some dSLR owners also depend on direct cable connections through a Firewire connection or, more commonly, through a USB cable. Both card readers and cable connections might use the latest USB 2.0 specification, or limp along with the slower USB 1.1 links. A few of the newest cameras use infrared transmitters to transfer photos from camera to computer. All these methods are affected by the size of the file: A JPEG image might be only a few megabytes in size, whereas a RAW file can easily be 5 to 10MB or more, and TIFF files can top 20MB — each. If you're in a hurry — for instance, you're covering a fast breaking news event for your local newspaper — you might find that a compromise in picture quality can save valuable time.

✔ **When working on your computer:** Huge image files take longer to load, longer to process in an image editor, and longer to save when you're finished with them. If you want to speed your image along to its final destination, such as your printer, smaller file sizes can be your friend.

Stop! What's That Sound?

For the digital photographer, no sound is sweeter than the authoritative clicks that resound when a picture is taken. Flipping mirrors and sliding shutter curtains mean that, once again, you've captured your vision as digital bits. Then, reality sets in — did you use the right shutter speed?

A speed that's too slow means any movement of the subject or the photographer's hands can result in shaky, blurry photos. A speed that's too high might remove all sense of movement, creating a sports picture, for example, that might as well have pictured a statue. A speed faster than your camera's electronic flash sync speed might mean your picture will show a shadow of the focal plane shutter rather than a complete frame. The right shutter speed with flash pictures can also mean that ambient light in the background produces a pleasing effect, but the wrong speed can produce ghost images.

As a digital SLR photographer, you have the responsibility to use the enhanced powers and control at your disposal to optimize your photos, and that includes choosing a shutter speed that's appropriate for the picture you want to create. Figure 14-2

Figure 14-2: A monopod steadied the camera, but the shutter speed had to be bumped from 1/30 of a sec (top) to 1/125 (bottom).

shows how changing from ⅟₃₀ of a second (top) to ⅟₁₂₅ of a second (bottom) can affect an image taken under existing light.

Working the Right F-Stop

Mark Twain never said, "The difference between the right f-stop and the almost-right f-stop is like the difference between lightning and a lightning bug." But, he might have said that if he'd been a digital photographer.

Sometimes, stopping down one or two aperture settings or opening up one or two stops can make a world of difference, so choosing the right f-stop can be an important part of optimizing your finished picture. Here are some examples:

- **A couple stops can boost sharpness.** Lenses designed especially for their speed — say, a 28mm f1.4 or a 400mm f2.8 lens is also designed to provide excellent sharpness when it's wide open. However, most other optics are their sharpest when they're closed down one or two f-stops from wide open. A 50mm f1.8 prime lens or an 80–200mm f4/f5.6 zoom lens that produce pretty good results at maximum aperture might excel with an aperture that's two stops smaller.

- **A few stops can help you stop camera or subject motion.** Going the other way, the ability to open up an extra stop or two can do your pictures a world of good if it lets you use a faster shutter speed. Try shooting a basketball game indoors at ISO 400 and settings of ⅟₆₀ of a second at f5.6. Then compare your results with similar pictures taken ⅟₂₅₀ of a second at a wider aperture like f2.8. If the second set of images are carefully focused, the subjects will be *a lot* sharper. It doesn't matter that your first batch of pictures has more depth-of-field (which I discuss in Chapter 6). You won't even notice that with all the subject blur.

- **A couple stops can stretch your depth-of-field usefully or trim it for creative effects.** This is especially true when shooting macro (close-up) photos, where depth-of-field is sharply limited. Stopping down or opening up an f-stop or two can produce dramatically different results.

- **Too small is as bad as too large.** Shooting wide open costs you depth-of-field and can impact lens sharpness, but using the smallest possible f-stop can be just as bad. After you stop down past f8 or f11, most lenses suffer from a phenomenon known as *defraction,* and any sharpness you think you gain in depth-of-field is lost to the resolution-robbing effects of too-small f-stops. It's almost as if your image had a fixed amount of sharpness, and the smaller f-stop is simply spreading it out over a larger range of depth. In addition, small f-stops can accentuate the appearance of any tiny dust motes on your sensor that, at larger apertures, are fuzzy and virtually invisible.

Focus Is a Selective Service

Knowing how to use the right aperture to control depth-of-field is only half the battle. You'll also want to explore exactly how you can *apply* that depth creatively.

Improve your photography by casting a wide depth-of-field (DOF) net to capture a broad range of subject matter, or focus in on a specific object by narrowing depth-of-field to a more selective range. Although there are many different techniques for emphasizing or de-emphasizing parts of an image, applying depth-of-field creatively is one that's easy to master and almost unlimited in its potential.

You need to become familiar with the DOF characteristics of each of your lenses, their zoom settings, and apertures. I'm not suggesting you memorize all kinds of figures and distances. Just work with, say, your favorite zoom lens and use photos you take or glimpses with the depth-of-field preview to know approximately the sharpness range at, perhaps, f2.8, f8, and f16 when shooting close up, at 5 to 10 feet, and at infinity using 25mm, 50mm, or 100mm zoom settings. Then you'll have a better handle on how focal length, aperture, and distance choices affect your shot before you frame a picture.

Playing the Angles

Good composition often involves playing all the angles — *all* of them. Don't be satisfied with the different perspectives you get with a 360-degree walk-around. Climb up on a nearby rock or ladder, stand on a chair, or experiment with the view from a handy balcony. Or, stoop down low, lay on the ground, or get *under* your subject to see what a worm's-eye view looks like. Everybody shoots flowers from above the blossoms; you can take a picture down at the flower's level, as shown in Figure 14-3.

You might be surprised at how different everything looks from a new vantage point. Even hackneyed and clichéd subjects can take on new life if you choose the right angle. If you find yourself at a popular tourist location and all the people clustered

Figure 14-3: Shoot flowers from the side rather than from above for a new perspective.

around a recommended "Picture Spot" while you're flat on your back on the grass, you're probably on the right track.

Through a Glass Brightly

There's a reason why digital SLR photographers frequently succumb to a compulsion called *lens lust,* which is the irrational need to add yet another interchangeable lens to one's camera bag, at the expense of luxury items such as food or clothing.

As I discuss in Chapter 6, lenses are the most powerful tools at your disposal, and you should discover how to leverage the capabilities of your optics even if you own only the lens that came with your camera kit. That lens is likely to be a zoom, which makes it many lenses in one, so even if your camera truly is a *single*-lens reflex, you can use lots of capabilities built into your lenses. Here are some of the capabilities that lenses have:

- ✔ **Make subjects appear to be closer:** Special macro lenses can capture life-size images of subjects from only a few inches away, but you'll find that many non-macro zooms and prime lenses focus close enough to provide a large image. The world of the close-up is one that's worth exploring, whether you're photographing flowers, insects, your stamp collection, or the texture of the rocks in your driveway. Figure 14-4 shows how a mundane object gains interest when photographed up close.

- ✔ **Bring distant things close:** When you want to keep your distance from an erupting volcano, capture images of timid wildlife from 50 yards away, or take soccer pictures from the stands that look like they were grabbed from the sidelines, a telephoto lens can do the job for you.

- ✔ **Make close things appear farther away:** When your back is up against the wall and you can't squeeze everything you want into your image, a wide-angle lens can make your subjects back off to a more manageable distance.

- ✔ **Flatter your portrait subjects:** A short telephoto lens or zoom setting in the 85mm to 105mm range (using 35mm equivalent focal lengths) provides a more flattering perspective of human subjects. Your victims will like the way their ears and noses don't look out of proportion. Depending on the lens cropping ("multiplier") factor of your camera, this 85mm to 105mm range might be 53mm–65mm (with a 1.6X factor) to 65mm–81mm (with a 1.3 factor). If you own a full-frame dSLR, there's no factor at all, and you can use your 85mm–105mm lenses. (See Chapter 1 for an introduction to the lens cropping effect.)

- ✔ **Insult or distort your subjects:** A wide-angle lens causes apparent distortion in portrait subjects that can be used for comical effect. With nonhuman subjects, you can have some creative fun by enlarging things that are very close to the camera while providing a seemingly distorted perspective on objects only a small distance away.

✔ **Compress distances:** Telephoto lenses tend to compress the apparent distances between objects, so you can make those utility poles seem as if they are right on top of each other, or those approaching cars separated by 10 to 20 feet look as if they're cruising along bumper to bumper.

✔ **Manipulate depth-of-field:** Telephoto lenses have less DOF at a given aperture, but wide-angle lenses have more. Choose your weapon and you're choosing the amount of depth-of-field you have to work with.

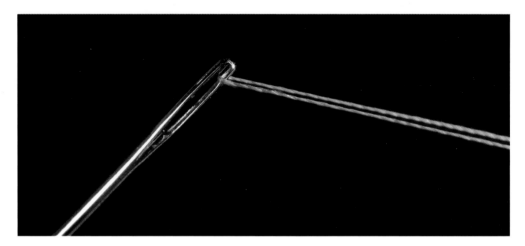

Figure 14-4: A needle and thread can create an interesting subject when photographed from an inch away with a macro lens.

Feel the Noize

If you're old enough to remember Slade or Quiet Riot, you'll know that "noize" rocks — as long as you're looking for a bit of multicolored speckly texture in your images. Like grain back in the film era, a bit of digital noise in your images can be used for artistic effect. Rather than avoid noise, you might want to enhance it. On the other hand, if you're looking for a satiny smooth finish on your digital images, you might want to *minimize* it. Fortunately, the techniques for adding or avoiding noise involve the same sets of concepts:

✔ **ISO setting:** To *increase* the amount of noise in your photos, switch to a high ISO setting, such as ISO 1600 or ISO 3200. The higher the setting, the more noisy speckles you'll see in your images. To *decrease* the amount of noise, use a lower ISO setting, such as ISO 100 or ISO 200.

✓ **Exposure time:** Longer exposures (from 1 second to 30 seconds or more) increase the amount of noise in an image as the sensor heats up and begins to register that heat as spurious image information. If you want to minimize noise, use a larger f-stop — if you can — to shorten the exposure time.

✓ **Software:** Applications such as Photoshop or Elements include Add Noise filters that you can use to spice up your photos with a little random grain (multicolored or monochrome, as you prefer). On the other hand, tools like Noise Ninja (www.picturecode.com) can remove excess noise to a certain extent when you *don't* want it. Chapter 11 offers an introduction to using noise filters in an image editor.

Editing, Retouching, and Compositing Images

Sometimes your best photographic techniques aren't enough to create the image you want. There's no shame in turning to an image-editing program to manipulate your photos.

High quality image editors can perform three main kinds of modifications:

✓ **Basic editing:** This kind of work includes fixing colors and tonal values, rotating or resizing images or portions of images, adding textures and special effects with filters, and other easy fixes.

✓ **Retouching:** If you're looking to remove red-eye effects, soften bad complexions, delete unwanted artifacts or people, and make other improvements to your images, the realm of retouching might be your best choice.

✓ **Compositing:** With this kind of editing, you combine several images into one, move objects from one place to another in your photograph, and create a brand new picture that might bear little resemblance to the originals.

Of course, there is a lot of overlap among what can be done with editing, retouching, and compositing, and sometimes you'll use all three when you work on a particular image. Figure 14-5 shows an image in which I used all three techniques.

In Chapter 11, you find an introduction to image editing and image editors. For more complete details on applying these modifications with a specific image editor, check out other *For Dummies* books, such as *Photoshop CS2 All-in-One Desk Reference For Dummies*, by Barbara Obermeier (Wiley).

Figure 14-5: Clouds, a satellite antenna, and a neighbor's house were edited from this image.

Reading the Funny Manual (RTFM)

If you're like me, you find the manual that's furnished with a digital SLR to be particularly unappealing when you first get the camera. The manuals are usually confusing and finding what you really need to know can be difficult. I'm always anxious to get shooting, and I've used enough different digital cameras that I can usually fumble my way through their operation without using the manual. As I familiarize myself with a dSLR for the first few weeks, I refer to the instructions only when I can't figure out how to do some particular task.

However, any dSLR is a complex machine, and after you become comfortable with its basic operation, the manual that perplexed you so much at first suddenly makes a lot of sense. You can find tricks you never thought of ("Oh, I can reformat a memory card by pressing these two buttons simultaneously!") and capabilities you didn't even know existed ("The depth-of-field button is *where?*").

So, the best advice I can give you for becoming an expert in the use of your particular digital SLR is that, *eventually* you'll want to Read the Funny Manual.

15

Ten Things You Never Thought of Doing with Your Digital SLR

*A*nybody can take her digital SLR, point it at something interesting, and come back with a good photo. It takes a genu-wine second-degree black belt photo master to turn the mundane into something special. One way to add excitement to your humdrum photos is to apply some techniques you probably never even thought of. This chapter provides a quick introduction to ten cool techniques.

Capturing the Unseen with Infrared Photography

If you're looking for a new type of photography to play with, infrared imaging with digital cameras can easily become your new playground. By ignoring visible light and capturing subjects solely by the infrared light they reflect, you can picture the unseen — in more ways than one. That's because, thanks to the magic of the digital SLR, you'll likely be shooting blind. The same techniques that shield your sensor from visible light also keep you from seeing anything through the viewfinder. Fortunately, workarounds exist.

Infrared photography lets you render foliage in eerie shades of white, and the sky in an unearthly black color. Human skin takes on a soft, fuzzy glow. You'll either love or hate the effects.

The first thing to do is to get your camera set up for infrared photography. Because digital camera sensors are highly sensitive to infrared illumination, most camera vendors try to filter this light out by placing a filter called a *hot mirror* in front of the sensor. Some hot mirrors are more effective than others.

You can test your dSLR for infrared compatibility by taking a picture of a TV remote control pointed at the camera with a button depressed. If a spot of light shows up in your image, your camera is sensitive to infrared light.

After you know whether your camera can take infrared photos, the following steps can help you get started:

1. **Get yourself a filter that blocks visible light while letting the infrared illumination through.**

   I like the Hoya R72 filter, but others have reported success using Wratten #87, #87C, #88A, and #89B filters.

2. **Infrared exposures are likely to be very long anyway (up to several seconds in duration), so be sure to use a tripod. Set up your camera on the tripod, compose your image, and *then* place the infrared filter on the lens.**

   Unfortunately, after you place the filter on your camera, the view through your finder is completely black.

3. **Set your white balance manually (check your camera's user guide to see how to do this) by using a subject that reflects a lot of infrared.**

   Grass is a good choice.

4. **Then, take a few pictures by using manual exposure.**

   I recommend using a small f-stop because the infrared focus point isn't the same as for visible light, and your autofocus mechanism won't work when the filter is in place anyway. Small f-stops lead to even longer exposures, but your tripod will keep the camera steady. Start with an exposure of 0.5 to 1 second, and then double the exposure time for each successive picture. You might be able to see an image on your camera's LCD after the shot and gauge exposure that way.

Initially, your infrared images will be highly tinged with red, as shown in the picture on the left in Figure 15-1. Play around with them in your image editor to adjust brightness and contrast, and color. (Chapter 11 introduces how to make these adjustments by using an image editor.) The picture on the right in Figure 15-1, for example, shows the same shot rendered only through the Red channel in an image editor (which indeed makes the image look gray, in case you aren't familiar with channels).

Figure 15-1: Infrared shots initially look, well, red! You can also produce an eerie gray image like the one on the right in an image editor.

Lighting for All in Tents and Purposes

One of the challenges of shooting close-up pictures of small objects is providing even lighting. You can arrange one or two (or even more) lights but might end up with unsightly shadows, harsh illumination, and reflections. There's a better way.

REMEMBER

Pros use handy setups called *tents* to provide soft, even illumination for their close-up pictures. These are exactly what they sound like — tent-like arrangements of translucent material, such as cloth, arranged to cloak your item so that it can be illuminated from all sides through the covering. Just remember to leave a hole big enough for your lens to shoot through!

You can make a tent out of coat-hangers and bed sheets, or use more elaborate devices. Plastic friction-fit plumbing pipes and joints make a good skeleton for tents of many sizes. You can assemble such a tent and tear it down on a moment's notice.

TIP

For small objects, I prefer a free-standing tent such as the one shown in Figure 15-2. I made it out of a translucent plastic milk bottle. I cut off the bottom so I could fit the tent over the object being photographed, and removed the spout and enough plastic from the neck to insert my dSLR's macro lens. My milk-bottle tent can be illuminated from all sides and creates a soft, even lighting effect like the one shown in Figure 15-3.

Figure 15-2: Cut up a gallon milk bottle to create a tent for shooting small objects.

Figure 15-3: Coin collections and other small, shiny objects are often best photographed inside a tent.

Turning Your $1,000+ dSLR into a Pinhole Camera

You probably paid at least a few hundred dollars for the lens mounted on your dSLR right now. How would you like to play with a "lens" that cost you, maybe, five bucks? Now you, too, can turn your $1000+ digital SLR into a pinhole camera by using the technique I explain in this section.

If you came to digital cameras from the film world, you might be way ahead of me. You likely experimented with pinhole cameras as you learned exactly how images are produced. You can also use digital cameras as pinhole cameras. All you need is a pinhole!

An easy way to create a pinhole "lens" is to poke a hole in a body cap that is used when no lens is mounted on your camera. (You might have to buy a real body cap if your camera came with a cheap plastic translucent cover instead.) The body cap already has a flange that fits your digital SLR's lens mount. Find the exact center of the cap and cut a hole in the center. That hole is likely to be too large: the smaller and more precisely-made your pinhole is, the sharper your pictures will be.

So, cover the hole you made with a piece of metal, as shown in Figure 15-4. Then, poke a tiny hole in the metal. I used a piece of aluminum foil, pierced with a sewing needle, but you can use a piece cut from a cookie sheet or other thin metal — the thinner the better. If you have a hobby hand drill with tiny bits, you can probably cut a precise hole in the metal sheet. Experiment with several different sizes until you get one that produces the sharpest image.

Figure 15-4: A hole pierced in a body cap can make a nifty pinhole "lens."

After you mount your pinhole lens, you can look through the viewfinder and see a fuzzy, dim image. If you have extension tubes, you can try mounting one between your camera body and your pinhole lens to change the "focal length" of the lens. The "f-stop" of the pinhole will be so small that you won't have to worry about focusing after you establish the correct distance away from the sensor to mount the pinhole. Virtually everything will be in focus.

Of course, your aperture will be so small you'll have to mount the camera on a tripod and shoot time exposures, even in bright daylight. Figure 15-5 shows an image exposed for 3 seconds at f-whatever, using my own pinhole rig. (Actually, a quick calculation based on the normal exposure times in bright daylight, I'd estimate that my pinhole is approximately f256!) I always use manual exposure to make my pinhole pictures. If you're using your camera's meter, you might need to cover the viewfinder eyepiece to keep extraneous light from venturing inside and affecting the metering system.

Figure 15-5: Pinhole photographs have a fuzzy, romantic look. Get used to it!

Warping Time with Time-Lapse Photography

Time-lapse photography is a great way to show a flower unfolding, the sun marching across the sky, the process of building construction, and, over the course of a year, the change of seasons. There are two ways to take time-lapse photos. One of them is pretty easy, works only with some dSLR cameras, and might require special software. The other way can be used with any dSLR, needs no special gadgets or applications, and is a whole lot of work.

The easy way usually requires tethering your camera to a computer through a USB cable, and working with software that can automatically trigger the camera to take a picture at intervals. The Nikon and Canon dSLRs have applications that can do this for you.

The images are automatically downloaded to the computer as they're taken, so you can take many more pictures in sequence than you could fit on a single memory card. Having your dSLR connected to an AC power source is a good idea because even cameras that use very little juice will eventually deplete their batteries if left on and connected to a computer for hours at a time. (Your dSLR uses much more power when linked to a computer than when operating in standalone mode.)

The other way to shoot time-lapse photos calls for more effort on your part. No special software is needed, nor do you need to connect your camera to a computer. Instead, you can use a digital tool to trigger each picture, that digital tool being the index digit of your right hand. Set your camera on a tripod and press the shutter release (or use a remote control/cable release) to take a picture at the interval you select. This can be a tedious process, and is actually best suited for longer-term sequences, such as construction progress pictures or the "changing seasons" shots shown in Figure 15-6.

To take a series like the one in Figure 15-6, you need to be able to set up your camera in the exact same spot at intervals. The easiest way to do this is to mount the camera on a tripod, and record the height the legs had been set, the extension of the center pole, and the tilt and angle of the tripod head. Then, mark the position of the tripod legs on the supporting surface. (I used bright orange paint on my driveway.) Then you can repeat your setup any time you want and take a series of pictures over the course of a few days or, in this case, a year. Be sure and use the same lens or zoom setting for each photo, too!

Figure 15-6: Spring and summer (top), fall and winter (bottom) through the magic of manual time-lapse photography.

Expanding Your Creativity with Slow Shutter Speeds

Ordinarily, blurry images are considered a bad thing. When I use a shutter speed that's so slow that my subjects are rendered as a big blur, I tend to say something like, "Oh, I *meant* to do that! I was showing the fleetingness of time against the backdrop of our fast-paced society." Yeah, that's the ticket.

On the other hand, you *can* get some interesting images by using a slow shutter speed if you allow some portions of your image to blur while other portions remain razor-sharp. The classic application of this concept is the photograph of the babbling stream, with the woodsy surroundings rendered in sharp detail, while the flowing water merges into a ghostly blur.

The secret, of course, is to mount the camera on a tripod and use a slow shutter speed. Anything that moves will be blurred, but the stationary surroundings will be, in contrast, very sharp. Figure 15-7 shows a carousel, with blurry steeds rushing by against a backdrop of light streaks caused by the illumination on the ride.

Figure 15-7: Oddly enough, a slow shutter speed can produce a feeling of action and movement in a subject.

If you look around you, you can find lots of subjects that can become more interesting if you let them blur a little. Be sure to mount the camera on a tripod (in this case, the camera was actually attached to a C-clamp with tripod-mount affixed to the railing around the carousel). Try different shutter speeds, reviewing your results on your dSLR's LCD, until you find the speed that produces the effect you want. Use shutter priority mode and select a range of speeds from ⅟₃₀ of a second to about 1 second.

Capturing an Instant in Time with Fast Shutter Speeds

Some subjects move so quickly that normally the human eye would never be able to observe them. However, a very fast shutter speed can freeze a moment in time. Falling water, breaking light bulbs, bullets penetrating an apple, and other events that are over in an instant lend themselves to hyper-freezing techniques. Figure 15-8 shows the ripples and splashes produced by a drop of water landing in a glass. I illuminated it by placing an electronic flash off to the left and triggering an exposure manually. This method involves a lot of trial and error, but, with digital cameras, you can easily take 30 or 40 pictures to get the exact one you want.

Figure 15-8: A tiny-fraction-of-a-second exposure can freeze the quickest action.

Most digital SLRs have shutter speeds of at least $\frac{1}{4,000}$ of a second; some have speeds of $\frac{1}{8,000}$ to $\frac{1}{16,000}$ of second. You can get even briefer "shutter speeds" by taking advantage of the fleeting duration of an electronic flash unit when used in close-up mode. Many strobes wink on and off in as little as $\frac{1}{50,000}$ of a second when used up close. That's because only a very quick flash is needed to properly expose an image from that range, but you can use the effect to stop action.

If you want to try freezing action with an electronic flash, use one that you can operate off-camera, connected with a cable. Or, try mounting your camera on a tripod, darkening the room, and shooting a time exposure. During the exposure, trip the flash manually by pressing the Test button. Because the room is dark, only the illumination from the flash is used for the exposure.

Making Your Own Effects Filters

Believe it or not, filters were originally something you put on the front of your lens — not a plug-in mini-application found in image editors such as Photoshop. Certainly, software filters can duplicate many of the effects of their glass or gelatin real-world counterparts, but that doesn't mean you have to abandon the joy of using real, actual filters on your lens. Lots of special effects are tricky to duplicate in an image editor, such as polarization to remove reflections, or split-filter gradients to even out the bright sky and dimmer foreground.

You don't even have to *pay* for special effects filters. You can make your own. Manufacture them out of ordinary, fairly useless filters like skylight or UV filters, or better yet, purchase a Series *x* adapter ring. Series adapter rings come in various sizes to suit the front filter diameter of your lens, with the *x* replaced by the number of the ring suitable for your lens, such as Series V, Series VI, Series VII, or Series VIII.

A Series *x* adapter ring comes in two parts. One part has a thread that screws into the front of your lens. The second part screws into the first part, usually with a filter of your devising between the two, forming a little sandwich of two metal rings and your custom filter inside.

The Roman numeral designations show the relative size of the ring set. For example, Series IX rings are sized to fit lenses with filter threads of 72mm, 77mm, and larger. Series VIII rings are good for lenses with 62mm to about 67mm filter threads. You can purchase step-up and step-down adapters so you can use, say, a Series IX ring on a lens with a 62mm thread. Mounting a larger ring on a smaller lens thread is always better, and you'll want to make sure the rings don't cause vignetting (darkening) in the corners of your image (which can be a particular problem with wide-angle lenses).

Here are some ideas for special effects filters that you can create on your own.

- **Starry night:** Use a piece of window screen cut to fit the Series rings to create a star filter that transforms each pinpoint of light into a star effect, as shown in Figure 15-9.

- **Color your world:** Cut a piece of gelatin filter material into a circle to fit in the Series ring to create a color filter.

- **Color your world times two:** Use two pieces of filter material of different colors to create a split-color filter. For example, you can use orange-red on top to give the sky a sunset color, and blue on the bottom to add cool tones to the foreground. The "real" (expensive) filters of this type have a smooth gradient between the colors, but a quick-and-dirty split filter approach can work, too.

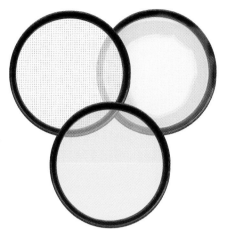

Figure 15-9: Create your own star filter (upper left), smudgy portrait filter (upper right), or split-field color filter (bottom).

- **Life's a blur:** Smear the outer edges of a piece of round glass (or another filter) with petroleum jelly to create a romantic blur filter. This method is great for portraits of females and teenagers with complexion problems.

- **Feature your filters:** Try a feather or other textured material to create interesting effects.

Shooting the Works!

You don't have to wait until Independence Day to shoot fireworks. Lots of other events and celebrations, including baseball games and auto races, are commemorated with an aerial display. Perhaps you've avoided shooting fireworks because you thought capturing skyrockets in flight was too difficult. Or, maybe you just wanted to watch the show rather than fiddle with your camera. I'm here to tell you that you can do both!

The secret to shooting fireworks is to do a little planning. Here are some tips:

- **Choose your spot.** You can position yourself up close and capture the display from underneath the exploding canopy, or get farther back and shoot the fireworks against a skyline. Both approaches work great. What you *don't* want is a view that is obstructed by buildings, trees, or very tall fellow observers.

- **Use a tripod.** Set your camera on a tripod so it will remain rock-steady during exposures that can last several seconds.

- **Check it out.** Take a few pictures at the beginning of the display and evaluate them to make sure your exposures are reasonable. Try 2 to 3 seconds at f8 for starters. Focus on infinity!

- **Go long.** Use longer exposures to capture multiple bursts in one frame, as shown in Figure 15-10.

- **Shoot RAW.** Use your dSLR's RAW option so you can adjust exposure and other parameters as the image is imported into your photo editor.

- **Don't use noise reduction.** If your camera kicks into noise reduction (NR) mode automatically, disable it. Don't manually activate NR, either. The extra time required to create the noise reduction "dark frame" will cause you to miss the next blast-off. Even a several-second exposure still looks good without this extra step.

- **Enjoy the show.** After you set up your camera and frame an area of the sky where the bursts will appear, just watch the display without peering through the viewfinder. Trigger your shots by pressing the shutter release button or using a remote control or cable release (if your dSLR can be used with one).

Figure 15-10: A long exposure can capture multiple bursts.

Going for Baroque

Normally, you'll want to set your camera's controls to get the best-exposed, most realistic image. However, at times you might want to go for baroque and get a really over-the-top image right in the camera. Simply adjust your settings to get some off-the-wall results. Of course, if you shoot RAW, you can manipulate your images when importing them to your image editor to get much the same effects, but adjusting the camera's controls is faster and repeatable.

Here are some things to try:

- **Boost saturation.** Set your camera's color saturation controls to the max to generate rich, unrealistic colors, as shown in Figure 15-11. Film photographers favored Kodak Ektachrome films for this very reason, and digital shooters can do the same thing electronically. Increasing saturation can also provide good color on dull, overcast days.

- **Enhance contrast.** Your dSLR probably has a contrast control intended to give you acceptable images of low-contrast subjects, but which can be subverted to produce high-contrast results of normal subjects. You lose detail in highlights and shadows, but that's what you're going for with this effect.

Figure 15-11: Crank up your color saturation to produce an off-beat look.

✔ **Add grain.** High ISO ratings can add unwanted noise to your images, except when it's *wanted* noise because of a creative decision. Crank your camera's sensitivity up all the way, and then experiment. In bright light, you generally have to use high shutter speeds, small apertures, or both, but most digital SLRs can shoot photos on the beach at high noon at ISO 1600, even if it means using $\frac{1}{4,000}$ of a second at f16.

Going Crazy with Your Image Editor

Many digital SLR users have more experience fiddling with images in Photoshop than they do taking pictures with a dSLR. After all, Photoshop has been around since 1990, and was an excellent tool for modifying scanned film images long before digital cameras began hitting their stride a decade later.

So, odds are, you have no fear of image editing and you might, in fact, be striving to create an image that's as close to your vision as possible *in the camera* in order to reduce the time you spend in post-processing.

All the more reason to take your image editor to its limit and work on special effects (like the one shown in Figure 15-12) that unleash your creativity.

Figure 15-12: Every picture tells a story, but even the best story can be spiced up with editing.

16

Ten Online Resources for Digital SLR Photography

*O*ne of the advantages of using a digital SLR is that, in terms of new ideas, new techniques, new applications, and new add-on gadgets, the sky is the limit. Certainly, an imaginative photographer will find it challenging to wring every last bit of potential out of a non-SLR digital camera, and can spend years doing so. But if the possibilities of an ordinary point-and-shoot camera are vast, the tricks you can do with a digital SLR are easily twice as vast. The expandability and versatility of a dSLR mean you have no excuse for doing things in a half-vast way (ahem).

One tool you'll want to avail yourself of is the Internet, with its unlimited treasure trove of ideas, showcases for your photos, equipment tests, and places to buy or sell dSLRs, lenses, and accessories. This chapter gets you started by introducing ten of the best online resources. (Although I give only ten sites the full feature treatment, I sprinkle in a couple bonus sites here and there.)

I provide all the links here, but you don't have to go to the trouble of typing them into your browser. Instead, go to www.dbusch.com/dslrlinks.htm, where you'll find a page full of clickable links for these sites and many more.

All Your PBase Are Belong to Us

www.pbase.com

A ton of image-hosting sites out there let you upload your photos to a Web page album so anyone with access to the Internet can view them. However, most of these are aimed at consumers, not serious photographers. Album and image size might be limited, and the things that you can do with the albums might be confined to a few levels of sharing (that is, you might be able to share with everyone in the world, with a fixed list of users, or only by invitation). These sites are great if you want to share a few pictures online and perhaps order some prints, personalized calendars, or photo coffee mugs.

PBase has become wildly popular for a good reason: It goes well beyond the album sites to provide true online photo galleries — and a lot more besides. Here's a sampling of the features:

- You can specify that the EXIF (image data) parameters of each photograph are available to viewers, so other photographers can see the settings you used to create a particular picture.

- A search engine enables visitors to look for photographs — including yours — by using specific keywords.

- You can upload batches of photos that have been compressed into archives (such as .zip files) to save time. (Most of the album sites ask you to upload non-zipped photo files individually, and limit you to five to ten images.)

- You can link galleries that you create. So if you start a gallery showing off your sports photos, you can subdivide it into football, baseball, tennis, or other appropriate categories.

- If you frequent any of the various online discussion forums, such as those shown in Figure 16-1, you can link directly to your photos.

- Many compatible sites can display PBase photos right in your postings, with buttons to zoom in and out.

PBase is even a terrific information resource. It publishes a magazine compiled entirely from the efforts of members. The premiere issue highlighted the work of two photographers and provided some useful tips on sensor cleaning.

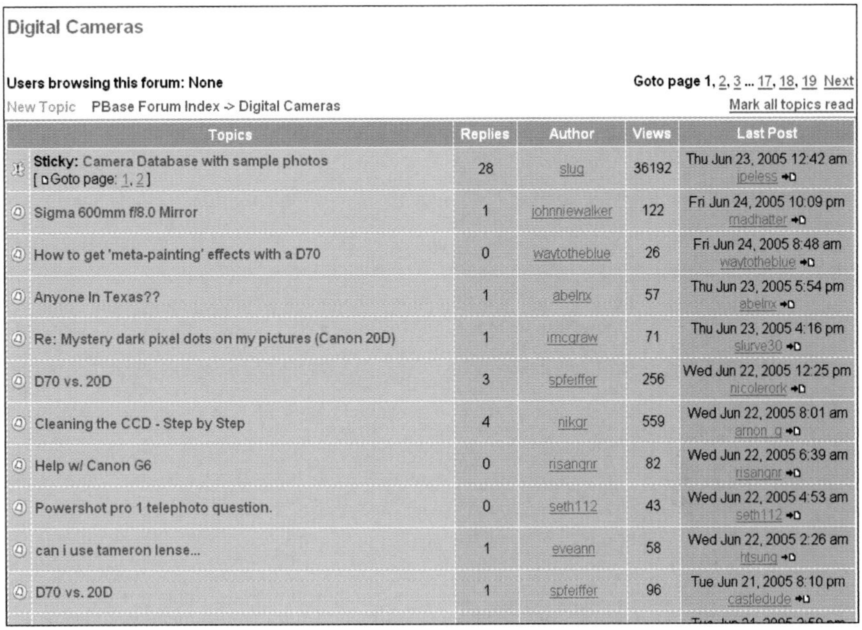
Digital Cameras

Users browsing this forum: None — Goto page 1, 2, 3 ... 17, 18, 19 Next

New Topic PBase Forum Index -> Digital Cameras — Mark all topics read

Topics	Replies	Author	Views	Last Post
Sticky: Camera Database with sample photos [Goto page: 1, 2]	28	slug	36192	Thu Jun 23, 2005 12:42 am jpeless
Sigma 600mm f/8.0 Mirror	1	johnniewalker	122	Fri Jun 24, 2005 10:09 pm madhatter
How to get 'meta-painting' effects with a D70	0	waytotheblue	26	Fri Jun 24, 2005 8:48 am waytotheblue
Anyone In Texas??	1	abelnx	57	Thu Jun 23, 2005 5:54 pm abelnx
Re: Mystery dark pixel dots on my pictures (Canon 20D)	1	imcgraw	71	Thu Jun 23, 2005 4:16 pm slurve30
D70 vs. 20D	3	spfeiffer	256	Wed Jun 22, 2005 12:25 pm nicolerork
Cleaning the CCD - Step by Step	4	nikgr	559	Wed Jun 22, 2005 8:01 am amon_g
Help w/ Canon G6	0	risangnr	82	Wed Jun 22, 2005 6:39 am risangnr
Powershot pro 1 telephoto question.	0	seth112	43	Wed Jun 22, 2005 4:53 am seth112
can i use tameron lense...	1	eveann	58	Wed Jun 22, 2005 2:26 am htsung
D70 vs. 20D	1	spfeiffer	96	Tue Jun 21, 2005 8:10 pm castledude

Figure 16-1: Forums in PBase are devoted to topics like Digital Cameras.

Of course, something this good isn't free. You can check out PBase for 30 days with 10MB of online disk storage. If you like it, a hefty 300MB of storage (enough for 800 images of an average 250 KB size) costs $23 a year (less than $2 a month) at the time of this writing. If you need 900MB of online space, that's $60 a year, and you can add more storage in 200MB increments for a reasonable cost.

Digital Photography Viewed and Reviewed

`www.dpreview.com`

An incredible free resource is Digital Photography Review (usually called just DPReview). DPReview is a top-notch site for information about any digital SLR camera. A British chap named Phil Askey publishes this site with help from a knowledgeable staff and thousands of avid fans and visitors.

Visiting DPReview needn't cost you anything but your time, which will be well-spent. However, you can donate funds through any credit card or PayPal, or you can support the effort by purchasing a t-shirt, coffee mug, tote bag, or whatever.

It's no exaggeration to say I spend a minimum of 30 minutes at this site virtually every day of the year. Here are the kinds of useful features at DPReview that will keep you coming back for more:

✔ **User forums:** You can find individual forums for all the key digital SLR cameras (as well as non-dSLRs) from Canon, Nikon, Konica Minolta, Pentax, Kodak, Fuji, and Sigma. There are even separate forums for topics such as Canon SLR Lens Talk, Nikon SLR Lens Talk, Lighting, Storage and Media, and Retouching. Those who own a particular camera model will enjoy the specialized forums for cameras such as the Nikon D70/D50, Nikon D1/D2, Canon 300/350, Canon 10D/20D, and so forth. Even with all these subdivisions, most of the forums have hundreds of fascinating posts a day. I spend most of my time on this site just trying to keep abreast of the interesting discussions.

✔ **Camera comparisons:** The site has separate pages for each digital camera vendor listing *all* the most recent models, with complete specifications for every camera and links to reviews. For example, the Nikon page lists 33 different Nikon models in detail and links to 17 discontinued models. You can compare the features of cameras from different vendors, too, as shown in Figure 16-2.

Be sure to use this trove of information to compare cameras. For example, if you want to know the sensor size of the Canon Digital Rebel XT compared to that of the Nikon D70s, simply retrieve that information with a couple clicks.

✔ **Comprehensive reviews:** The DPReview evaluations of cameras are among the most complete and thorough available on the Internet. For example, the review of the Pentax *ist DS is 25 pages long and includes a description of every feature, screen shots of each menu, tests, sample images, and an evaluation of the software that comes with the camera. You can even listen to the sound the shutter makes if that's important to you. These reviews don't appear the instant a camera comes on the market, but they're worth waiting for.

✔ **Daily news updates:** The main page provides a listing to the main digital photography news stories of the day and more than a few rumors. You can find things like notices of the latest firmware updates for your camera, new product introduction announcements, and other breaking stories.

✔ **An online glossary:** Wonder what *bokeh* is? You can find a glossary on the DPReview sight that explains this and just about any other term you care to look up.

As I write this, DPReview is fast closing in on 500 *million* visitors since it began keeping track in January 1999. You should jump on the bandwagon, too. Visit www.dpreview.com.

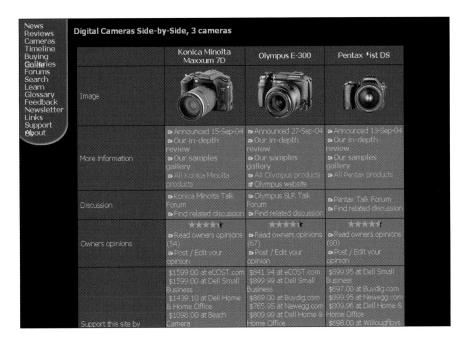

Figure 16-2: DPReview's Side-by-Side comparison feature lets you pit one camera's feature against another's.

For the Shutterbug in You

www.shutterbug.net

If you're an old-line photographer, someone who was a serious photo hobbyist back when people had to use something called *film,* you'll appreciate the full-spectrum viewpoint provided by this venerable resource. It's an online adjunct to *Shutterbug* magazine, and as such covers digital photography in depth as well as recent and classic film cameras, photo techniques, and other topics of interest.

Like DPReview, Shutterbug's strength lies in its forums, which, like the magazine and Web site, span a range of interests. You can find forums dedicated to Nikon, Canon, Pentax, Olympus, and Konica Minolta digital SLRs. Shutterbug also offers several forums for the film SLR counterparts (always a good source for information about compatible lenses and accessories), along with forums for inkjet, dye sublimation, and traditional silver halide printing. Color management, lighting and exposure, and collectible cameras are also covered.

Whereas DPReview's product evaluations are mostly devoted to digital cameras, Shutterbug looks at all kinds of items, including equipment bags, gadgets, books, and photo shows. You can find interesting monthly columns, too.

Pop Goes the Photo!

www.popphoto.com

Popular Photography & Imaging magazine has been the most authoritative resource for serious amateur photographers for longer than most of us have been alive. Indeed, long-time editor and columnist Herbert Keppler, who has been providing insights since the 1950s, understands the progress that has been made in the photographic industry because he's *lived* through much of it.

The addition of a Web site as a supplement to the magazine's coverage and increasing emphasis on digital photography prove that venerable doesn't have to equal stodgy or old-fashioned. Pop Photo remains as up-to-date as the latest digital camera, and most of the time, is several steps ahead of the technology in its predictions. (In the interests of full disclosure, I should point out that I am a contributor to *Popular Photography & Imaging* from time to time — but I've been a subscriber and avid reader ever since I was in high school.)

The Popular Photography Web site's strength is its authoritative voice when it comes to the technology. The editors really, *really* understand all the finer points of digital and conventional photographic imaging, and their lab tests of equipment are unmatched. When you read the performance figures on various lenses or other equipment, you have information at your fingertips that you can use to go out and make purchases with confidence.

Nowhere else can you find solid information available in such depth. Can a 16.2MP digital SLR produce better results than a fine-grain ISO 100 film? What are the seven most significant breakthroughs in tripod design? What are the some of the best photos taken in the last year? The answers are all available at the Popular Photography Web site. The site offers forums, of course, but it also provides lots of tips and tricks, how-to's, workshops, and videos.

News Groupies

Internet newsgroups, known to old-timers as *Usenet,* is a wonderful, unbridled resource where anything goes. Groups with names like `rec.photo.digital`, `rec.photo.digital.slr-systems`, or `rec.photo.digital.rangefinder` remind you of the Old West, full of gunslingers and common folk, sheep-herders and cattlemen (think Canon users versus Nikon gunslingers). The only law in the land of Usenet anarchy is whoever has the most time to spend posting.

Newsgroups are a little like the online forums sponsored by DPReview, Shutterbug, or Pop Photo, only less focused. Posts range far and wide, and you're likely to see hundreds of different topics and comments in a particular group on virtually anything — in a single day. One key strength of Usenet is this diversity: You're bound to stumble across information you'd never pick up anywhere else in a refreshing, serendipitous way. Another advantage is the potential for speed: If you have a question, you can post it on a news-group and sometimes get an answer in minutes.

Newsgroups operate in a way that's a little different from purely Web-based resources. The information doesn't reside on a single, central Web server as it does with pages that you access through a browser, such as Internet Explorer. Instead, messages are received by a loosely connected network of news servers scattered around the world. The news servers might be operated by your ISP for free access by the ISP's customers. AOL, Roadrunner, and other ISPs all operate their own news servers. They also decide which newsgroups to carry. Or, you can access newsgroups through free or fee-based services such as TeraNews or GigaNews. These sources often carry a larger and more varied selection of newsgroups than those offered by ISPs, and keep the post-ings available for longer periods of time.

The most common way to access newsgroups is through a special program, or *client,* called a newsreader. Among the most popular newsreaders are Free Agent and the newsreader built into Outlook Express. However, you can also search through newsgroup postings with a Web browser by accessing Google Groups (`http://groups-beta.google.com`).

After you launch your newsreader, you need to tell it which news server to use, connect to that server, and download a list of groups available from that source. (Sources can number 50,000 or more!) Choose which groups you want to monitor by *subscribing.* Then you can download the available message headers (titles of the posts), sort through them, and mark specific messages for retrieval.

You can sort messages by parameters, including author and date, but mes-sages are most frequently listed by *thread,* that is, all the messages stemming from an original post. Viewing threads lets you follow a discussion easily. At any time, you can respond to a post by typing a message of your own.

After you send your reply, it will be uploaded to your particular news server, and then, in minutes or hours, be distributed (or *propagated*) to all the other news servers that carry that particular newsgroup.

Although the process might sound complicated, newsgroups are a great resource for collecting a lot of varied information on many different topics. Figure 16-3 shows a typical newsgroup search conducted from Google.

Figure 16-3: Google newsgroup searches can yield lots of good information.

Landscapes Can Be Luminous

`www.luminous-landscape.com`

Calling The Luminous Landscape a Web site devoted to landscape and nature photography is a little like calling the Encyclopaedia Britannica a collection of articles. This site is, above all, amazingly comprehensive, with more than 2,000 *pages* of information, articles, tutorials, product reviews, and photographs.

This site has everything you'd want to know about nature photography, but goes far beyond that. Here are some of the features to check out:

- ✔ The site's *Understanding* series of tutorials covers everything from SLR viewfinders and how they work to sensor cleaning. You can discover how to use unsharp masking, work with histograms, and use polarizing filters effectively.

- ✔ The *Tutorial* series covers digital workflow, pinhole photography, high dynamic range photography, and other topics.

- ✔ You can find lists of workshops occurring around the world. (China, Africa, Antarctica, Ireland, and Iceland are just a few destinations where these workshops have been held in the past.)

- ✔ The descriptions of prime shooting locations for nature photography help you find new places to take photos.

- ✔ Oh yeah — and don't miss the essays, regular columns, and hundreds of product reviews on cameras, tripods, and other essentials.

If you're interested in nature, landscape, or documentary photography, you must visit this site. However, everyone from sports photographers to portraiture specialists can discover something by stopping by.

Photos That Don't Bite

www.bytephoto.com

I include BytePhoto because it's a slightly lesser-known site that deserves a little more attention, if only for its quirkiness. It includes lots of features but is especially strong as a portal to other sites. For example, BytePhoto offers online galleries, but you can also find links to sharing services, including SmugMug (www.smugmug.com), which is the strongest competitor to PBase. BytePhoto gives you links to other interesting pages on external sites, a Google search box for combing the Net, and a ton of ads with interesting offers you might want to jump to.

BytePhoto offers news, reviews (not especially great, but interesting), and photo contests. You can also find tutorials on image editing, Photoshop Actions (macros), and the usual collection of forums. If you have old gear to unload or things to buy, you might find the classified ads useful. (One of the site's forums contains the ads.) You might need to use the home page's search box to find a particular feature, but it's worth the look.

Cult of Personality

As you search the Web, you'll find a ton of sites founded and operated by individuals, such as www.kenrockwell.com (good stuff, but focusing mostly on Nikon and *highly* opinionated), www.fredmiranda.com, and www.robgalbraith.com (discussed next).

Rob Galbraith

www.robgalbraith.com

Rob is probably best known for his exhaustive evaluation of CompactFlash (CF) and Secure Digital (SD) card performance data. He has tested virtually every CF and SD card available, with just about every camera on the market. There are more than 20 pages of tables and data to pore through. If you want to know how a SanDisk Ultra II 1GB CompactFlash card performs with a Canon EOS-1D Mark II, you'll find that information. These tests are quite literally the bible of the industry.

The site also includes a good list of links to other useful Web pages, from the American Society of Media Photographers (ASMP) to *National Geographic.* Rob's site offers forums (especially strong in the professional digital photography arena), news and reports, links to software upgrades, and the usual array of ads that help pay for the cost of publishing all this information online.

Most photographer-run sites focus more on promoting the photographer than providing solid information, but this is one exception.

Charmin' Miranda

www.fredmiranda.com

Another photographer who believes it is better to give than receive is Fred Miranda. His gorgeous site is bursting with valuable information, all arranged logically and easy to access. Lots of digital photographers agree: On a recent night when I logged in, nearly 1,500 *other* photographers were also using the site at that exact moment!

Of course, Fred does hawk some amazing software, but in an unobtrusive way. You almost have to stumble across the FM Software offerings, mostly Photoshop plug-ins and Actions that do tasks such as reduce noise, resize photos, or manage workflow.

You'll be highly engaged by the forums, shown in Figure 16-4, which are some of the best available online with contributions from more than 70,000 members. You can also find useful articles and reviews, as well as image hosting. Even if you don't want to set up showcases of your own, you'll definitely want to browse the hosted galleries. You can get lots of ideas by viewing other photographers' best efforts.

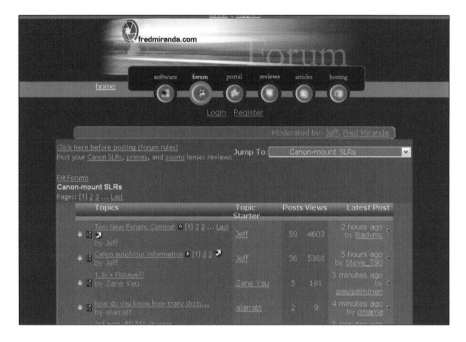

Figure 16-4: The forums are one of the more engaging parts of Fred Miranda's Web site.

Don't Miss eBay

www.ebay.com

Once called "the nation's garage sale," eBay is one online resource that really pays — if you have old equipment to unload. It's also a great place for registered members to locate hard-to-find camera equipment at reasonable prices. Although www.keh.com, a real camera dealer in Atlanta, www.bhphotovideo.com, and www.adorama.com (both reliable dealers in New York City) are the go-to organizations for much new and used stuff, nothing beats eBay for variety, and, if you get caught up in bidding, excitement.

I know whereof I speak. I've had more than 8,000 transactions on eBay myself, and I ended up writing a book about my experiences, *The eBay Myth Buster,* available from the same John Wiley & Sons folks who brought you this tome.

eBay is a great place to locate new and used equipment at a price you're willing to pay, especially if you do some research ahead of time and have a good idea of what an item is truly worth. The venue does best with supplies (such as ink for inkjet printers), older cameras and lenses, and difficult-to-find accessories. For example, when I picked up a used 170–500mm zoom lens from my local camera dealer, no lens hood was available for it. The lens hood I found on eBay was delivered to me in less than a week for quite a bit less than my dealer would have charged for a special order.

Perhaps you're looking for older, manual-focus lenses that are compatible with your dSLR. An MF macro lens for $150 probably performs as well as a new AF version for two or three times as much, and you can probably get away with manual focus for precision close-up work anyway.

Perhaps you're upgrading to a new camera and want to sell your old one. Your dealer or a company like KEH will be glad to buy it from you, but they must offer enough less than the camera's worth to allow for some profit when they resell. Peddle the camera on eBay and your net might be a lot more than you would have gotten as a trade-in or selling outright with a dealer.

Ever since I went all-digital, I've been slowly selling off my film cameras on eBay. Figure 16-5 shows an edited version of an eBay auction I conducted for a beloved old half-frame camera I wanted to relocate in a new home.

Figure 16-5: Sell your old film gear on eBay and use the proceeds to buy new digital stuff!

Here are a few keys to using eBay successfully:

- **Check the seller's feedback.** Each eBay ID has a Feedback Rating number next to it, which represents the net number of positive feedbacks (that is, positives minus negatives) received. Click the number to view the actual feedback comments. Sellers or buyers with 50 to 100 or more positives and no negatives are probably reliable. Those with fewer feedbacks or a few negatives might also be good eggs, but be sure to check a little further.

- **Pay for your items by using your credit card through a service like PayPal.** Although eBay provides a modicum of buyer protection, if you use your credit card through PayPal you have two extra levels of security. If a deal goes awry, PayPal might be able to get you a refund. If not, you can go directly to the credit card company and frequently get a chargeback that way. Scams are fairly rare on eBay in the overall scheme of things. If you avoid deals that seem too good to be true (for example, a Nikon D70s for $200) you won't easily fall victim.

- **Don't expect sensational deals on cameras or lenses that have just been introduced.** It's unlikely that "used" ones will be available in any case, and the new ones are probably being sold by dealers who have a profit margin to make. New cameras are likely to be no more than about $50 cheaper than you'd pay locally (if that), but you can save on local sales tax, unless your are a New York resident. In most cases, you'll do better on newly introduced equipment at B&H Photo or Adorama.

- **When purchasing used equipment, see whether you can get a money-back guarantee or an inspection period.** This gear is frequently sold as-is, which can be okay if the seller is well-respected (has a lot of positive feedback), but risky if the seller is new.

Visit www.ebay.com to explore the offerings available. You can pick up a copy of my eBay book through my Web site at www.dbusch.com, or visit your local or online bookstore.

Appendix

Glossary

additive primary colors: The red, green, and blue hues that are used alone or in combinations to create all other colors that you capture with a digital camera, view on a computer monitor, or work with in an image-editing program such as Photoshop. See also *CMY(K) color model*.

AE/AF lock: A control that lets you lock the current autoexposure and/or autofocus settings prior to taking a picture, freeing you from having to hold the shutter release partially depressed.

ambient lighting: Diffuse, nondirectional lighting that doesn't appear to come from a specific source but, rather, bounces off walls, ceilings, and other objects in the scene when a picture is taken.

analog/digital converter: The electronics built into a camera that convert the analog information captured by the sensor into digital bits that can be stored as an image bitmap.

angle of view: The area of a scene that a lens can capture, determined by the focal length of the lens. Lenses with a shorter focal length have a wider angle of view than lenses with a longer focal length.

antialias: A process that smoothes the rough edges in images (called jaggies or staircasing) by creating partially transparent pixels along the boundaries. Your eyes merge the semitransparent pixels into a smoother line.

aperture priority: A camera setting that allows you to specify the f-stop that you want to use, with the camera selecting the required shutter speed automatically based on its light-meter reading. See also *shutter priority*.

artifact: A type of noise in an image or an unintentional image component produced in error by a digital camera during processing.

aspect ratio: The proportions of an image as printed, displayed on a monitor, or captured by a digital camera.

autofocus: A camera setting that allows a digital SLR to choose the correct focus distance for you, usually based on the contrast of an image (the image is at maximum contrast when in sharp focus) or a mechanism such as an infrared sensor that measures the actual distance to the subject. Cameras can be set for single autofocus (the lens is not focused until the shutter release is partially depressed) or continuous autofocus (the lens refocuses constantly as you frame and reframe the image).

autofocus assist lamp: A light source built into a digital camera that provides extra illumination that the autofocus system can use to focus on dimly lit subjects.

averaging meter: A light-measuring device built into a camera that calculates exposure based on the overall brightness of the entire image area. Averaging tends to produce the best exposure when a scene is evenly lit or contains equal amounts of bright and dark areas that contain detail. A digital SLR uses very sophisticated exposure-measuring systems based in center-weighting, spot-reading, or calculating exposure from a matrix of many different picture areas.

backlighting: A lighting effect produced when the main light source is located behind the subject. Backlighting can be used to create a silhouette effect or to illuminate translucent objects.

barrel distortion: A lens defect that causes straight lines at the top or side edges of an image to bow outward into a barrel shape. See also *pincushion distortion.*

blooming: An image distortion caused when a photosite, or pixel, in an image sensor has absorbed all the photons it can handle, so that additional photons that reach that pixel overflow to affect surrounding pixels, producing unwanted brightness, blown highlights, and overexposure around the edges of objects.

blur: To soften an image or part of an image by throwing it out of focus or by allowing it to become soft due to subject or camera motion.

bokeh: A buzzword used to describe the aesthetic qualities of the out-of-focus parts of an image. Some lenses produce good bokeh, and others offer bad bokeh. *Boke* is a Japanese word for "blur," and the *h* was added to keep English speakers from rhyming it with "broke." See also *circle of confusion.*

bounce lighting: Light bounced off a reflector, including a ceiling and walls, to provide a soft, natural-looking light.

bracketing: Taking a series of photographs of the same subject at different settings for various elements, including exposure, color, and white balance, to help ensure that one setting will be the correct one. A digital SLR allows you to choose the order in which bracketed settings are applied.

buffer: The digital camera's internal memory, which stores an image immediately after it is taken until the image can be written to the camera's nonvolatile (semipermanent) memory or a memory card.

burst mode: The digital camera's equivalent of the film camera's motor drive, used to take multiple shots within a short period of time.

calibration: A process used to correct for the differences in the output of a printer or monitor when compared to the original image. After you calibrate your scanner, monitor, and/or image editor, the images you see on-screen more closely represent what you'll get from your printer, even though calibration is never perfect.

Camera RAW: A plug-in included with Photoshop CS and Photoshop Elements that can manipulate the unprocessed images captured by digital cameras, such as a digital SLR's RAW files.

camera shake: Movement of the camera, aggravated by slower shutter speeds, which produces a blurred image.

CCD (charge-coupled device): A type of solid-state sensor that captures the image. It is used in some scanners and digital cameras, such as the Nikon D70, Konica Minolta Maxxum 7D, and others. See also *CMOS*.

center-weighted meter: A light-measuring device that emphasizes the area in the middle of the frame when calculating the correct exposure for an image.

chromatic aberration: An image defect, often seen as green or purple fringing around the edges of an object, caused by a lens failing to focus all colors of a light source at the same point. See also *fringing*.

circle of confusion: A term applied to the fuzzy disks produced when a point of light is out of focus. The circle of confusion is not a fixed size. The viewing distance and amount of enlargement of the image determine whether you see a particular spot on the image as a point or as a disk.

close-up lens: A lens add-on that allows you to take pictures at a distance that is less than the closest-focusing distance of the lens alone.

CMOS (complementary metal-oxide semiconductor): A method for manufacturing a type of solid-state sensor that captures the image, used in scanners and digital cameras such as the Nikon D2X and Canon dSLRs.

CMY(K) color model: A way of defining all possible colors in percentages of cyan, magenta, yellow, and frequently black. Black is added to improve rendition of shadow detail. CMYK is commonly used for printing (both on press and with your inkjet or laser color printer).

color correction: Changing the relative amounts of color in an image to produce a desired effect, typically a more accurate representation of those colors. Color correction can fix faulty color balance in the original image or compensate for the deficiencies of the inks used to reproduce the image.

compression: The reduction of a file's size by encoding with fewer bits of information to represent the original. Some compression schemes, such as JPEG, operate by discarding some image information, but others, such as TIF, preserve all the detail in the original, discarding only redundant data.

continuous autofocus (AF-C): An automatic focusing setting in which the camera constantly refocuses the image as you frame the picture. This setting is often the best choice for moving subjects. See also _single autofocus._

contrast: The range between the lightest and darkest tones in an image. A high-contrast image is one in which the shades fall at the extremes of the range between white and black. In a low-contrast image, the tones are closer together.

dedicated flash: An electronic flash unit designed to work with the automatic exposure features of a specific camera.

depth-of-field: A distance range in a photograph in which all included portions of an image are at least acceptably sharp. With most dSLRs, you can see the available depth-of-field at the taking aperture by pressing the depth-of-field preview button, or you can estimate the range by viewing the depth-of-field scale found on many lenses.

diaphragm: An adjustable component, similar to the iris in the human eye, which can open and close to provide specific-sized lens openings (or f-stops) to control the light striking the sensor or film.

diffuse lighting: Soft, low-contrast lighting.

digital processing chip: A solid-state device found in digital cameras that's in charge of applying the image algorithms to the raw picture data prior to storage on the memory card.

diopter: A value used to represent the magnification power of a lens, calculated as the reciprocal of a lens's focal length (in meters). Diopters are most often used to represent the optical correction used in a viewfinder to adjust for limitations of the photographer's eyesight, and to describe the magnification of a close-up lens attachment.

equivalent focal length: A digital camera's focal length translated into the corresponding values for a 35mm film camera. You can calculate this value for lenses by multiplying the actual focal length of the lens by 1.3, 1.5, 1.6, or some other factor appropriate to a particular camera.

EXIF (Exchangeable Image File Format): A variation on JPEG, EXIF is used by most digital cameras and includes information such as the date and time a photo was taken, the camera settings, resolution, amount of compression, and other data. This format was developed to standardize the exchange of image data between hardware devices and software.

exposure: The amount of light allowed to reach the film or sensor, determined by the intensity of the light, the amount admitted by the iris of the lens, and the length of time determined by the shutter speed.

exposure program: An automatic setting in a digital camera that provides the optimum combination of shutter speed and f-stop at a given level of illumination. For example, a dSLR's sports exposure program uses a faster, action-stopping shutter speed and larger lens opening instead of the smaller, depth-of-field-enhancing lens opening and slower shutter speed that might be favored by the camera's close-up mode at exactly the same light level.

exposure values (EV): EV settings are a way of adding or decreasing exposure without the need to reference f-stops or shutter speeds. For example, if you tell your camera to add +1EV, it provides twice as much exposure, either by using a larger f-stop, a slower shutter speed, or both. This feature is usually available as a separate setting, allowing the user to override an automatic camera setting.

fill lighting: In photography, lighting used to illuminate shadows.

filter: In photography, a device that fits over the lens, changing the light in some way. In image editing, a feature that changes the pixels in an image to produce blurring, sharpening, and other special effects.

flash sync: The timing mechanism that ensures that an internal or external electronic flash fires at the correct time during the exposure cycle. A digital SLR's flash sync speed is the highest shutter speed that can be used with flash, ordinarily from $\frac{1}{180}$ to $\frac{1}{500}$ of a second. See also *front-curtain sync* and *rear-curtain sync*.

focal length: The distance between the film and the optical center of the lens when the lens is focused on infinity, usually measured in millimeters.

focal plane: A line, perpendicular to the optical access, which passes through the focal point. It forms a plane of sharp focus when the lens is set at infinity.

focus lock: A camera feature that lets you freeze the automatic focus of the lens at a certain point when the subject you want to capture is in sharp focus.

focus servo: A digital camera's mechanism that adjusts the focus distance automatically. The focus servo can be set to single autofocus (AF-S) or continuous autofocus (AF-C).

focus tracking: The ability of the automatic focus feature of a camera to change focus as the distance between the subject and the camera changes. One type of focus tracking is predictive, in which the mechanism anticipates the motion of the object being focused on, and adjusts the focus to suit.

fringing: A chromatic aberration that produces fringes of color around the edges of subjects, caused by a lens's inability to focus the various wavelengths of light onto the same spot. Purple fringing is especially troublesome with backlit images.

front-curtain sync: The default kind of electronic flash synchronization technique, originally associated with focal plane shutters. The focal plane shutters consist of a traveling set of curtains, including a front curtain (which opens to reveal the film or sensor) and a rear curtain (which follows at a distance determined by shutter speed to conceal the film or sensor at the conclusion of the exposure).

To take a flash picture, the entire sensor must be exposed at one time to the brief flash exposure, so the image is exposed after the front curtain has reached the other side of the focal plane, but before the rear curtain begins to move.

Front-curtain sync causes the flash to fire at the beginning of this period when the shutter is completely open, in the instant that the first curtain of the focal plane shutter finishes its movement across the film or sensor plane. With slow shutter speeds, this feature can create a blur effect from the ambient light, showing as patterns that follow a moving subject with the subject shown sharply frozen at the beginning of the blur trail. See also *rear-curtain sync.*

frontlighting: Illumination that comes from the direction of the camera. See also *backlighting.*

f-stop: The relative size of the lens aperture, which helps determine both exposure and depth-of-field. The larger the f-stop number, the smaller the f-stop itself.

graduated filter: A lens attachment with variable density or color from one edge to another. A graduated neutral density filter, for example, can be oriented so the neutral density portion is concentrated at the top of the lens's view with the less dense or clear portion at the bottom, thus reducing the amount of light from a very bright sky while not interfering with the exposure of the landscape in the foreground. Graduated filters can also be split into several color sections to provide a color gradient between portions of the image.

gray card: A piece of cardboard or other material with a standardized 18 percent reflectance. You can use gray cards as a reference for determining the correct exposure or for setting white balance.

high contrast: A wide range of density in a print, negative, or other image.

highlight: The brightest parts of an image that contains detail.

histogram: A kind of chart showing the relationship of tones in an image by using a series of 256 vertical bars, one for each brightness level. A histogram chart, such as the one a digital SLR can display during picture review, typically looks like a curve with one or more slopes and peaks, depending on how many highlight, midtone, and shadow tones are present in the image.

hot shoe: A mount on top of a camera used to hold an electronic flash, while providing an electrical connection between the flash and the camera.

hyperfocal distance: A point of focus where everything from half that distance to infinity appears to be acceptably sharp. For example, if your lens has a hyperfocal distance of 4 feet, everything from 2 feet to infinity would be sharp. The hyperfocal distance varies by the lens and the aperture in use. If you know you'll be taking a shot without warning, sometimes it's useful to turn off your camera's automatic focus and set the lens to infinity, or better yet, set the hyperfocal distance. Then, you can snap off a quick picture without waiting for the lag that occurs with most digital cameras as the autofocus locks in.

image rotation: A feature that senses whether a picture was taken in horizontal or vertical orientation. That information is embedded in the picture file so that the camera and compatible software applications can automatically display the image in the correct orientation.

image stabilization: A technology (called *vibration reduction* by Nikon and *anti-shake* by Konica Minolta) that compensates for camera shake, usually by adjusting the position of the camera sensor or lens elements in response to movements of the camera.

incident light: Light falling on a surface.

International Standards Organization (ISO): A governing body that provides standards used to represent film speed or the equivalent sensitivity of a digital camera's sensor. Digital camera sensitivity is expressed in ISO settings.

interpolation: A technique that digital cameras, scanners, and image editors use to create new pixels required whenever you resize or change the resolution of an image based on the values of surrounding pixels. Devices such as scanners and digital cameras can also use interpolation to create pixels in addition to those actually captured, thereby increasing the apparent resolution or color information in an image.

jaggies: A staircasing effect of lines that aren't perfectly horizontal or vertical, caused by pixels that are too large to represent the line accurately. See also *antialias*.

JPEG (Joint Photographic Experts Group): A file format that supports 24-bit color and reduces file sizes by selectively discarding image data. Digital cameras generally use JPEG compression to pack more images onto memory cards. You can select how much compression your camera uses (and therefore how much information it throws away) by selecting from among the Standard, Fine, Super Fine, or other quality settings offered by your camera. See also *RAW*.

Kelvin (K): A unit of measurement based on the absolute temperature scale in which absolute zero is zero. You use it to describe the color of continuous spectrum light sources, and you apply it when setting white balance.

lag time: The interval between when you press the shutter and when the picture is actually taken. During that span, the camera might be automatically focusing and calculating exposure. With digital SLRs, lag time is generally very short; with non-dSLRs, the elapsed time can easily be 1 second or more.

latitude: The range of camera exposures that produces acceptable images with a particular digital sensor or film.

lens flare: A feature of conventional photography that is both a bane and a creative outlet. It is an effect produced by the reflection of light among internal elements of an optical lens. Bright light sources within or just outside the field of view cause lens flare.

lighting ratio: The proportional relationship between the amount of light falling on the subject from the main light and other lights, expressed in a ratio, such as 3:1.

lossless compression: An image-compression scheme, that preserves all image detail. When the image is decompressed, it is identical to the original version.

lossy compression: An image-compression scheme, such as JPEG, that creates smaller files by discarding image information, which can affect image quality.

macro lens: A lens that provides continuous focusing from infinity to extreme close-ups, often to a reproduction ratio of 1:2 (half life-size) or 1:1 (life-size).

matrix metering: A system of exposure calculation that looks at many different segments of an image to determine the brightest and darkest portions.

midtones: Parts of an image with tones of an intermediate value, usually in the 25 to 75 percent range. Many image-editing features allow you to manipulate midtones independently from the highlights and shadows.

mirror lock-up: The ability to retract the SLR's mirror to reduce vibration prior to taking the photo (with some cameras) or to allow access to the sensor for cleaning.

neutral color: A color in which red, green, and blue are present in equal amounts, producing a gray.

neutral density filter: A gray camera filter reduces the amount of light entering the camera without affecting the colors.

noise: In an image, pixels with randomly distributed color values. Noise in digital photographs tends to be the product of low-light conditions and long exposures, particularly when you have set your camera to a higher ISO rating than normal.

noise reduction: A technology used to cut down on the amount of random information in a digital picture, usually caused by long exposures at increased sensitivity ratings. In a digital camera, noise reduction involves the camera automatically taking a second blank/dark exposure at the same settings that contains only noise, and then using the blank photo's information to cancel out the noise in the original picture. The process is very quick, but it does double the amount of time required to take the photo.

normal lens: A lens that makes the image in a photograph appear in a perspective that is like that of the original scene, typically with a field of view of roughly 45 degrees, roughly the same as the human eye.

overexposure: A condition in which too much light reaches the film or sensor, producing a dense negative or a very bright/light print, slide, or digital image.

pincushion distortion: A type of lens distortion in which lines at the top and side edges of an image are bent inward, producing an effect that looks like a pincushion.

polarizing filter: A filter that forces light, which normally vibrates in all directions, to vibrate only in a single plane, reducing or removing the specular reflections from the surface of objects.

RAW: An image file format that includes all the unprocessed information captured by the camera. RAW files are very large compared to JPEG files, and must be processed by a special program (such as Nikon Capture or the Adobe Camera RAW filter) after being downloaded from the camera.

rear-curtain sync: An optional kind of electronic flash synchronization technique, originally associated with focal plane shutters.

Rear-curtain sync causes the flash to fire at the end of the exposure, an instant before the second (or rear) curtain of the focal plane shutter begins to move.

red eye: An effect from flash photography that appears to make a person's eyes glow red, or an animal's yellow or green. It's caused by light bouncing from the retina of the eye, and is most pronounced in dim illumination (when the irises are wide open) and when the electronic flash is close to the lens and therefore prone to reflect directly back. Image editors can fix red eye through cloning other pixels over the offending red or orange ones.

RGB color mode: A color mode that represents the three colors — red, green, and blue — used by devices such as scanners or monitors to reproduce color.

saturation: The purity of color; the amount by which a pure color is diluted with white or gray.

selective focus: Choosing a lens opening that produces a shallow depth-of-field. Usually this is used to isolate a subject by causing most other elements in the scene to be blurred.

self-timer: A mechanism delaying the opening of the shutter for some seconds after the release has been operated.

sensitivity: A measure of the degree of response of a film or sensor to light, measured with the ISO setting.

shadow: The darkest part of an image, represented on a digital image by pixels with low numeric values.

sharpen: To increase the apparent sharpness of an image by boosting the contrast between adjacent pixels that form an edge.

shutter: In a conventional film camera, the shutter is a mechanism consisting of blades, a curtain, plate, or some other movable cover that controls the time during which light reaches the film. Digital cameras might use actual mechanical shutters for the slower shutter speeds (less than $\frac{1}{500}$ of a second) and an electronic shutter for higher speeds.

shutter priority: An exposure mode in which you set the shutter speed and the camera determines the appropriate f-stop.

single autofocus (AF-S): An automatic focusing setting in which the camera focuses once when the shutter release is partially depressed.

slave unit: An accessory flash unit that supplements the main flash, usually triggered electronically when the slave senses the light output by the main unit, radio waves, or infrared signals.

slow sync: An electronic flash synchronizing method that uses a slow shutter speed so that ambient light is recorded by the camera in addition to the electronic flash illumination. With slow sync, the background receives more exposure for a more realistic effect.

specular highlight: Bright spots in an image caused by reflection of light sources.

spot meter: An exposure system that concentrates on a small area in the image.

subtractive primary colors: Cyan, magenta, and yellow, which are the printing inks that theoretically absorb all color and produce black. In practice, however, they generate a muddy brown, so most printers include black to preserve detail (especially in shadows). The combination of the three colors and black is referred to as CMYK. (K represents black, to differentiate it from blue in the RGB model.)

time exposure: A picture taken by leaving the shutter open for a long period, usually more than one second. The camera is generally locked down with a tripod to prevent blur during the long exposure.

time-lapse photography: A process by which a tripod-mounted camera takes sequential pictures at intervals, allowing the viewing of events that take place over a long period of time, such as a sunrise or flower opening. With a digital SLR, time-lapse photography is often accomplished by connecting the camera to a computer with the USB cable and triggering the pictures with special software.

TTL (through the lens): A system of providing viewing and exposure calculation through the actual lens taking the picture.

underexposure: A condition in which too little light reaches the film or sensor, producing a thin negative, a dark slide, a muddy-looking print, or a dark digital image.

unsharp masking: The process for increasing the contrast between adjacent pixels in an image. This increases sharpness, especially around edges.

vignetting: Dark corners of an image, often produced by using a lens hood that is too small for the field of view or generated artificially by using image-editing techniques.

white balance: The adjustment of a digital camera to the color temperature of the light source. Interior illumination is relatively red; outdoor light is relatively blue. Digital cameras often set correct white balance automatically or let you do it through menus.

Index

• E •

• *G* •

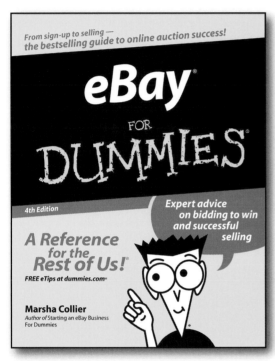
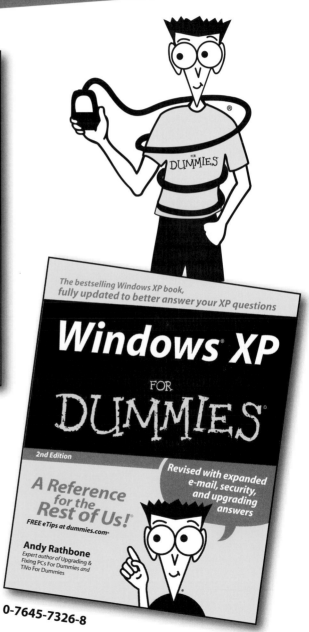

Don't forget about these bestselling For Dummies® books!

0-7645-8958-X

0-7645-8996-2

Don't forget about these bestselling For Dummies® books!

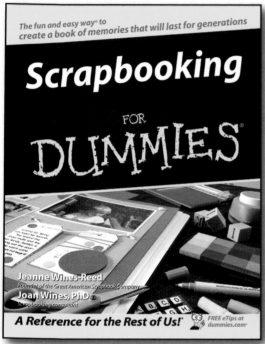

0-7645-7208-3

0-7645-4116-1